GOD AND THE FASCISTS

GOD AND THE FASCISTS

The Vatican Alliance with
MUSSOLINI, FRANCO, HITLER, AND PAVELIĆ

Karlheinz Deschner

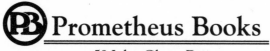

Prometheus Books

59 John Glenn Drive
Amherst, New York 14228–2119

Published 2013 by Prometheus Books

God and the Fascists: The Vatican Alliance with Mussolini, Franco, Hitler, and Pavelić edited by Peter Gorenflos, translated by Richard Pepper—First English Translation. Copyright © 2013 by Peter Gorenflos. First published October 1965 by Hans E. Günther Verlag, Stuttgart, with original German title, *Mit Gott und den Faschisten*, by Karlheinz Deschner, © Karlheinz Deschner. October 1965 by Hans E. Günther Verlag Stuttgart.

Cover design by Nicole Sommer-Lecht
Cover images © 2013 Media Bakery; image of Francisco Franco
© Bridgman Art Library/Peter Newark Pictures

Inquiries should be addressed to
Prometheus Books
59 John Glenn Drive
Amherst, New York 14228–2119
VOICE: 716–691–0133 • FAX: 716–691–0137
WWW.PROMETHEUSBOOKS.COM
17 16 15 14 13 5 4 3 2 1
Library of Congress Cataloging-in-Publication Data

Deschner, Karlheinz.
    [Mit Gott und den Faschisten. English]
    God and the fascists : the Vatican alliance with Mussolini, Franco, Hitler, and Pavelic / by Karlheinz Deschner ; translated into English by Richard Pepper.
        pages cm
    Includes bibliographical references and index.
    ISBN 978-1-61614-837-9 (pbk.)
    ISBN 978-1-61614-838-6 (ebook)
    1. Fascism and the Catholic Church. 2. Pius XI, Pope, 1857–1939. 3. Pius XII, Pope, 1876–1958. I. Title.

BX1377.D413 2013
282.09'04—dc23

2013022365

Printed in the United States of America

For Lena and Steff Kager
and all good heathens

For Else and Sepp Schmidt
and all good Christians

―――――――――――――――――――――――――

*"It has been an old, time-honored custom of the Holy Mother Church
to make use of the Devil in the service of God!"*

―Upton Sinclair

CONTENTS

Foreword by the Editor to the 2013 Edition   11

Preface to the Original 1965 Edition   19

Chapter 1: The Vatican and Italian Fascism   23
- Prehistory   23
- The Beginnings of Cooperation between the Vatican and Fascism   28
- The First Service   31
- The Lateran Pacts   33
- The Nazis' Reaction to the "Reconciliation" with the Fascists   38
- The Abyssinian War—with Papal Approval and the
  Complete Support of the Italian High Clergy   41
- Almost the Entire Italian Episcopate Supported the Fascist Raid   44
- "Ave Maria"   46

Chapter 2: The Vatican and the Spanish Civil War   51
- The Causes   51
- From the Foundation of the Republic until the Outbreak of the War   55
- Hitler's Germany and Italy Helped the Catholic Rebels to Win   61
- The "Dear Son" of the Pope—a Devoted Friend of Hitler   64
- Russia's Help for the Republic   66
- Concerning the "Christian" Crusade against the "Godless Reds"   67
- Republican Crimes and the Church's Martyr Legend   73
- The Crimes of the Franco Rebels   76
- Franco and the Vatican   79
- "Peace in Order, Honor, and Well-being"—Pope Pius XII   84

Chapter 3: The Vatican and Hitler's Germany   87
- National Socialism Assumes Power   87
- The Enabling Act   91

The Catholic Parties Dissolved Themselves on Church Orders   94
The Concordat with Hitler's Germany   95
All the German Bishops Called for Cooperation with Hitler
   in 1933 because the Vatican Wanted It   102
Leading Catholic Theologians Also Supported Hitler   107
The Alleged Scapegoat: German "Milieu Catholicism"   112
1. Under Hitler, the German Bishops Never Protested
   against Him or His System   114
2. The German Catholic Martyrs under Hitler Are Witnesses
   against the Church   118
The "Lion of Münster"   120
The German (and, after 1938, Also the Austrian) Catholic Bishops
   Supported One of the Greatest Criminals in World History with
   Increasing Intensity until the Final Years of the Second World War   125
Bishop von Galen Authorizes the "Oath to the Flag" as a Pledge
   of Allegiance to Hitler   133
The German Bishops Supported Hitler Even More Intensely during
   the War   136
The Flexible Cardinal Faulhaber (or, How to Survive for
   Two Thousand Years)   141
Prelate Neuhäusler's Résumé   147
The German Catholic Press Also Interceded for Hitler's War   148
A Brief Sidelong Glance at the German Protestant Church in
   Hitler's Reich   149

Chapter 4: The Vatican and the Second World War   155
   What Did Pacelli Want?   155
   The German Invasion of Czechoslovakia   157
   Danzig   162
   The German Invasion of Poland   164
   The Pope's "Efforts to Make Peace" and Italy's Entry into the War   166
   The German Invasion of Norway and the Occupation of the
      Netherlands, Belgium, and France   170
   Closer Affiliation to the Victorious Führer   173
   The German Invasion of the Soviet Union   175

Papal Policy in the Final Years of the War   179
The Turnabout of the Catholic Church after Germany's Defeat   182
The Protector and Shield of the Fascists to the Very End   184

Chapter 5: The Vatican and the Croatian Atrocities   **187**
The Papacy and the Balkans up to the First World War   188
Pacelli's Threat   191
A Papal Blessing for Criminals   193
"Further Work"   195
Even the Germans Protested   198
Concentration Camp and Caritas   200
The Deeds of the Ustaša Were Deeds of the Church   201
The Franciscans' Leading Role   203
The Primate of the Croatian Catholics, Archbishop Dr. Stepinac,
    Also Supported the Murderers   205
The Most Bloodthirsty Criminal of All Satellite Countries Was
    Protected and Blessed by the Catholic Church Right to the End   208
Did the Pope Know Nothing?   209

Appendix   **215**
Discussion about Karlheinz Deschner's Critical Church History,
    Abermals krähte der Hahn (*And Again the Cock Crew*) in
    Die Tat, Zurich   215
Abermals krähte der Hahn as reviewed by Theologians   234
Abermals krähte der Hahn as reviewed by Rationalists and
    Free Religious   238
Other Reviews   239

Notes   243

Bibliography   277

FOREWORD BY THE EDITOR TO THE 2013 EDITION

W hy, after almost fifty years, should there be a reprint of Karlheinz Deschner's work *God and the Fascists* (*Mit Gott und den Faschisten*)? Because it is very topical. Because it is, fully unfairly, in danger of being forgotten. Because it disrupts a process of suppression, or better, indeed the deliberate policy of disinformation, pursued by the Vatican. It reminds us of the Vatican's collaboration not only with Hitler, the greatest criminal of all time, but also with Mussolini, Franco, and the little-known Pavelić, the Fascist leader in Croatia who, along with Cardinal Stepinac, was responsible for the concentration and death camp of Jasenovac, of whose existence only few people know today.

Because the web of lies spun by the Vatican is exposed. It has been trying to position itself as an anti-Hitler resistance organization for decades, although according to Cardinal Faulhaber, Pius XII was "the best friend, indeed, the only friend of the new Reich at the beginning," especially in the unstable initial phase of National Socialism, when history could have taken a completely different course! Because it is not a fashionable book that caters for a trendy opinion for reasons of accommodation but presents and summarizes historical facts precisely and in great detail and draws conclusions that are comprehensible to everyone. Daniel Jonah Goldhagen clearly considers it unnecessary to quote Deschner at all in his book *A Moral Reckoning: The Role of the Catholic Church in the Holocaust*, despite Deschner being able to provide much more information using much less ink nearly forty years earlier. And because it is also exciting to read, like a novel but where every line is the truth and every reader is considerably more intelligent and enlightened after reading it than he or she was before and may also be shocked to see the extent of the collaboration between the Nazis, all the Fascists, and the Vatican! In short, because it exposes a historical lie. The lie of the Catholic resistance.

Let us not forget that it was the French Revolution that showed the Catholic Church where its boundaries were and thereby put an end to its feudal power—albeit, unfortunately, only half-heartedly. But still, the Spanish Inquisition did not sentence the last heretic—the schoolteacher Caetano Ripol—to death at the gallows, followed by a "symbolic burning," until July 26, 1826, almost half a century after the Bastille was stormed! After the revolution, Napoleon's troops occupied the Papal States at the end of the eighteenth century—which had arisen from bloody wars and been legitimized by a forged document, the so-called Donation of Constantine—arrested Pius VI, and took him to Valence as a prisoner. The Congress of Vienna restored the Vatican State again in 1815 with a reduced territory, but in 1870, after the occupation by Italian troops, it finally disappeared in the new Italian state. Those responsible were then excommunicated . . . and could not have cared less.

The increasing power of the bourgeoisie, the development of the European national states, the emancipation movement, the natural sciences and progress through technological developments increasingly forced Catholicism onto the back foot in the second half of the nineteenth century—it tried desperately, and in vain, to take up the fight against "modern rationalism" with the first Vatican Council and restore the beleaguered papal authority by means of the dogma of infallibility. But time was against Catholicism. Under Bismarck, nearly two thousand Catholic clergy were imprisoned or given hefty fines in the *Kulturkampf* ("battle of the cultures") for interfering in state affairs; the United States broke off diplomatic relations with the Vatican on February 28, 1867 (and did not restore them until 1984 under Ronald Reagan). The "Roman Question" had arisen: How could the Holy See be saved from ultimate, and at that time foreseeable, downfall? How, and with whose aid, could its former power be restored? This problem was exacerbated by the growth of the decidedly anticlerical workers' movement after the debacle of the First World War, which was committed to enlightenment and the principle of equality.

This is the starting point of Karlheinz Deschner's book *God and the Fascists*. The aim of this new edition, published by Prometheus Books, is to ensure it is not forgotten. With richness of detail, historically founded, and by mining a vast number of sources, it proves that after the First World War, the chance was seized to turn the wheel of history back together with the rising Fascist movements. For fear of a victory of the workers' movement across Europe—according to the Soviet model—the Vatican, together with the reactionary property-owning classes and their henchmen—the Fascists—entered an alliance that was intended to secure the existence of both. This unholy Catholic alliance with the supposedly lesser—Fascist—evil led to the greatest catastrophe in human history: the Second World War and the Holocaust.

After the Catholic party "Partito Popolare" was dissolved by Pius XI, the curia paved the way for Benito Mussolini and Italian Fascism. As a reward, they received—by means of the Lateran Pacts—the Vatican State back, a sovereign, stately construct, albeit reduced in size, and the monstrous sum of one billion lire in state bonds and 750 million lire in cash. These assets formed the basis of the Vatican Bank, which is under strict observation from the American supervisory authorities today because of its machinations, suspicion of money laundering, and proximity to the Mafia.

And the Vatican helped the Nazis to power according to exactly the same pattern and under the same premises. The Catholic Centre Party—the oldest party in Europe led by Prelate Kaas, a close friend of Cardinal Secretary of State Eugenio Pacelli, the Pope's second-in-command—concurring with the Enabling Act of March 24, 1933, and then dissolving itself cleared the way for Hitler. The subsequent dictatorship set the catastrophe in motion. The historical lie that nobody at the time knew who they were dealing with is clearly disproved by Karlheinz Deschner. Because the first concentration camps had been built before the Enabling Act—not for the Jews at this point, but for political opposition—basic citizens' rights were suspended and the boycott of Jewish businesses, doctors, and lawyers was called for. Hitler's *Mein Kampf* could not have been unknown to Eugenio Pacelli: the same Eugenio Pacelli who had been the papal nuncio in Berlin until 1929 ("the best-informed diplomat in Germany") and then made a career in the Vatican, first as cardinal secretary of state, then as pope. Pope Pius XII. He, who had the reputation of being an outstanding connoisseur and friend of Germany, harvested the fruits of that collaboration on July 20, 1933, in the form of the concordat with Nazi Germany. This treaty under international law still has constitutional status in the Federal Republic of Germany to this day (Article 123.2 of the German Basic Law). It regulates the friendly relations between the Holy See and the German Reich; state religious education was introduced under it, with a status equal to that of the other subjects taught, the payment of salaries from religious-education teachers to bishops by the state from public tax revenue is guaranteed and church tax collected by the state—to this day, let it be noted—a new phenomenon that was to have far-reaching consequences. Workers must publicly declare their religious confession, losing their previously constitutional right to keep this silent, and employers are obliged to take part in the collection of the ecclesiastical obolus. A church state was born! The Hitler concordat meant that the clergy's robes were afforded the same protection as military uniforms, priests were exempted in advance from military service—they knew what was coming—the dissolution of the Centre Party was retrospectively justified and a great deal more.

Karlheinz Deschner describes how the collaboration of the German episcopate with the Nazis—which could only happen with the approval of the curia—lasted until the end of the Second World War, how vicars, priests, and bishops prayed for Hitler's Reich every Sunday all across the land, which was also regulated in the concordat (Article 30), and agitated in favor of the war, how churches and cathedrals were decorated with swastikas on Hitler's birthday, and the papal nuncio personally congratulated the Führer, full of pride, on his fiftieth birthday in 1939—half a year after the Kristallnacht! In the so-called church struggle, which is supposed to have been the expression of church resistance, the church stood up only for its own interests, never against Hitler, never against the war, and never for the Jewish population. And even after the military defeat of Nazi Germany, the Vatican helped high-ranking Nazi functionaries to flee to South America with the help of the ratline, with which Mengele, Eichmann, and many other criminals escaped the Allies' justice.

What did Benedict XV, Pius XI, and Pius XII dream of? They dreamt of a Catholic continental Europe in a united military battle against the godless Soviet Union, as degenerated as it may already have been by Stalin's influence (read Arno Lustigers *Stalin and the Jews: The Red Book*). They dreamt of the end of

Orthodoxy, the end of communism, and the Catholicization of Russia. And of a neutral, Anglican Great Britain and a neutral United States. Because a military conflict within the western camp made the outcome of the war unpredictable. After the military defeat of France, this dream seemed to be well within reach, and in 1940 the whole world was convinced that Hitler would win the war. The realization of the curia's dream had, with Hitler's help, come within their grasp.

We learn from Karlheinz Deschner how the invasion of the Soviet Union on June 22, 1941, was openly welcomed, not only by the German episcopate, and how unlimited their enthusiasm for Hitler and agitations against Russia were. And Pius XII—who allegedly did too little against Hitler and said too little—spoke in a radio address one week later of "rays of light that raise the heart to great, holy expectations: great bravery and courage in defending the foundations of Christian culture and optimistic hope for their triumph," by which he intended to express, according to embassy counselor Menshausen, the hope that the great sacrifices demanded by this war would not be in vain and would, should Providence so wish, lead to victory over Bolshevism. In this "war between worldviews," which had been so longed for by the Catholics and which Hitler also called it, the Holocaust was viewed as a kind of collateral damage. There may even have been a secret feeling of satisfaction in light of the two thousand years of Christian anti-Judaism. Had Hitler not, in April 1933, already coquetted before high Catholic functionaries—as Deschner reports—and much to their delight, that his "treatment of the Jewish Question" was merely a continuation of medieval Catholic tradition?! In any case, the pope never condemned the Nazi pogroms against the Jews, not even when the Jews were rounded up before his eyes, so to speak, and taken away. Today's propagated idea of a Judeo-Christian West is based on a syncretism swindle.

The Vatican was even more deeply involved in Fascist crimes in Croatia, where the Franciscans played a leading role in the atrocities perpetrated there, which were so brutal that even the Germans complained. Ante Pavelić, the leader of the Croatian Fascists, called the Ustaša, coined the slogan that a third of the Orthodox population of Yugoslavia should be forcibly converted, a third expelled, and the other third murdered. Seven hundred fifty thousand Serbs fell victim to this regime with clerical help, and often after brutal torture, as did 80 percent of the Jews in Yugoslavia. The Primate of the Croatian Catholics,

Archbishop Dr. Stepinac, collaborated with Pavelić from the first minute to the last. After his conviction as a war criminal, the Ustaša leader managed to escape, initially to South America, with the help of the ratline. He was accompanied by the former contact man between the Croatian archbishop Stepinac and the Vatican, the priest Krunoslav Draganović, who was, among other things, responsible for the deportation of Jews and Serbs during the war as a "resettlement officer" and was later one of the key figures in the organization of the ratline. He later fled to Franco's Spain, where he found refuge in a Franciscan monastery in Madrid. This war criminal died on December 26, 1959, and received the blessing of the Holy Father on his deathbed. Stepinac was the only high cleric who was at least partly brought to justice for his deeds. The sentence: sixteen years' imprisonment with forced labor. After six years of imprisonment, he was released early. Today's theologians may claim that this verdict was based on a "misunderstanding." But it is no misunderstanding that Yad Vashem rejected the obscenity of an application to grant him the title and honor of a "Righteous among the Nations" twice, in 1970 and 1994. He was beatified by Pope John Paul II in 1998.

In his résumé at the end of the book, Karlheinz Deschner says, in 1965, "If one considers the attitude of Eugenio Pacelli to the politics of Mussolini, Franco, Hitler, and Pavelić, it hardly seems an exaggeration to say: Pius XII is probably more incriminated than any other pope has been for centuries. He is so obviously involved in the most hideous atrocities of the Fascist era, and therefore of history itself, both directly and indirectly, that it would not be surprising, given the tactics of the Roman Church, if he were to be canonized."

And now the beatification is already under way, less than fifty years later! If Hitler had won the war, one may wish to add, then he would presumably have long since attained the same Catholic honors.

And Franco's support from the Vatican in the Spanish Civil War—and before—is also a theme of this rewarding book, this irreplaceable source of information.

Let us now return to the present, to the constitutional knock-on effects of the church's collaboration with Fascism in Germany. One has to only compare this close interrelationship between church and state, this still-surviving German church state—which, under the Weimar Constitution and the federal constitution of Germany, should never have been permitted—with the constitutions of France and the United States, in which the separation of church and state is clearly stipulated. It then becomes clear how far Germany is today from being a modern democracy. It is a country in which the churches, on the basis of regional concordats, have places in all radio and television broadcasting councils, in nearly all newspaper editorial offices, in countless other influential institutions, and—some quite openly, others well hidden—at the levers of power. It then becomes clear what massive favors Hitler and Mussolini did the Vatican with this special answer to the Roman Question, with the restoration of its statehood, its assets, and its public influence, which were in a state of dissolution in the second half of the nineteenth century. And at what cost to the rest of the world!

Karlheinz Deschner's book is an important contribution to enlightenment, a jewel for anyone who seeks historical truth; it is an antidote to the historical lie of Catholic resistance to Adolf Hitler and provides a fundamental contribution to the current debate on the rehabilitation of the Pius Brotherhood (fronted by Richard Williamson, who denied the Holocaust), the planned beatification of Pius XII, the scandal surrounding the Vatican Bank, the reintroduction of the Good Friday Intercession, and the role of the Vatican in the world in general.

Anyone who is looking for the historical Ariadne's thread in the labyrinth of church heteronomy will go nowhere without Karlheinz Deschner's book *God and the Fascists*. I would, at this juncture, recommend to anyone who wishes to find out more, many historical layers deeper, for example, about the historical origins of Christianity, Hyam Maccoby's superb, central work *The Mythmaker: Paul and the Invention of Christianity* (1986), in which he proves that Christianity is not founded on the Jewish Jesus but the Greek Paul, who composed a highly virulent mythical mix of gnosis, mystery cults, and the story of Jesus and, therefore, started off two thousand years of Christian anti-Judaism, which culminated in the Holocaust.

The other Ariadne's thread from the religious labyrinth—the subjective, "psychological" one—can be found by anyone looking for it in Sigmund Freud (e.g., *Totem and Taboo*, *The Future of an Illusion*, *Moses and Monotheism*), and more especially in the pioneering study of religion by Fritz Erik Hoevels, "'Bhagwan' Rajneesh and the Dilemma of any Humane Religion" in *Mass Neurosis Religion*, published by Ahriman International, which is now also to be credited with the republishing of Deschner's masterpiece *God and the Fascists*. Both authors make it clear how small the eye of the needle is through which human society must pass if the aims of enlightenment, reason, freedom, the principle of equality, and maximum happiness for the maximum number of people are to become reality, how many archaic and yet real power structures must be broken in order to achieve this.

May the interested reader convince himself or herself of the topicality of this book nearly fifty years after *God and the Fascists* was first published. It is thrillingly written and a literary achievement of the first rank.

Editor's note: Brackets indicate editorial changes made by either Karlheinz Deschner or me.

Peter Gorenflos
Berlin, Germany

PREFACE TO THE ORIGINAL 1965 EDITION

While at least the collaboration of the church with the Nazi regime has become more common knowledge in recent times—almost a quarter of a century after the event is late enough, I should say—there are still many circles not aware that the Catholic hierarchy systematically supported all the Fascist states from their beginnings and therefore carry a great responsibility for the deaths of sixty million people.

The collaboration of the Vatican with Fascism had already begun in 1922, even before the famous "March on Rome," which Mussolini himself had, as is well known, participated in in the sleeper from Milan, and led to the Second World War via the Lateran Pacts and the raid on Abyssinia, which was a shining success, carried out with the help of pictures of the Madonna and poisonous gases.

In Spain, the bishops, also supported by the pope, called for a Christian "crusade" against the legally elected republican government as early as 1933, a crusade at whose forefront the troops of the heathen Hitler and the atheist Mussolini fought from 1936 to 1939, as did Franco's 150,000 Mohammedans and the Foreign Legions—their motto was "Long live death! Down with intelligence!"

In Germany, the Vatican's cooperation with Hitler started, in all probability, before the "seizure of power," but in any case directly afterward and culminated not in 1933/34 but, despite the struggle between the church and the state, the so-called *Kirchenkampf* (which was fought almost exclusively for purely Catholic interests) not until the middle of the war, after the attack on the Soviet Union, which the Catholic Church had been longing for with a passion, as the mutual pastoral letters of the German and Austrian bishops, which could never have been written without curial approval, prove.

While the relationship of Pius XI and Pius XII to Mussolini, Franco, and Hitler is discussed in the first three chapters, the final two deal with the behavior of the Vatican in the Second World War and papal policy in Yugoslavia, where from 1941 to 1945, also with the full support of the Catholic clergy, 299 Orthodox churches were destroyed, 240,000 Orthodox Serbs violently converted to Catholicism, and around 750,000 Orthodox Christians, frequently after brutal torture, were murdered; incidentally, this did not become known in German-speaking countries until 1962, when it was exposed in some circles at least by my church history, *Abermals krähte der Hahn* (*And Again the Cock Crew*).

I have taken up the theme investigated in the final part of that work once again and expanded in particular the sections on Italian Fascism, the Spanish Civil War, and the Croatian atrocity. But the chapters on Hitler's Germany and the Second World War have been revised. So this is not merely a new book in appearance.

However, when I realize all the distortions and lies with which my church history has been defamed—read pars pro toto the review by the Protestant vicar Wolfgang Hammer in the appendix—I am certain that the lies will continue. What else would there be to do other than to be silent at best? Or to silence me.

But slander from a church that not only persecuted and massacred millions in the Middle Ages but "repeatedly" and "most insistently" supported probably the greatest criminal of all time in the twentieth century; which in 1933 "would not withdraw the powers of the Church from him at any price," but on the contrary, wanted to procure everyone for his "great development work," which in 1935 "strictly [rejected] any action or position taken against the state by its members" and also promised "to support the ruler of the German Reich . . . with all means necessary" in 1936, which, one year before the war broke out, accompanied Hitler's "work for the future with their highest blessings." And, when the war started, the church ordered the Catholic soldiers "to do their duty out of obedience to the Führer and be prepared to sacrifice their entire person," which followed his invasion of the Soviet Union in 1941 "with satisfaction" and affirmed: "We have repeatedly[!], and in the summer pastoral letter, called upon our believers to fulfill their duty with loyalty, to stand firm courageously, work in willingness to sacrifice and fight with all their might[!] in the service of our people in the most serious times of war," only to condemn Hitler and the Nazis as soon as they collapsed. Well, I consider slander by a church like this an honor.

I would like to thank all readers to whom I am connected by the struggle against lies and barbarism for their participation in my work and their help in its dissemination.

1

THE VATICAN AND ITALIAN FASCISM

"We shall always remember with gratitude that which has happened for the benefit of religion in Italy, even if the good deeds performed by the party and the regime were not smaller—indeed, they may even have been greater."

—Pope Pius XI, 1931[1]

"Your Excellency! The priests of Italy invoke over your person, your work as the restorer of Italy and founder of the Reich and the Fascist government the blessing of the Lord and an eternal halo of Roman wisdom and virtue, today and forever. Duce! The servants of Christ, the fathers of the peasantry honor you loyally. They bless you. They swear loyalty to you. With pious enthusiasm, with the voice and heart of the people we call: hail the Duce!"

—Father Menossi, January 12, 1938, Palazzo Venezia,
to which seventy-two bishops
and 2,340 priests broke out into shouting: "Duce! Duce! Duce!"[2]

PREHISTORY

"It was all about earthly and temporary things, about kings and king-doms, trials and disputes. Hardly any discussion of spiritual affairs was permitted."

—Bishop Jakob von Vitry, in the thirteenth century[3]

The poor Son of Man possessed nothing he could lay his head on. And his disciples should pronounce the gospel without money in their belts. He would only allow them a walking staff and sandals, according to Mark.[4] According to Matthew and Luke, he even forbade these.[5] The biblical Jesus demands the renunciation of all possessions,[6] and in the primitive Christian community, where his teachings and the style of his shared life with his disciples had to have the most continuing effect, there was also more than a hint of communism or, as Troeltsch puts it,[7] the religious communism of love. And the New Testament even observes: "All the believers were one in heart and mind. No one claimed that any of their possessions was their own, but they shared everything they had . . . there were no needy persons among them. For from time to time those who owned land or houses sold them, brought the money from the sales and put it at the apostles' feet, and it was distributed to anyone who had need."[8]

But while Early Fathers such as Cyprian and, in particular, the noble Basil praised the communism of original Christianity,[9] and while doctor of the church John Chrysostom was still preaching that "the community of property is more an adequate way of living for us than private property, and it is in accordance with nature,"[10] the loving communist seed of Christianity had already progressed to becoming "the most gigantic exploitation machine," as Kautsky wrote, "that the world has ever seen."[11]

There is, admittedly, little known of the origin and distribution of church property. Until the fifth century, the Christian writers remained almost completely silent about a development that could not be reconciled with the evangelical ideal of poverty. Under Constantine, at the beginning of the fourth century, when the church suddenly surrendered the pacifism that it had represented for centuries,[12] the money rain had definitely already begun. The emperor donated gold, churches, and palaces; his Christian successors awarded new endowments and immunities; what had previously flowed into sacred heathen sites was now being received by the Catholics. It also confiscated the temples and church property of the "heretics."[13] And the assets that were left to it by clerical dignitaries, monks, and slaves[14] constantly increased their possessions, especially as it became a custom to choose bishops from rich families. But many laypeople also left capital to the church since it was seen as the best guarantee of reaching eternal salvation.

After 475 CE, the Church of Rome gave a quarter of the entire church income to the bishop. The clergy received a quarter; the lower clergy, however, also had to depend on outside earnings. A quarter was distributed among the poor and a quarter used for maintaining church buildings.[15] But it seemed as if the pope was consuming all four parts for himself alone for years.[16] Gradually the ownership of massive property developed, which was termed *patrimonium ecclesiae* or *patrimonium St. Petri*. The Roman Church not only had massive possessions in Italy but also in Sicily, Corsica, Sardinia, Dalmatia, Africa, and even in the Middle East. After the fifth century, the bishop of Rome, whose "predecessors" had to preach the gospel barefoot and without money, had become the biggest landowner in the Roman Empire.[17]

Then, during the reign of Steven III in the eighth century, a religious war led to the creation of the Papal States, those grotesque monstrosities that would separate the north and the south of Italy for more than a millennium. By using the carrot of heaven and the stick of hell and presenting a letter from St. Peter himself, the pope drove the Frankish ruler Pepin, whose usurped royal dignity the church had recognized and whose predecessor it had put in the monastery, to two crusades against the Lombards, who were threatening Rome. In 756 Pepin gave the conquered territories to St. Peter and his alleged[18] successors, who thereby not only had massive estates but also had their own army at their disposal.

Now, however, the newly formed Papal States, which had arisen through two bloody wars, were given a more ideal origin. While Pepin still reigned, the so-called *donatio Constantini*, the Donation of Constantine, was fabricated, which was to tie in with the legend of Sylvester. According to this legend, the terrible persecutor of Christians, Constantine(!), was healed from leprosy, converted, and baptized by Pope Sylvester I, and, as a reward, Constantine richly thanked the pope by granting him imperial titles and rights not only with the Lateran, as was actually the case, but also with the city of Rome and even "all the provinces of Italy and the Western lands."[19]

This notorious document, which presented the Papal States as a gift from the first Christian emperor, dated and signed personally, played a crucial role in the popes' battles with the emperors as "classic evidence." And with a view to this document, anyone who misappropriated curial property or even favored any such action in any way whatsoever was condemned by the church.[20]

Hadrian I, who, out of fifty-five letters he wrote to Charlemagne, wrote forty-five that almost exclusively concerned the papal territories,[21] was the first pope to refer to the forgery. In the twelfth century, it went into the *Decretum Gratiani*, which received the first place in the *Corpus Iuris Canonici*, the valid law book of the church until 1918. After the followers of Arnold of Brescia had already recognized the fraud, it was finally uncovered in 1440 by the papal secretary and humanist Laurentius Valla in a document that was published by Ulrich von Hutten in 1519. Roman Catholic historiography, however, did not admit the forgery until the nineteenth century. The Papal States, which had been considerably expanded under Innocence III at around 1200, were lost to the popes during their sojourn in Avignon. But by the beginning of the sixteenth century under Julius II, they had achieved their greatest expansion. The pope, who also took up arms to fight in the campaigns, went to war in almost every year of his reign. At the end of the eighteenth century, Napoleon's soldiers occupied the territory, Pius VI was taken to Valence as a prisoner, and the Papal States were divided up between France and Italy. Although they were restored by the Congress of Vienna in 1815, they were finally absorbed into the kingdom of Italy in 1870.

For at that time, the Italians occupied Rome on September 20, 1870, and declared it to be their capital. The pope, who had raised the white flag after a brief cannonade, lost his army and his "worldly" rule and even had to be protected by Italian troops from the enraged populace.

While the king moved into a papal palace on the Quirinal, Pius IX locked himself in the Vatican, sent all government mediators away, excommunicated all those involved in the "usurpation" of Rome on November 1, 1870, and regarded himself as a "prisoner."

Thereupon, Italy generously regulated the position of the pope with the Law of Guarantees of May 13, 1871. It declared his person to be "holy and invulnerable," guaranteed him authority over all Catholic superiors, permitted him a bodyguard, and gave him the use of the completely tax-exempted Vatican buildings and gardens, the Lateran, and the Castel Gandolfo, including the museums, libraries, and collections located there; these would, however, remain the sovereign territory or property of Italy. Furthermore, he was guaranteed complete freedom to exercise his spiritual office, the representatives of foreign governments at the Holy See were granted all the privileges usually accorded to diplomats, and Italian officials were banned from intruding into the papal palaces. And finally, as compensation for the loss of Papal State income, there was a tax-free endowment of 3.25 million lire in the form of an annual pension; however, this was declined by Pius IX and his successors—the "gifts of love" from the believers all over the world who were lamenting them as "prisoners" amounted to more.

The liquidation of the Papal States and the occupation of Rome by the Italians, the "crime," as Pius IX put it,[22] led to the so-called Roman Question, for whose solution, according to the statement of the Italian politician Francesco Crispi, a man who had an inclination toward mediation, the greatest statesman of all time would be required.

During the First World War, for which the Vatican was partly responsible,[23] the pope understandably did not sympathize with Italy. He supported the Central powers, which is why the Catholic French and Belgians in particular continuously cursed him as a "Boche" and the diplomats of Germany and Austria who had been accredited to him had to leave Rome in 1915. Indeed, the Italian government even made it a condition of their participation in the war, in the papal clause of the London agreement, that the Vatican stay away from the peace negotiations![24] But on the other side of the Central powers, the thought of a new Avignon was propagated during the war. The handover of one of the old spiritual principalities of Salzburg, Trento, Bressanone, or Liechtenstein to the pope as a papal state was considered. There was also discussion in this regard about one of the Calabrian or Dalmatian islands as well as Elba.[25] But all plans of this nature remained unfulfilled after the Central powers' cause was lost and because the Vatican had supported them during the war, in particular in 1917, when the nuncio Pacelli conducted intensive peace negotiations on their behalf,[26] the victorious states did not even think of lifting a finger to help the pope. And apart from that, Britain was antipapal; France, anticlerical; Russia, Bolshevist. And since in Italy itself the liberal regime seemed to be tipping toward a socialist or communist one, there was hardly any hope for a solution to the Roman Question.

In this nearly hopeless situation, the Vatican made its first contacts to a man to whom Konrad Adenauer sent a telegraph in 1929 saying that his name would be entered into the history of the Catholic Church written with golden letters[27]—Benito Mussolini.

THE BEGINNINGS OF COOPERATION BETWEEN THE VATICAN AND FASCISM

"I decorate myself with the curses of priests as I would with a fragrant wreath."

—Benito Mussolini, 1920[28]

"I recognize that the Latin and world-dominating tradition of Rome has its modern incarnation in Catholicism."

—Benito Mussolini, 1921[29]

"Mussolini is making quick progress."

—Cardinal Ratti, 1921[30]

Pope Pius XI, elected at the fourteenth ballot in 1922, had already been following the new party *Partito Fascista* with great interest as Cardinal Archbishop Ratti of Milan. It has, in fact, even been claimed that his predecessor, Benedict XV, had, in the last days of his life, "sent special attestations of his favor" to the then director of the Milan journal *Popolo d'Italia.*[31]

Mussolini was certainly an atheist. His first essay, published in 1904 and titled "There is No God," was about the nonexistence of God. He called him a "monstrous product of human ignorance," and Jesus, if he ever even existed, "a small and mean (*piccolo e meschino*) person."[32] And as late as 1919 the author of the anti-Catholic novel *The Cardinal's Mistress* drew up a strictly antichurch manifesto and swore in 1920 that he would literally spit on all dogmas. "There is no God," he professed. "From an academic point of view religion is nonsense; in practice it is immoral and the people it attaches itself to are sick."[33] "Never," stresses G. A. Borgese in his excellent Mussolini book, "had a vendetta been declared so ruthlessly on Christian ethics and religiousness as by the Fascist theory of state and war. A merciless fight between the two powers seemed inevitable."[34]

But only one year later, in the summer of 1921, the Fascist leader announced "that the only universal idea that exists in Rome today is the one that emanates from the Vatican."[35] And on February 5, 1922, on the day Achille Ratti was elected pope, Mussolini, accompanied by two friends, rushed to St. Peter's Square, where the presence of the president, vice president and secretary of the Fascist Party attracted considerable attention. "Hardly had he arrived at the square," one of his companions said, "that the Duce was deeply moved by the grandiose spectacle presented by the incredible size of the crowd and the majesty of the Vatican building, which at this moment appeared even more solemn since it enveloped a deep secret within its walls. For a while the Duce remained silent, moved, as if he wanted to quantify the force of the picture before him, then he said: 'It is incredible that the liberal governments have not realized that the universality of the papacy, the heir to the universality of the Roman Empire, represents the greatest glory of the history and tradition of Italy.'"[36]

Shortly after, Mussolini wrote in a letter: "As a citizen of Milan I share the joy of all Milanese about the election of Cardinal *Ratti* as Pope. Apart from the characteristics that I would call religious he also possesses those that make him agreeable to the mundane world. He is a man of profound historical, political and philosophical education who has seen much of other countries and is very familiar with the situation in Eastern Europe. I am of the view that relations between Italy and the Vatican will improve with Pius XI."[37]

What was Mussolini thinking of? Had he been converted? Had he become a theist or even a pious Catholic? Not at all! He thought no differently of Catholicism than he had done when he assumed power. Even his public speeches confirm this. Even his major chamber report about the Lateran Pacts, that pitiful capitulation to the Vatican, is peppered with anti-Catholic digs.[38] Mussolini not only rightly said of Christianity that, although it came into being in Palestine, it did not become Catholic until it reached Rome. He also bluntly declared at this solemn moment: "It is peculiar that I have had to have more Catholic newspapers confiscated in the last three months than in the previous six years put together!"[39] And time and again he would speak some harsh words against the papacy and described himself as a Ghibelline and an unbeliever.[40]

But on the other hand, Mussolini knew that religion, as he had himself stated in his first atheist piece of writing, is "a trick of kings and oppressors to keep their subjects and slaves under control."[41] And since the Duce had also given up Marxism in favor of an antisocialist and antiliberal position, since he was no longer demanding conscientious objection in fiery speeches or calling on working women to throw themselves in front of transport trains,[42] Cardinal Achille Ratti was already able to say in 1921, a year before he was elected pope: "*Mussolini is making quick progress and will crush everything that gets in his way with elemental force. Mussolini is a wonderful man. Did you hear? A wonderful man!* He is a new convert. He comes from the extreme left and has the driving zeal of the novice. . . . The future belongs to him."[43]

So began the cooperation between the Vatican and Fascism *before* the "March on Rome." Pius XI hinted at two years of negotiations concerning Mussolini's suggestions as early as December 23, 1922.[44] And Mussolini stressed later that he had not waited for the Lateran Pacts with his policy on religion. "It starts in 1922, indeed in 1921! Read the speech I gave at the Chamber in June!"[45]

After all, there were a lot of commonalities. Both sides fought against communists, socialists, and liberals. Both exercised authoritarian rule. The Grand Council of Fascism was also a clear imitation of the so-called Sacred College, and the Duce's successor was determined as clearly as that of the pope.[46] Since Mussolini also abolished the freedoms of press and assembly, had crucifixes brought back to the classrooms, reintroduced religious education, protected the Catholic holiday processions, and released churches and monasteries that had been confiscated shortly afterward, they would have come to an agreement even if the atheist had not prayed to Madonna before a gathering of Fascists.[47]

"A product composed of clericalism and militarism"—this is how Fascism was described at an early stage by Francesco Nitti, the previous Italian prime minister,[48] of whom Curzio Malaparte, head of the journal *Stampa* under Mussolini, wrote that the strict, straight, decent Nitti represented Protestant moralism with his modest living habits, but what Italy now needed "to become great is Catholic immoralism."[49]

Before he came to government, Mussolini had had a secret meeting with Cardinal Secretary of State Gasparri at the house of the Catholic senator Count

Santucci in Rome—a meeting that is vividly reminiscent of Hitler's with the papal confidant von Papen, the "alter ego of Monsignor Pacelli,"[50] at the house of the Cologne banker von Schroeder before the Nazis' seizure of power (p. 89). "After this discussion," said Cardinal Gasparri, "I knew that we would get what we wanted through this man if he came to power."[51]

And since Mussolini could hardly achieve his goals without Vatican help— "Five minutes of fire," said Pietro Badoglio, chief of the general staff at the time, "and we'll hear nothing of Fascism ever again"[52]—the Duce collaborated with the curia before the "March on Rome," which he, as we have already noted, traveled to in a sleeper.[53] As early as October 22, 1922, the Vatican called on the Italian hierarchy not to identify with the (anti-Fascist) Catholic Party but to remain neutral, which was undoubtedly tantamount to supporting Mussolini,[54] who assumed office on October 28.

Nearly three months later, on January 20, 1923, the cardinal secretary of state started secret talks with him.[55] The Vatican committed to shutting down the *Partito Popolare*, the Catholic Party, since they could expect a much more radical attack on liberals, democrats, and communists by the Fascists. Mussolini guaranteed their abolition and the preservation of church "rights."

THE FIRST SERVICE

> *"Mussolini . . . did not, after his march into Rome, send some ridiculous delegation to the Vatican or seek to buy the friendship of the powerful High Priest with tactless attentions. He took the right way by first settling the debts in the territories of the higher and highest."*
> —*Bayerischer Kurier*, Munich[56]

> *"He recognized what none of the statesmen of Europe had since Metternich: that the Vatican is primarily a spiritual power, a religious power, which must not be approached with political and material things."*
> —Baron von Cramer-Klett in the *Münchener Zeitung*[57]

The first service the ex-socialist rendered to the Holy See was a financial one. He saved the "Banco di Roma," to which the curia and many of its prelates had entrusted large amounts of money, from bankruptcy by stepping in with approximately 1.5 billion lire at the expense of the Italian state.[58] (The Pacelli family, closely related to Italian and international monopoly capital, still has considerable influence on this bank today. Just as the three nephews of Pius XII, Marcantonio, Carlo, and Giulio Pacelli, who were high dignitaries of the Vatican under his papacy and at the same time presidents and supervisory board members of important banks and monopoly companies,[59] were involved in nearly all the major Italian financial scandals of the post-war period. Their income during their papal uncle's time in office amounted to around fifty million dollars.[60])

After the "Banco di Roma" was bailed out, the songs of praise to Mussolini from the Italian bishops, including the pope, began. Cardinal Vannutelli, the deacon of the so-called Sacred College, went as far as to declare to Mussolini's face that he was "chosen to save the nation and restore its happiness."[61] "When Fascists were attacking and murdering members of the Catholic Party at that time, including priests such as Father Don Minzoni, the pope did not utter a syllable in protest."[62] On the contrary, he crucially accommodated Mussolini at the same time. Because when the latter wanted to abolish parliament by means of electoral reform in early 1923, an act bitterly opposed not only by liberals and democrats but also by the founder and leader of the Catholic Party—Sicilian clergyman Don Sturzo—and 107 Catholic members, the pope ordered Don Sturzo to resign on June 9, 1923, and even pushed for the dissolution of the Catholic Party.[63] Although it did continue to exist for a while, it was affected considerably by the removal of its leader. And directly afterward, the highest representatives of the Catholic hierarchy, especially those who were in the know about the pope's new policies, quite openly briefed for Mussolini; indeed, the archbishop of Florence, Cardinal Mistrangelo, showered him with thanks in a public speech ten days later, embraced him, and kissed him on both cheeks.[64]

Now the Fascist "revolution" in Italy was certainly one of the most bloodless of all; it all happened in accord with the previous ruling powers, the monarchy and, in particular, the church, and those who resisted were allegedly "loosened" quickly with castor oil.[65]

But still, several thousand also died at the hands of Fascist terror. Communists and socialist workers were shot outside the cities at dawn. More highly placed opponents, including previous friends of Mussolini, were dragged out of their beds at night and slaughtered in front of their wives and children.[66] An unknown number were incarcerated or sent to desolate islands, including men such as Rossi, Fancello, Bauer, and Vinciguerra. Many went into exile. The author Lauro de Bossis flew from France to Rome, threw flyers over the city, and disappeared without trace forever. The author Carlo Rosselli, one of the most important Italian emigrants, was assassinated along with his brother thirteen years to the day after a crime committed by Mussolini that nearly cost him his career.

For on June 10, 1924, the young criminal law teacher and socialist leader Giacomo Matteotti, Mussolini's bitterest opponent, was abducted by Fascists and gruesomely murdered. Matteotti, who came from a family of big land-owners, had selflessly helped the countless unusually poor peasants in his province and sacrificed all of his assets for his social work.[67]

The outrage in Italy was extraordinary. As the documents show, the murder, which Catholic journals later wanted to hang on the Freemasons,[68] was ordered personally by Mussolini.[69] His career seemed over. There were calls for the king to depose him. But Pius XI once again took the Duce's side and even ordered all the priests to leave the Catholic Party, which was as good as dissolving it. The pope had thereby as good as eliminated one of the most important obstacles to a Fascist dictatorship; on December 20, 1926, he announced to the world: "Mussolini has been sent to us by Providence."[70]

For at the time, those negotiations whose conclusion would forge even closer links between the Vatican and Fascism were already taking place.

THE LATERAN PACTS

"For a government to undertake to study a reform of the state church laws and heed the warning of the Pope were things that had not been experienced in Italy for more than a century in the church policies of the various successive governments."

—Francesco Pacelli, 1929[71]

"Before God and his Holy Revelations I swear and promise on the occasion of my nomination as bishop to remain loyal to the Italian

state. I swear and promise to respect the King and the government,
which was formed in accordance with the constitutional basis of the
state and have them respect the clergy under my charge. I swear and
promise that I will not take part in any consultations or agreements
that could damage the Italian state or public order and I will not
permit any of the clergy under my charge to take part. I will make
every effort to serve the well-being and the interests of the Italian state
and counter any danger that could threaten it."

— oath of loyalty that the Italian bishops had to swear to the
Fascist state because of the concordat.[72]

Tellingly, the negotiations began in 1926. Because this was the year the pope finally surrendered the Catholic Party, the liberals and socialists, who had just received more than 50 percent of all votes, were banned, their newspapers suppressed, their leaders arrested, and, in general, all legal guarantees were abolished. So it was definitely no coincidence that the negotiations began at the same time as the Fascist dictatorship with what the dictator himself called the totalitarian fascistization of the state.[73] Because after Mussolini had achieved his aims with the help of the pope, the pope should then—remember the words of Gasparri (p. 31)—achieve his with Mussolini's. And Francesco Pacelli asks: "How could Jesus Christ, the son of the living God, not hear the prayers of his representative?"[74]

And indeed, he did hear them. It did, however, take place in secret for a long time. The draft solution to the Roman Question, drawn up at the end of February 1926, was not transferred to the chamber, "a position," as Francesco Pacelli said in 1929, "that is beyond praise."[75]

The consistorial advocate Pacelli, a brother of the later Pope Pius XII, negotiated for the Vatican; his friend, State Councilor Domenico Barone, for the Fascists. After Domenico Barone's death, Mussolini conferred with Pacelli himself and did so, as the Catholic newspaper *Bayerischer Kurier* wrote, "mostly at night."[76]

The significance of the lawyer Pacelli in this context can hardly be overestimated. Barone said to Mussolini on this matter in the summer of 1926: "I think I did my duty when I drew Your Eminence's attention to the possibilities that exist of an agreement about the regulation of the relations between the Italian state and the Holy See. I did this on the basis of a tip I had received from a prelate who has a high position in the Vatican and on the basis of the talks I had with the advocate Francesco Pacelli on his initiative. The latter is, of the legal representatives of the Holy See, the one who enjoys the complete trust of the Holy Father most directly."[77] And indeed, Francesco Pacelli was received no less than 150 times by the pope, according to his own reckoning.[78] And Mussolini also emphasized Pacelli's "very large role" in the pacts[79]; he later received the title of margrave after their ratification, and in 1940, after his brother was appointed pope, Pacelli was elevated to the title of hereditary prince. His sons are the abovementioned three papal nephews with whom Pius XII let the nepotism of the Renaissance hierarchs bloom in its full glory once again.

The agreement signed on February 11, 1929, increased the standing of the Fascists phenomenally on the one hand, as soon later the concordat with Hitler's Germany would the prestige of the Nazis; on the other hand, it provided great benefits to the Roman curia. It relinquished the restoration of the Papal States once and for all—for almost one and a half millennia the allegedly indispensable basis of their independence and freedom that had cost countless wars—and recognized the Kingdom of Italy under the dynasty of the House of Savoy with Rome as its capital, it is true, but in return, the pope received unlimited territorial and personal sovereignty over the Vatican City and, as additional compensation, the monstrous sum of one billion lire in government bonds and 750 million lire in cash.

Mussolini had solved the Roman Question by accommodating the church all the way. The Fascist state had made possible what the protest of four popes to the liberal Italian state could not because it still needed the support of the curia. It was, as former Italian prime minister Francesco Nitti wrote, quite simply *"a capitulation of the Italian government."*[80] "Because what benefits does the Italian state have?" asks Nitti in an enlightening essay. "Nothing but the recognition of the real situation that has existed since 1870. Who would ever have believed that Rome would once again be ruled by the Pope? *Not even anyone in the Vatican would have believed it.* I have been talking with the leading persons from the Church about the Roman question for thirty years. Nobody has ever seriously asked me for Rome or even the tiniest plot of Italian soil. But what has the Vatican now actually received? A territory, albeit a very small one, but recognition as a sovereign state. It has also received a sum whose amount is unique in the history of the Church . . . the capital of a world bank."

Nitti, originally a professor of finance in Naples, then expands: "I am the only person who knows the financial position of the Church outside the Vatican. I have documents regarding their precise income and expenditure. I was Treasury Minister during the war when the income of the different funds was being checked. I was Prime Minister when the capital tax was introduced. I have no right to make documents public that are not intended for the public; but I do have the right to say that *this remuneration*, which is unprecedented in history, is *absolutely inexplicable*."[81]

Apart from the political pact, the Fascists also concluded a concordat with the curia in which they also made unusual concessions. Catholicism became the state religion, church marriage equal to civil marriage, divorce impossible, and religious education compulsory at all elementary and high schools as the "foundation and crowning achievement of public education." Antichurch books, newspapers, and films were banned; criticism and insulting of Catholicism were made punishable by law. Indeed, the state committed itself to coordinating its entire legislation with canon law. Of all the concordats that Pius XI had concluded until that time (with Latvia in 1922, Bavaria in 1924, Poland in 1925, Lithuania in 1927), the concordat with Fascist Italy was the most beneficial to the curia. As Francesco Nitti wrote, it extinguished two centuries of domestic development and abolished the intellectual independence of the country.[82]

The church rejoiced. On February 13, 1929, the pope once again praised Mussolini as the man "who was sent to us by Providence" and shortly after ordered the clergy to say a prayer "for the King and the Duce" (*"Pro Rege et Duce"*) at the end of daily mass.[83]

On February 17, there were particularly solemn services in all the major cities in Italy in the presence of prominent prelates, high-ranking party leaders, and the military. Fascist and church flags were flown next to each other, bands played the national anthem and hymns, and the bishops gave sermons in which they glorified the pope and Mussolini.[84]

On March 9, Pius XI received the diplomatic corps accredited to him and declared himself to be "extremely happy." It was the most pleasant and gratifying audience he had ever given.[85] And on the same day the cardinals wrote to him in a message that Mussolini was governing "on behalf of Divine Providence."[86]

And of course the entire Catholic world was jubilant, especially pious Germany, where a second Fascist state would soon do its deal with the church.

Konrad Adenauer, the meritorious sponsor of the Nazi Party (p. 93), sent the Duce a moving congratulatory telegram.[87] And such a forthright admirer of Hitler as Cardinal Faulhaber (p. 141 ff.) was already welcoming the pact with Mussolini "with trumpets of joy." "What the first Peter experienced," said Faulhaber in a sermon, alluding to the liberation of Peter in the Bible, "has been repeated with his successors throughout world history and today with the 261st Peter. . . . Now the prayer of the Church has been heard. The hour of redemption has arrived. The angel of God has struck at the door of the Vatican prison with a hammer: open up, ye ancient gates! How this answer to our prayers must strengthen *our trust in prayer*! . . . No, it is not a dream. The iron door that leads from the Vatican into the city has opened, and let us say with Peter: *The Lord* has brought this about . . . , *the Lord*, who has rescued the successors of Peter from their imprisonment. It is not the work of Man, it is a *deed of God*."[88] Which was bitingly commented on by the journal *Altkatholisches Volksblatt*: "It is more amusing that Mussolini has suddenly turned into Christ Himself."[89]

If influential German Catholics such as Faulhaber and Adenauer were already enthusing, the Catholic press were in no way going to fall behind. They praised the fraternization of the Vatican and Fascism as "the greatest and most joyous event the world has seen for a century,"[90] as the "hour of God"[91]; Mussolini was the cutter of the Gordian Knot, the "Alexander of this deed,"[92] "the worldly Pontiff of Italy," the "fire of good will," "the genius of politics."[93] Only he, "who lived in the closest relationship . . . with Roman Catholicism was called upon to solve this question which no liberal had dared to tackle so energetically."[94] "The House of Piedmont has been ashamed by the Duce Mussolini,"[95] and so on, and so forth.

The Berlin Catholic *Germania*, Franz von Papen's paper, wrote tellingly: "It is not only the Italian clergy who are now admiring the great statesman that is Mussolini, who has freed Italy from the prevalence of freemasonry and broken the chains of the church, but laypeople and former supporters of the *Popolare* party are now admitting that he has given the flag of Fascism unprecedented success in just a few years, the kind of success the Italian People's Party was only hoping to achieve in decades."[96] This was why Pius XI dropped them. He had made the right calculations. And in 1933 he tried, with the support of Pacelli, von Papen, and Kaas, to do the same in Germany by sacrificing the Centre Party! Both times the pope pushed for the dissolution of the Catholic Party to help Mussolini take up the reins of power there and Hitler here.

THE NAZIS' REACTION TO THE "RECONCILIATION" WITH THE FASCISTS

> *"I see a time when the Pope will one day welcome the Church being protected from the centre parties by National Socialism."*
> —Adolf Hitler, 1929[97]

It is worth reading the articles in which the *Völkischer Beobachter* delivered polemics against "the pious paper of the Bavarian People's Party," the *Bayerischer Kurier*, after the Lateran Pacts had been concluded.[98] Hitler's later organ of government was suddenly able scornfully to play the pope and the cardinal of Munich against the Bavarian Catholic Party, the sister party of the German Centre Party!

Pius XI's avowal, "We have been supported by the other side in the noblest of fashions. And perhaps it also required a man like this one, who did not possess the bias of the liberal school of thought, for whose adherents that order, or rather lack of it, all those laws and regulations were false gods and as such were felt all the more untouchable the uglier and more wrong they were,"[99] must, of course, have been massively encouraging to the Nazis, who fought against all liberal forces as much as the Vatican. And so the *Völkischer Beobachter* triumphantly rejoiced in spaced letters: "This clear denunciation of liberalism and its democratic system by the Pope is more or less the exact opposite of the statements made in this Catholic Munich paper."[100]

Directly after this, the *Völkischer Beobachter* enjoyed a second triumph by quoting from Cardinal Faulhaber's speech exactly what Catholic newspapers had sometimes withheld: "The partner on the other side was a man sent by

Providence, as the Holy Father put it, one of the great men of world history whose state policy is not swamped by a plethora of constitutional paragraphs, whose vigor is not chained up by a hundred-strong parliament"—golden words that meant all the more to the Nazis since Faulhaber himself, completely in keeping with the *Bayerischer Kurier*, which had previously condemned nationalism. Now the *Völkischer Beobachter*, once again in spaced letters, determined *"that the highest authorities of the Catholic Church think differently about Fascist state ideas than the scribes of the Bavarian People's Party*. And, therefore, they also think differently about the idea of a nationalist state in general, because when the Cardinal praises the Roman Event not only as a work of divine Providence and the intelligence of the Curia but also as the result of a state policy whose anti-parliamentarian character, determined by the national dictatorship, is expressly emphasized, this also means a clear condemnation of the parliamentary democratic system, i.e., the very system the paper of the Bavarian People's Party 'continues' to express its sympathy for."[101]

This brief polemic already shows the development of church policy. First the Vatican crossed over to the Fascists, then the episcopate (represented here to a degree by the cardinal from Munich) quickly changed its stance while the paper representing the views of the Catholic people in general still supported the parliamentary system.

Something very similar happened just four years after Hitler seized power. The German bishops, his avowed opponents, suddenly stood together to support him while the Catholic parties, too slow to understand, were dissolved summarily on the orders of the Vatican.

The *Völkischer Beobachter* in 1929 stated: "If the words of the Pope and Cardinal are to have any meaning, then it can only be the solemn recognition of Fascism, the recognition of a nationalist state concept."[102]

Hitler also said immediately that if the Catholic parties persisted in preferring democracy, it would be contradictory to the spirit of the Lateran Pacts. "This means these organs are having the impudence to subject the ideological opinion of the Holy Father to correction for their own party political reasons."[103] Hitler not only said "Everything that makes Italy strong today is good for us. For this reason we most cordially welcome the current government in Italy," but also the following striking sentence: "I see a time when the Pope will one day welcome the Church being protected from the centre parties by National Socialism."[104] The pope, then, really dropped the Catholic parties in 1933 because he was hoping to make progress with the Nazis as he had with the Fascists.

—⁂—

There was certainly still the occasional dispute with Mussolini, above all concerning the education of the youth, which representatives of feeble worldviews were still constantly claiming for themselves. Because the younger and more inexperienced the individuals, the more easily they can be won over; that is why the church violates them before they are even capable of self-consciousness, let alone independent thought, that is, immediately after birth or, by means of "intrauterine" baptism, even in the mother's womb.[105]

It was impossible to avoid conflict entirely between two such totalitarian institutions as the Vatican and Fascism. They started especially at the beginning of the thirties. But Pius XI, who complained bitterly about it in his encyclical "Non Abbiamo Bisogno," would not entertain condemning the party. "We have not only distanced ourselves from formal and detailed judgments, but have actually come to the conviction that compromises are possible. We have therefore favored compromises that others deemed unacceptable. It is not Our intent to condemn the party and the regime. . . . We make every effort only to condemn those things in the manifesto and actions of the party that are in opposition to Catholic teaching and practice."[106]

Incidentally, the curia also worked according to this principle in the *Kirchenkampf* with Hitler. It never attacked his regime as such, only its infringement of *Catholic* interests. Here it was above all Eugenio Pacelli who mediated. In early 1932, Mussolini also asked the cardinal to intervene, and he would not have asked for nothing, especially as he (as Hitler did later) threatened to make sexual scandals public. "Pacelli's procedure," it said in German newspapers at the time, "made an excellent impression and convinced Mussolini that lasting agreement was now to be reckoned with."[107] For this, Cardinal Secretary of State Pacelli even received the Order of Annunciation, which had not been awarded to his predecessor Pietro Gasparri until the Lateran Pacts had been concluded.[108]

In the following years, during which Hitler's terror began in Germany, the Fascists and clergy cooperated as united. The pope and the Duce praised each other, and Italian children said the prayer that had been composed by the church: "Duce, I thank you for making it possible for me to grow up strong and healthy. O dear God, protect the Duce so that Fascist Italy may keep him for a long time."[109] In fact, the books in Italian primary schools at the time consisted of one-third parts of the catechism and prayers and two-thirds glorification of Fascism and the war that was about to be unleashed.

THE ABYSSINIAN WAR—WITH PAPAL APPROVAL AND THE COMPLETE SUPPORT OF THE ITALIAN HIGH CLERGY

> *"In view of the fateful bond between Italy and the Vatican, the Italians deserve the honorary title of 'Assistants and Helpers of God.' We work together with God in this national and Catholic[!] mission of good, especially at this moment at which the flag of Italy carries forward the cross of Jesus on the battlefields of Ethiopia in triumph. . . . Peace and divine protection to the brave army that sheds its blood for the sake of opening the gates of Ethiopia to the Catholic faith and Roman culture!"*
>
> —Cardinal Ildefonso Schuster of Milan[110]

> *"Pacelli [the later pope, KD] has always stood for good relations with Mussolini and Fascist Italy. In particular, he has promoted and supported the national position of the Italian clergy in the Abyssinian conflict."*
>
> —Count du Moulin, head of the Department of Vatican Affairs at the German foreign office, March 3, 1939[111]

The main reason for the invasion of Abyssinia, which had been accepted into the League of Nations in 1923 under the patronage of the Fascist government, was the excessive population of Italy. Italy was a "people without space" and, for this reason, as it said in countless Catholic newspapers, not least in the Vatican Jesuit newspaper *Civiltà Cattolica*, the Abyssinian adventure was morally justified.[112]

For this paper, which has been reproducing the official opinion of the "Society of Jesus" for more than a century and is one of the most important church journals, clarified the moral preconditions of economic colonization just at the time of the Abyssinian War in such a way "that Catholic moral theology definitely does not condemn every violent act of economic expansion." On the contrary, a state that has exhausted its resources and tried all peaceful ways may "attain its right through violent conquest" in cases of extreme need.[113] And the need for space in Italy, incidentally, was by no means so great. In fact, there was a great deal of undeveloped land there, even though it did belong to the great landowners, including the church, with whom the Fascists had to keep in, though. When in 1936 a representative of the "New Statesman" asked the minister of agriculture, Rossoni, one of Mussolini's closest colleagues, why the undeveloped land was not divided up, he received more or less evasive answers and drew his own conclusion: *the Fascist revolution failed to resolve the agricultural question because of the regime's bond to the powers of financial capital and the landowning classes* and, since the Italian dictatorship could not carry out the agricultural reform that was so urgent, a solution in Abyssinia had to be sought. This war was a "replacement" for agricultural reform.[114]

A further reason for war was Italy's need to spread the blessings of the Christian Western culture. "It is Italy's mission," wrote the Viennese Catholic journal *Schönere Zukunft*, for instance, "to carry *Christian culture and Occidental* [Western] *civilization to the center of the black part of the earth* and thereby help the Abyssinian people achieve morality and wealth."[115] And so they started with bombs and grenades and, as even the Catholic *Germania* reported, sprayed gas from the army airplanes of the "assistants and helpers of God," so that, before long, thousands of poisoned Abyssinian women and children were lying in the English military hospitals.[116]

"Furthermore," admits *Schönere Zukunft*, "the credibility of the Italian state leadership, which had earned the eternal thanks of the Catholics [i.e., the Vatican, KD] by means of the conclusion of the Lateran Pacts and the re-Catholicization of the country that resulted from it, demanded obedience to the demands that this state leadership made on the strength of its own responsibility."[117] This was indeed the point of the matter. For *manus manum lavat*. And what Caesar renders unto the pope, let the pope render unto Caesar.

In his book *La preparazione e le prime operazioni*, with an introduction by Mussolini, the Italian marshal de Bono states bluntly that he suggested the war to Mussolini in 1932 and the latter had been secretly preparing it since 1933 without consideration of the stance of Abyssinia, also by bribing the lower lieutenants of Negus, the Emperor of Abyssinia.[118]

On September 4, 1935, the Italian delegate of the League of Nations in Geneva, Baron Aloisi, refused to negotiate with Abyssinia. Italy was now at best prepared only to negotiate *about* Abyssinia.[119] But that was also a lie. Because Mussolini wanted the fight. He wanted to conquer. "No," he declared, "even if Abyssinia were handed to me on a silver plate, I want it by means of a war."[120] The Vatican was completely in agreement with the Fascist raid.

On August 27, when the Italian war preparations were running at full speed, the pope announced—interwoven in many calls for reason and peace—that a defensive war(!) for the purposes of the expansion(!) of a growing population could be just and right.[121] The Viennese Catholic journal *Reichspost* published the following commentary on this from a *"competent source"*: "Rarely has the Holy Father spoken so precisely and referred so clearly to a current situation as on the danger of war between Italy and Abyssinia. This makes it clear how much this question is on the Pope's mind, how much he has thought about it. By clearly[!] declaring a *defensive war* and, beyond this, even a colonial war as long as it is kept within reasonable limits and is for the benefit of a growing population, to be not unjustified, Pope Pius XI consciously wants to grant Italy a natural law within these paraphrased limits—and as part of this incomplete human right a right also to conduct an Abyssinian expansion."[122]

Soon after the pope's speech, four weeks before the invasion, the cardinal's legate once again celebrated Mussolini as "the man of Providence" at the national Eucharist Congress.[123] And since it was the League of Nations that was dealing with the Abyssinia problem and the Duce was being condemned from almost all sides, nineteen archbishops and fifty-seven bishops sent him a telegram, published in the *Osservatore Romano*, that read: "Catholic Italy prays for the increasing size of its beloved fatherland, which is more united than ever under your government."[124]

Two days later, on September 7, the pope once again sought to influence the not very belligerent Italians, the numerous Catholic delegates at the League of Nations debate, and the world in general by declaring that although he prayed for peace, he still wished that "the hopes and rights . . . of the Italian people would be satisfied and recognized in justice and peace."[125]

So the position of the Italian bishops was absolutely clear.

ALMOST THE ENTIRE ITALIAN EPISCOPATE SUPPORTED THE FASCIST RAID

> *"The bishops led by example."*
> —The Catholic *Schönere Zukunft*, Vienna[126]

> *"The responsibility of the Pope and the Vatican will not be affected by this."*
> —*Katholisches Kirchenblatt*, Berlin[127]

The most absurd apologies have always thrived best on church ground. But all attempts to exculpate the pope are in vain because his own words are a testament to the contrary. Quite apart from the fact that the bishops can do only what he wants. Or should they collect gold, bless weapons, and give martial speeches in Italy, of all places, if the pope has banned it? If he really desires peace?

Even Catholic papers flatly admitted that Pius XI had permitted colonial war.[128] "The conscience of the world has condemned Italy's vigorous approach," Gert Buchheit also wrote in 1938. "What did the papacy do? . . . The Church demanded that the bishops hand in their gold crosses and chains. The balance of power in the College of Cardinals was shifted towards the Italian members by means of new nominations. Yes, the Pope even gave the Duce the frozen assets in Germany so that Italy could purchase the necessary raw materials—and church leaders in other Catholic countries acted in the same way as Rome. Thousands of missionaries, priests, chaplains, etc., prayed not only for the victory of the Italian weapons, but they even supported the motherland of the Church directly and indirectly through their propaganda from the pulpit or, as in Canada, by an energetic protest against the Canadian delegate at the League of Nations when it applied for sanctions to be toughened. In one fell swoop unexpected allies appeared all over the world—and why? Because Italy had made its peace with the Church."[129] Exactly. Which is why it could now wage its war on Abyssinia.

When it started on October 3, 1935, the enthusiasm of the high clergy was almost boundless. While fifty-two League of Nations states condemned the Italian actions as an illegal war of aggression, the episcopate in the land of the pope supported the party speakers from their pulpits and called upon the people to donate for victory. The prelates themselves offered up their golden bishop's crosses, necklaces, rings, medals, and watches, and some, such as Cardinal Lavitrano of Palermo, placed their gifts personally in the hands of the Fascist party secretary.[130] The entire Italian press glorified their sacrificial joy.[131]

In addition, one appeal and pastoral letter followed the next. The royal archbishop of Florence declared it the duty of every good citizen and Christian to support the government.[132] The cardinal archbishop of Genoa had his clergy urge the people to donate metal.[133]

The archbishops of Messina and Brindisi protested against the sanctions from England and called upon their diocesans to imitate the ancient Romans' courage to sacrifice.[134]

There was special applause for the archbishop of Monreale, who even instructed churches, monasteries, and places of pilgrimage to place their gold and silver votive offerings on the altar of the fatherland.[135] These and other treasures were used to buy, among other things, the most corrupt characters among the tribal chiefs and church dignitaries of Abyssinia.[136]

The archbishop of Parma exhorted the Catholics to march at the head of the most zealous and loyal citizens, and he did not hesitate to say, "the Fatherland is in a *state of siege*."[137]

The bishop of Cremona banned "pointless discussions on the justification of the war" and concluded by decreeing prayers for the government, the soldiers, and even the Abyssinian people.[138]

The fact that the hypocrisy of these circles is boundless is also shown by the pastoral letter of Bishop Cola from the Umbrian dioceses of Nocerae Gualdo, who praised the Fascist slaughter as "a just and holy matter" and declared that Italy had "a great civilizing mission to fulfill for the semi-feral and mentally and religiously backward people."[139]

The archbishop of Taranto, after reading a mass on a submarine, called the aggression "a holy war, a crusade."[140]

The archbishop of Milan, Cardinal Schuster, who blessed the troops that were marching out in front of Milan Cathedral, compared Mussolini with Caesar, Augustus, and Constantine and taught Italian schoolchildren that the work of the Duce was "God's answer from Heaven."[141]

Many other high clergy blessed cannon and bomber airplanes during the campaign and endorsed the war in the name of the Catholic Church.[142]

According to Professor Salvemini from Harvard University, at least seven Italian cardinals, twenty-nine archbishops, and sixty-one bishops supported the Fascist raid immediately, ignoring the concordat concluded in 1929 that strictly banned the bishops from any political activity.[143]

The Virgin Mary played a special role in the Ethiopian War.[144] And since she has played this role—something that is relatively little known—in many other slaughters in the history of Christianity (which is overrich with war) and may well continue to do so, let us take a brief excursus, which shows how even moving images—"a beautiful invention," as Goethe called the Mother of God[145]—are satanically perverted in Catholicism.

"AVE MARIA"

> "If you fulfill my requests, Russia will be converted and there will be peace. If not, Russia will spread its errors throughout the world and bring about wars and persecution of the Church; many good people will be martyred; the Holy Father will have to suffer greatly; several nations will be destroyed . . ."
>
> —from the prophecy of Our Lady of Fatima[146]

Many things are Janus-faced in the Catholic Church; Mary is one of them. Her beautiful face (as shown, for example, in Stephan Lochner's beautiful *Madonna in Rosenhag*), surrounded by angels making music, and which one knows from flower-decorated statues and from atmospheric May devotions in twilight village chapels, is just one side. The other is revealed by the book published in 1953 *with permission to print from the church*, which is tellingly dedicated to Pius XII, "the greatest champion of peace[!]," "Mary saves the Occident [West]. Fatima and the 'victor in all God's battles[!]' in the fight for Russia." This "ideological preparation for World War III"[147] reveals "the Marian dynamic of history from the beginning of time to our days," the "history of Our Blessed Virgin Mary of Victory," the "strong woman," the "woman who crushed the serpent's head," the "arch-strategist," and the "decisive moments of Christianity."[148]

After a short statement at the beginning of the introduction stating that the American defense budget is bigger than ever, the discussion of the actual theme begins with the Council of Ephesus in the year 431. The writer forgets to mention, among other things, only that massive amounts of money in bribes, which the patriarch of Alexandria gave to all kinds of people—from high state officials and the wife of the Praetorian prefect to influential eunuchs and chambermaids—which exhausted his coffers to such an extent that he had to borrow more than one hundred thousand pieces of gold, despite being rich, and still did not have enough.[149] Nonetheless, "a first victory for Mary,"[150] and a bloodless one to boot, which cannot be said of most of the others with all the will in the world. Charles Martel, a passionate admirer of Mary, slaughtered three hundred thousand Saracens at Tours and Poitiers with the help of the Blessed Mother in 732.[151] Charlemagne, who, despite his numerous wives and other women, always bore Mary's image on his breast, pinned victory upon victory onto his flag with her help, the most significant of which was, of all places, at Lourdes![152] In 1212, King Alfonso of Castile, flying Mary's banner, defeated a superior army of Moors at the time of the Feast of the Scapular of Our Blessed Mother. The result: "The bodies of more than 100,000 Moors."[153] There was a battle under the Queen of Heaven's banner at Belgrade in 1456, on the day of the Transfiguration of Christ and just after the Feast of the Dedication of Saint Mary Major. The result: eighty thousand dead Turks.[154] Then came the naval victory of Lepanto in 1571. With the help of the papal navy and passionate prayers to Mary from Pius V, 167 galleys were conquered, sunk, or burned and eight thousand Turks were killed. The consequence: the Feast of the Rosary was founded.[155] Then "General Tilly and his 32 victories under the sign of Our Dear Lady of Altötting."[156] This "great admirer of the Blessed Mother" was always victorious, "apart from the once," when he was unfairly defeated by the heretic Gustav Adolf and died.[157]

The series of wonderful Marian victories continues throughout the pious history of the West. Most of the decisive slaughters took place on Marian feast days or at least "three days before her solemnity," "two days before the birth of Mary," "on the day after Assumption Day," "on the eve of the Feast of the Rosary,"[158] and so on, until Napoleon and Hitler, the latter of which, as we finally discover here, was basically defeated by only Mary and Pope Pacelli.[159] Because as "a truly Marian Pope," Pius XII, "when the people of the Occident [West] . . . were under deadly threat," called upon "the Catholic world to consecrate the Queen of the Rosary and launch a powerful crusade of prayer" in 1942, and behold, Marian victories came one after the other—just not on the side of the Axis powers Pacelli had intended them for.

And on October 31, 1942, just as the pope was consecrating mankind to the immaculate(!) heart of Mary, came the first breakthrough by the British at El Alamein.[160] The next Marian victory: Stalingrad! On the Feast of Candlemas.[161] And then came the liberation of Tunis and North Africa on Our Lady of Fatima Day. The surrender of Italy on the Birth of the Blessed Virgin Mary. The final defeat of Germany and a ceasefire on the Feast of the Appearance of the Archangel Michael (patron of Germany!) on Mount Gargano.[162] And then the victory over Japan after the first atom bombs were dropped—a Marian victory! The Japanese surrender on Assumption Day![163]

Where this "Marian dynamic of history" might lead was prophesied by Our Lady of Fatima in all clarity in case Russia should not be converted: "*several nations will be destroyed . . .*"[164] Do the insane make history?

But in Abyssinia, Mary was still definitely on the right side. The Italian soldiers sent postcards from the war, on which there was a star-garlanded Madonna with Child looking down upon the tower of an armored car flanked by advancing infantry and surrounded by gun smoke. The title: "Ave Maria."[165]

The cardinal archbishop of Naples, Ascalesi, organized a procession from Pompeii to Naples under the image of the Blessed Mother, with military machines dropping flyers glorifying the Holy Virgin, Fascism and the Ethiopian War at the same time.[166]

Indeed, they even sent images of Madonna to Africa, such as the "Madonnina d'Oltremare," to which miraculous characteristics were ascribed in Italy. It was taken, after being blessed by the military vicar general Rusticoni and the cardinal of Naples, on board the *Conte Grande*, accompanied by prominent Fascists.[167] Cannons and poison gas were sent with other ships, or even on the same one,[168] and the half-naked Abyssinians, who had neither gas masks nor shelters, unsuspectingly fell victim to the bringers of Catholic culture. After the so-called Battle of Amba Aradam, an Italian captain counted more than sixteen thousand butchered "enemies." They lay there, dead or half-dead, where the skin-burning, lung-tearing gas that was sprayed from the air had reached them, and they were all eliminated in the most hygienic possible way—that is, by flamethrowers.[169]

In the middle of the war, a cycle of conferences began in the Sala Borromini, one of the largest and most popular lecture halls in Rome, at which the highest dignitaries of the curia and leading Fascists would speak in turn. Cardinal Secretary of State Eugenio Pacelli, the great admirer of Mary, started with a lecture on "Rome's holy destiny," dwelling on the Lateran Pacts with "words of high recognition," and, in general, presenting "unusually obvious proof of the wish for Vatican-Italian solidarity."[170]

After Abyssinia had been subjugated—90 percent as a consequence of the powerlessness or complete absence of the Abyssinians[171]—and after hordes of monks and nuns followed the Catholic armies, the bishops, cardinals, and vicars apostolic from Milan to Addis Ababa celebrated the "religious significance" of the March on Rome and the "new Roman Empire, which will carry the cross of Christ all over the world under the leadership of this wonderful man, the Duce."[172] And the pope also shared in the "triumphant joy of the truly great and good people about the peace, which," he said on May 12, 1936, "as one may hope and agree, will be an effective contribution, a prelude to true peace in Europe and the whole world."[173]

The next prelude to true peace, which would soon be followed by further preludes, began in Spain in the same summer.

THE VATICAN AND THE SPANISH CIVIL WAR

"The Vatican was determined to use force after it had turned out that the Church policy to obtain power politically had failed in Spain as it had in other countries.

The Vatican established close connections not only with Mussolini, but also with Hitler in Franco's interest. It made an agreement with him in which he would, in return for the help in Spain, commit himself to unleashing a large-scale campaign against Bolshevism throughout the Catholic world."

—Avro Manhattan[1]

THE CAUSES

"The Spanish hierarchy is seriously threatening the interests of the Catholic Church in Spain and all over the world."
—French cardinal Verdier[2]

". . . leaving workers and tenant farmers in their misery and unconcerned about their fate; instead of becoming the people's spiritual leaders we became its social irritation."
—Don Gallegos Rocajul, canon of the Cordoba cathedral[3]

"Money is very Catholic."

— Spanish proverb

The clergy in Spain has had a special power since ancient times. Fighting heresy was already rigorous there in ancient times; persecutions of Jews took place over long periods of time,[4] slavery lasted until the eighteenth century,[5] and the Inquisition thrived as in no other country.

So the wealth of the Spanish Church was no surprise. In the sixteenth century, it is said that it owned half of the national income,[6] and even at the beginning of the nineteenth century, it still owned six million hectares of land—17 percent of the total land area—in addition to gifts from high-born grandees, mostly confiscated "heretics' estates."[7] Although they were then dispossessed of most of their property, they still, after the Third Carlist War (1872–1876) in which they (also) played a leading part, received new gifts and sinecures, which they mostly invested in banks, railways, mines, shipping companies, and textile factories.[8] The Jesuits, the Vatican's elite troops who were said even to have run dance halls and cinemas,[9] controlled a third of the entire Spanish capital in 1912.[10] Then, before the republic decreed the laws on church possessions at the beginning of the thirties, the "Society of Jesus" named a stooge as its representative, who had directorships in forty-four major associations and trading companies—trams, railways, shipping companies, banks, hydroelectric plants, mines, construction companies, and wireless, among others.[11] And at the same time two-thirds of the population were suffering from endemic malnutrition![12]

The high clergy, in cahoots with the aristocracy and big business, sunned themselves in the glory of their business connections and let the people go to rack and ruin. They were completely in agreement that 4 percent of landowners owned more than two-thirds of developed land while the other 96 percent had to make do with the other third.[13] And it did not bother them that of 1,026,412 agriculturalists who were liable to pay tax, 847,548 had daily earnings of less than one peseta,[14] which corresponded to ten cents at the time; indeed, nor did they care that in some parts of the country conditions were the same in 1936 as they were at the time of the Romans.[15]

While most of the major agrarians regarded their properties as "a kind of distant colony"[16] and hardly ever saw them, living instead in expensive coastal resorts or in Paris, their workers toiled almost like serfs from dawn until dusk, and entire areas succumbed to hunger. "People," the *Neue Zürcher Zeitung* wrote in the summer of 1936, "live in caves, straw huts, in ditches covered with branches."[17]

And they fed, as Pastor Fliedner's gazette *Blätter aus Spanien* reported, "on bread and onions, and not infrequently on bark and grass."[18]

They lived, as the Spaniards said themselves, "on miracles."[19] Even the pious Berlin paper *Germania*, which had no qualms in calling "freemasonry the primary cause of today's troubles" when the catastrophe broke out, followed by godlessness and the twelve thousand divorces in Madrid,[20] considered it "impossible to find suitable words to convey the misery of the majority of the Spanish rural population."[21]

But the wages of the factory workers, who mostly had no other clothing than their blue overalls and a pair of canvas shoes, were pitiful and could still be pushed even lower, since the workers had no social legislation to support them.[22]

And the church, of course, had not the slightest interest in educating the people. As in the Papal States, the percentage of illiteracy was one of the highest in Europe, and even today [that is, circa 1960], almost 5.5 million people cannot read or write in Catholic Italy.[23] In Spain more than 60 percent of the population were illiterate in 1870,[24] and as late as 1930 there were still eighty thousand children not receiving school education in Madrid alone,[25] and those who did spent a great deal of their time praying to the rosary.[26] Because, as Bravo Murillo said when he was chosen to approve a school for six hundred workers: "We don't need people who can think but oxen that can work."[27] The church, whose scholars were talking solemnly about the language of the angels at Spain's biggest university in Salamanca at the times of Goethe and discussing whether heaven consisted of wine-like liquid or bell metal, fought bitterly against liberalism in Spain in the nineteenth and twentieth centuries, which had already defeated them in France, Germany, and Italy. In 1910, for example, the teacher and confessor of the young king threatened to have any Spaniard sitting at a table with Protestants excommunicated.[28] The question "What kind of sin do you commit if you vote for a liberal candidate?" was answered by the catechism of 1927: "In general, a deadly sin." And the answer to the question "Is it a sin for Catholics to read a liberal newspaper?" was: "They may read the stock market news."[29] Because, as a well-known saying went at the time, *"El dinero es muy católico"* ("money is very Catholic").

Among the lower clergy, most of whom were paupers themselves, there were many who had a social conscience. As early as 1861 the Jesuit Vicente in

Valencia had founded the *Centros Católicos de Obreros*, a Catholic trade union, but this folded in 1874. And when the Jesuits Ayala and Abreu founded a workers' organization on a Christian basis in Barcelona before the First World War, it was quickly made impossible to operate. Both priests were exiled.[30] A draft law on agrarian reform brought before the *Cortes*, the Spanish parliament, from the Catholic side in the 1930s could not be pushed through either. A lot of lies were disseminated about the failure of these attempts. "The truth is," writes the Jesuit Johannes Reisberger, "that years ago far-sighted priests in Spain had to give up their social foundations, which had been greeted with enthusiasm by the people, *because that is what the responsible bishops wanted.*"[31]

Even a higher Spanish clergyman, Don Gallegos Rocaful, admitted in a Swiss newspaper after the start of the Spanish Civil War: "Founding a workers' association alone was reason enough for the strictest of police measures, arrests and *years* of false imprisonment. The Church remained silent. Any socio-political activity was *strictly* forbidden by the clerics. . . . Above all, there was *never any spiritual care for laborers in the whole of Spain. Any clergyman who engaged with the lower classes in any way was sent to the country immediately* and the rural parishes in Spain are such that they can really only be ministered to with a great spirit of penance. It must almost be taken for granted that under such conditions of a workforce completely neglected in terms of pastoral care there could be no saints and only few who were Christians despite everything—*the vast majority are unbaptized because their parents would never have been able to pay the baptism charge*. But somehow, in this people of mansards and tiny basements, the right idea came about that the clergy were failing to carry out a mission for them and were unfairly evading and neglecting them. And nothing is more terrible once it has broken out than the hate of the child that avenges the right for love it has never received."[32]

Hidden mostly between hypocrisy and lies, even some Catholic papers hinted "that the Catholic parties and leaders of the people in question have missed an opportunity and clearly allowed social divides, untenable in the long term, to widen"[33]; that "the crisis is primarily of economic and social character" and Catholicism bears "the heaviest of shared responsibilities"[34]; "that the Catholic Church in Spain has brought serious blame upon itself."[35] "Every victory of Bolshevism is a memorial stone to our failings."[36] And the Jesuit Marina wrote in the April 1936 edition of the Spanish Jesuits' journal *Razon y Fe*: "The moment has arrived when we can see, if we look in depth, the monstrous moral and religious misery of our people and must beat our breast with the deepest of shock at the guilt we all undoubtedly share in this collapse."[37]

The failure of the Spanish hierarchy was discussed so globally that not even the pope could remain silent. Since self-awareness has always been the weakest side of the Catholic Church, no admission of guilt was to be expected from Pius XI; but hardly was such a tactless defense either. "It has been said in recent days," he said on September 14, 1936, to Spanish refugees, "that religion and the Catholic Church have shown themselves to be too weak and ineffective to counter this devastation and horror. But this is disproved by the words of Manzoni's work: 'One never needs to retreat into examples to justify the Church. It is sufficient to research its basic principles.'"[38] Yes, examples from its practice are mostly fatal for the church. This is why it so prefers to refer to its theories, to which it pays such scant regard in practice. Jesus, with his teaching "Ye shall know them by their fruits!" was once again of a different view than the pope, who could hardly invoke the fruits of Spanish Catholicism.

FROM THE FOUNDATION OF THE REPUBLIC UNTIL THE OUTBREAK OF THE WAR

> *"These people were treated like dogs until they learned to bite."*
> —*Der Bund*, Bern, September 12, 1936

The Spanish Church, on whose instigation thousands of people were still being tortured with medieval methods in prisons and hundreds were shot before the First World War, had been losing influence on the people decade by decade as an ally of the propertied classes. By 1910 more than two-thirds of Spaniards were no longer practicing Catholics. And at the beginning of the thirties, of eighty thousand people in a district of Madrid, only 3.5 percent still attended service, 25 percent of the children were not baptized, and 40 percent died without receiving the sacraments.[39] In several villages in Andalusia, only 1 percent of men went to church, and in some places, the priest was reading his sermon alone.[40]

The people were increasingly turning to the liberal, socialist, and radical socialist parties, and finally the military dictatorship of General Primo de Rivera, approved by King Alfonso XIII, collapsed in 1923. At the municipal elections on April 12, 1931, a massive majority voted the monarchy out and declared the republic.

At the parliamentary elections in June 1931—"undoubtedly the freest and most proper in Spanish history"[41]—the coalition of bourgeois republicans and socialists won 377 seats while the right-wing parties, represented by the high clergy, the grandees, the officers' corps, and the upper classes, won only 60 seats. On December 9, 1931, the new constitution was accepted by the constituent *Cortes*. The role of the head of cabinet was assumed by the former Augustinian pupil from the college of the El Escorial monastery, Manuel Azana y Diaz, an author and an avowed enemy of the church, who remained prime minister in 1933 and also presided over the Spanish Republic during the civil war.

The new government had some enormous difficulties to overcome. It was sabotaged by the extreme Left and the Right, and it could not afford to make itself unpopular at any price if it was to continue to exist in order to achieve anything of significance, which meant that it continuously lost authority, especially on account of its concessions. On top of this, the country was on the verge of bankruptcy as a consequence of the prevailing conditions and the general economic crisis. Despite this, 7,000 schools were built under Minister of Education Marcelino Domingo in the first year of the republic alone and 2,500 in the second year.[42] By the end of 1932, there were already seventy thousand pupils attending high school, up from twenty thousand.[43] A very modern divorce law was passed, as well as new criminal law and laws about civil marriage, forced labor, arbitration committees, minimum wages, and rights for women, and other legal improvements. "Reforms that had required more than half a century elsewhere had been pushed through in two years."[44] The new constitution, which guaranteed freedom of speech and freedom of the press, declared all citizens equal and abolished titles of nobility, envisaged the separation of church and state. It withdrew education and care from the clergy, dissolved the Jesuit order, banned monks and nuns from trading, and secularized marriage. But the government, despite the rigorous anticlerical clauses in the constitution, was by no means antireligious or even intent on turning Spain into an anti-Christian country. It allowed the church to spread its teachings everywhere and guaranteed freedom of faith and conscience.[45] Even the *Völkischer Beobachter* spoke of "Church facilities continuing to thrive all over the country despite all the restrictions" in 1935.[46]

After the abolition of the monarchy, the Spaniards boasted that no people on earth had ever brought about such an elementary change of system as "gallantly" and "humanely."[47] The introduction of the bourgeois regime had hardly cost a drop of blood. And the anticlerical forces also undertook no violence directly after the election victory.

But when the hostilities began, they were started by the church. "The first shot in the fight that was to last until the Civil War," writes Hugh Thomas, whose book about the Spanish Civil War is one of the most objective presentations, "was fired by Cardinal Segura, Archbishop of Toledo and Primate of the Church of Spain, with his biting pastoral letter at the beginning of May."[48] Shortly after this "clearly anti-republic pastoral letter"[49] was published, and after the almost simultaneous release of an interview with the king, who had fled to Paris, there was unrest in Madrid that quickly spread all across the country. The anger of the demonstrators was tellingly directed against the Catholic Church, which was allied so closely with the monarchy and aristocracy, and which replaced them to an extent in Spain when the throne had been abolished. In the center of Madrid, a Jesuit church was burned down in broad morning daylight and "The People's Tribunal over Thieves" was written in chalk on the walls of the ruin.[50] In six major cities alone, more than one hundred churches and monasteries were completely destroyed.[51]

The Spanish episcopate immediately tried to regain its original position. It publicly agitated against the government—"the red Antichrists," as Cardinal Segura put it—in the following years, by calling for "an end to the enemies of the Kingdom of Jesus Christ."[52] It looked to supporters of the old regime, the major landowners and the aristocracy, and the most backward parts of the peasant population, of which, thanks to Catholic education, 80 percent were still illiterate in 1930.[53] As early as 1933, the Spanish bishops (in a pastoral letter) and the pope (in an encyclical dated June 3) demanded a "holy crusade for the complete restoration of Church rights."[54] The episcopate called for a revolt against the government both verbally and in writing. At the same time, Eugenio Pacelli also stepped in. It is little known that the *Confederación Española de Derechas*

Autonomas (CEDA), which arose from *Accion Popular*, a kind of Spanish Center Party financed by rich "right-wingers" but aimed at winning over the people, was founded in 1933 on the instigation of the papal secretary of state.[55]

CEDA, which was sponsored by the Vatican and Fascist groups abroad,[56] the high clergy, and leading members of the army and big landowners in Spain, opposed in particular Marxism and the liberal influence of the Freemasons, who, incidentally, announced in the Madrid edition of the newspaper *ABC* on October 20, 1936, that they were "absolutely on the side of the people's front, the legal government and against fascism,"[57] and the lodges of other countries supported them in this.[58]

The leader of the CEDA, whose foundation was initiated by Pacelli, was José Maria Gil Robles, an admirer of Hitler and militant Catholic raised by Salesians who was credited by the *Völkischer Beobachter* in 1935 with "above all possessing an organ with the strength that enables him to shout down even the most burdensome and loudest Marxist shouters."[59] Heavily influenced by Fascism, Gil Robles—whose supporters called him "*Jefe*" ("Chief") at the elections, in analogy to "Führer" and "Duce"—described his political manifesto, which was predetermined by the encyclicals of the previous popes, as "Christian-Social."[60]

Even before the uprising began, the youth organization of Gil Robles's CEDA joined the *Falange Española*, the Fascist party of Spain, which was founded in 1933. Its founder and leader, José Antonio, the son of the dictator Primo de Rivera, was closely connected to the upper classes and the church and had already informed Franco in a letter dated September 24, 1934, that he would support a military coup to restore "the lost historical destiny of the country."[61] It was that much easier for the Catholic youth organization to go over to the Spanish fascists because it could already be rightly demonstrated as being of "clearly fascist character."[62] As on the other side, every member of the *Falange* had to go to mass, confess and receive communion, at least during the civil war."[63]

The leader of the Catholic youth who had gone over to the *Falange*, Ramón Serrano Suner, a brother-in-law of Franco's and a friend of Mussolini's and Hitler's, later became Spanish interior secretary and secretary of state, and he was decorated with the Grand Cross of the Order of Pius IX by Pope Pacelli at the end of 1942. Two months earlier, Suner had said to a Danish newspaper correspondent that there were already fifteen thousand Spaniards on the eastern front, and their number could be increased to one million, if necessary.[64] At the end of 1933, the right-wing parties, which had opposed all the measures of the government, attained the majority in parliament, whereupon the church- and Fascist-friendly government of Lerroux (-Gil Robles) liquidated the few social and political achievements of the young republic in the "two black years." The execution of the law on agriculture was refrained from and wages were reduced until they were lower than they were at the time of the monarchy.[65] The replacement of faith schools by state ones was postponed, and the Jesuits, whose order remained formally banned, were even allowed to take up their teaching activities again. Countless men and women lost their jobs and livelihoods because of the big landowners, and many of them ended up in prison without trial simply for being members of the left-wing parties.[66] In October and November 1934 alone, thirty thousand people were incarcerated for political reasons, and they were often tortured.[67] The journalist Luis Sirval, who had reported on the tortures, was imprisoned and murdered by three officers.[68] Unemployment reached one million.[69]

The monarchists, who were collaborating with the high clergy, also reappeared under the new rulers. After 1933 the Carlists trained troops in the north. Their military chief, the ambitious colonel Enrique Varela, known as "Uncle Pepe," "rode through the Pyrenean villages, disguised as a priest, like a missionary of the Civil War."[70] And as early as March 31, 1934, the leader of the monarchist group in parliament, Antonio Goicoechea, visited Mussolini accompanied by several Carlists. The partner of the pope, "sent by God," promised the Spanish rebels two hundred machine guns, twenty thousand hand grenades, and other material after the putsch started. They also received 1.5 million pesetas the next day.[71]

The increasing influence of the church's and Fascist powers had not only led to a series of strikes, mass demonstrations, and local uprisings, but it also caused the workers and farmers, the urban middle and lower-middle classes, as well as the socially sensitive intelligentsia, to form the "People's Front" on January 16, 1936. On the other side, the *Falange*, the monarchists, and Carlists, the agriculturalists, the CEDA, and other right-oriented circles came together to form the "National Front."

At the elections on February 16, which ran "perfectly," according to the

London Times,[72] the People's Front won 268 seats; the Right, 140; and the Center, 70. And this was despite the Catholic Church's efforts, moving heaven and earth to throw excommunications at the "Reds" and even ordering nuns living in the strictest enclosure, who had not even been allowed to leave the nunnery when their parents died, to go and vote.[73]

The overwhelming victory was the answer to two years of the clerical rule of violence. While the reactionary groups were dumbstruck, the Left celebrated. "The masses processed along the streets of Madrid for days," Pastor Fliedner's *Blätter aus Spanien* reported, "but just as at the time the republic was declared, it was in a completely orderly fashion. No shot was fired, no blood flowed, and no church was plundered or burned. The joy at the victory had devoured any thoughts of revenge and hate."[74] But this did not last long. The opposition rose up against the "Reds," as Cardinal Goma y Tomas had summarily referred to the republican parties in a pastoral letter from January 24, 1936.[75] There were provocations, attacks, shootings, hundreds of partial and general strikes, and hundreds of assassinations and murders on both sides. There were new wage cuts, rent hikes, and evictions to the extent that even Gil Robles spoke of the "suicidal egotism" of the employers,[76] who were turning tenants and day laborers out onto the streets: "Let the republic feed you!"[77]

Now the workers had started burning down churches again in many places; some of them were also burning down the *Falange* in order to blame the destruction on the anarchists.[78] Quite apart from the fact that many churches served nonchurch purposes or were destroyed by rebel airplanes during the civil war. The Catholic Friedrich Prinz zu Loewenstein wrote after his visit to Spain in autumn 1937, "I have repeatedly been to churches that have been used as fortresses by the Fascists; I have seen numerous churches in Madrid that were not military objects and were easily recognizable as churches—but they were still reduced to ashes by Fascist airplanes. It can also no longer be denied that numerous churches were used as operation bases against the people and the state during the uprising of July 18, 1936."[79]

The actual cause of the uprising was the People's Front election victory in February. But Franco succeeded in the bloody coup only with the help of the Fascists.

HITLER'S GERMANY AND ITALY HELPED THE CATHOLIC REBELS TO WIN

"There would be no Franco today without the support of the two countries."

—Adolf Hitler on September 28, 1940[80]

"He [Franco] would even have accepted help from the headhunters of Borneo to defeat his own people."

—Charles Duff[81]

The "Nationals," who had risen with the blessing of the church on July 17, 1936, had been expecting a quick success—but they were disappointed. Indeed, by the end of July, their situation was desperate. "Franco's rebel army was facing certain defeat."[82] Because although the majority of the army and Spanish Civil Guard had gone over to them, and although they had the better strategy and better-trained troops, the government, with the help of the fanatically fighting people, put down one uprising after another in Madrid, Barcelona, Albacete, and other cities. Even the opponents conceded that the People's Front had the better fighting spirit. "Write it down in your diary," said Mussolini to Ciano, "I prophesy the defeat of Franco. . . . The Reds are fighters, Franco is not."[83] And the German embassy also reported from Madrid on July 25 that the rebels were having a much lower impact than the government troops, the resistance of the people in urban and rural areas was very strong, and even the spiritual, moral, and propagandist balance of power was shifting toward the government. "It has at its disposal a manifesto that grips the masses. Defense of the republic, freedom, progress, defense against political and social reaction. . . . The red militia are filled with a fanatical fighting spirit and fight with extraordinary bravery with the losses that accompany that. However, these can be replaced easily from the masses while the rebels, who only have contingents of their units at their disposal, generally lack such reserves. Unless something unexpected happens, the success of the military rebellion is not foreseeable; prolonged duration of the fighting, however, is."[84]

The unexpected happened on the same night on which this report was wired to Berlin: Hitler decided to support the rebels.[85]

Nazi circles had already agreed to provide reinforcements to the Spanish opposition before the putsch.[86] General Sanjurjo, who was to lead them, went to Berlin directly before the rise to power[87] but suffered a fatal accident while flying back. So Franco sent a delegation that was received by Hitler after a performance of *The Valkyrie* in Bayreuth on July 26, 1936, where he promised immediate help at the insistence of Göring.[88] "Franco had his troops in Africa," Göring reported at the Nuremberg trials, and "couldn't cross because the fleet was in the hands of the Communists. . . . The crucial task was to get the troops in particular to Spain."[89]

At the end of June, twenty German transport airplanes flew to Morocco carrying Franco's "army of redeemers," his Mohammedan Moors and his legionnaires, under the motto "Long live death! Down with intelligence!"[90] to rescue the Catholic West by carrying them across the sea, whereupon they carried out their first heroic deeds in Seville. "The entire workers' district—despite being virtually unarmed—resisted to the end. The massacre in the district of San Julian was especially terrible. The legionnaires drove all the men they found here onto the streets and stabbed them there with knives. The lower part of Triana [the workers' district of Seville] was then leveled by artillery bombardment."[91] More than twenty thousand men arrived in Spain across the first "air bridge" between the end of July and September, which led Hitler to say in 1942: "Franco should erect a monument to [the] Ju 52. The Spanish Revolution has this airplane to thank for its victory."[92]

Soon after the transport airplanes were supplied, the Nazis sent fighter planes, warplanes, and reconnaissance planes, as well as tanks and flak.[93] Four cargo planes now took off for Spain every week, and about every five days, a German ship went there. All in all, 170 German cargo steamers arrived there during the civil war.[94]

Initially, Hitler's supplies arrived mostly via Portugal, a particularly clerical country that was dedicated to "Our Dear Lady of Fatima" by the Portuguese bishops in 1931, whose dictator supported the rebels wherever he could.[95] As early as August 1, Salazar promised to help them "with all means available."[96] He not only let them conspire and set up a weapons-purchasing depot in Lisbon, but he also had Hitler's war material quickly transported on to Spain and also supplied twenty thousand Portuguese to fight on the side of the rebels.[97]

Catholic Ireland quickly sent a brigade for the "Christian Crusade" under O'Duffy. But when they were supposed to fight alongside Franco's Mohammedans, who had been dressed in monks' habits for the sake of appearances, the Irish could no longer be used for the holy war and were hardly deployed in battle.[98]

Hitler had already delivered eighty-seven airplanes, forty-one combat vehicles, twenty-four antitank guns, fifty mortars, two hundred twelve machine guns, ten thousand hand grenades, twenty-two thousand bombs, thirty thousand guns, and seventy-five million cartridges to Franco's Catholic Spain by October 1936.[99] This was augmented at the beginning of November by a closed air corps, the Legion Condor, which initially comprised 4,500 men.[100] Franco, however, continued to make new demands to the end and was also able to push them through, although Berlin was beginning to get fed up with the Spanish Civil War because the most important things had already been tried out: Stukas, Heinkel bombers, Messerschmitt fighters and 88 mm flak. "Hopefully enough Germans will come," said the British ambassador in Spain, who was unswervingly in favor of the rebels, "to put an end to the war."[101]

Along with the Nazis, the Italians also hurried to Franco's help; in 1934, they had also supported the Spanish conspirators with weapons and gold.

On August 5, the "Day of the Madonna of Africa," 2,500 soldiers and their equipment arrived in Spain from Morocco by ship under the protection of Italian fighter planes.[102] On September 2, the first Fascist militia arrived and, at about the same time, Mallorca fell into Italian hands.[103] It was expanded to form a military and naval base for the Fascists, which led to the terrible slaughter of Spanish workers.[104] The Italian newspaper *Roma fascista* wrote on September 2, 1936: "The comedy of non-intervention is at an end. It had never started for us . . . fascism is once again rank and file . . . we are fighting in Spain, which is the liveliest part of our war at the moment and has been going on for more than seventeen years. . . . Today, Franco is the leader of the revolution that has turned out to be the sister of our revolution and we are, as soldiers bearing arms, with him and his legionnaires."[105]

It is said that there were already forty thousand Italian soldiers fighting in Spain in January 1937[106]; later it was 110,000.[107] The Italians supported Franco increasingly during the war and even made offered deals off their own bat.[108]

They knew, after all, as the Italian ambassador said in Paris, that Franco's forces were "not sufficient to conquer the whole of Spain."[109]

Hitler and Mussolini provided material support above all. Their constant supplies prevented, for instance, the collapse of the start of the rebellion in 1937 after three vain attempts to conquer Madrid. And the Fascist supplies made it possible for the rebel air force, which was hardly disturbed by the republicans at all, to drop an average of ten thousand bombs every day for five weeks during the Battle of the Ebro.[110] All in all, the German and Italian civil war aid amounted to more than one billion reichsmarks.[111]

THE "DEAR SON" OF THE POPE— A DEVOTED FRIEND OF HITLER

As the Italians shouted "Du-ce, Du-ce!" the nationalist Spaniards, after the rebel had been declared head of state in Burgos on October, called "Fran-co, Fran-co!" And instead of the Nazi slogan "One People, One Reich, One Leader," posters in Nationalist Spain were proclaiming: "One State—One Country— One Chief!"[112]

Just few days after Franco's seizure of power, a German embassy counselor conveyed Hitler's congratulations. The general, who held a reception for this occasion in Salamanca, where he resided in the archbishop's palace,[113] thanked the German dictator for his "valuable material and moral help" and expressed the hope that soon his own flag would be waving next to the banner of the culture that the Führer was already pushing forward.[114]

On November 18, Hitler and Mussolini broke off relations to the Spanish Republic and recognized Franco's "government," which promised close economic and political cooperation in a secret agreement with Mussolini on December 1, 1936, and Hitler in March 1937.[115] The rapid rapprochement of Germany and Italy that was a consequence of their mutual intervention in Spain, the "bulwarks of culture and Christianity," as Franco called them at the time,[116] was certainly one of the most momentous international events of the Spanish Civil War. In October the Italian secretary of state had a meeting in Berlin, and directly after, in a speech in Milan's cathedral square, Mussolini coined the phrase "Berlin-Rome Axis."[117] In later years, too, just to preempt it briefly here, Franco made no bones about his sympathy for the Fascists, and especially not for Hitler. When he was awarded the Golden Grand Cross of the German Eagle in 1940, the commander in chief of Spanish Catholicism was "proud to have had the Legion Condor, the glorious herald of your victories of today, under my command in the first battles of this great conflict."[118]

Franco wrote to Hitler on February 26, 1941: "Like you, I am also of the conviction that a historical mission makes us inseparable, you, the Duce and me"; he tactfully did not mention the pope but, in conclusion, promised the "dear Führer" once again "to put myself on your side with full determination, bound to a mutual destiny whose avoidance would be a surrender of oneself and a betrayal of the good cause that I lead and represent in Spain. There is no need for me to affirm my belief in the victory of your good cause, which I will always loyally adhere to. Warmest greetings, Your sincere friend."[119]

When Hitler invaded the Soviet Union, the Spanish clergy propagated real crusaders' enthusiasm, and Franco placed submarine and air bases, monitoring services, and war material at Germany's disposal.[120] He sent the "Blue Division," which consisted of forty-seven thousand soldiers, to Russia, after the Spanish bishops and priests had blessed them for their "holy task" and handed over the medals dedicated to the "heroic Catholic crusades against the Reds,"[121] but he was farsighted enough not to declare war. Yes, the "ungrateful coward," as Ribbentrop said, "who has us to thank for everything and now doesn't want to join in any more"[122] (while Hitler was now saying that such a man would not even have become county leader under him), had already ordered everyone back to Spain in 1943, when he saw that the war was lost for the Fascists, and suddenly sought contact with the leading circles of Britain and America—and by doing so, he behaved exactly the same as the Vatican (p. 179).

But then, in 1945, when the news of Hitler's "heroic death" reached Madrid, the Spanish Fascists lined up to sign their names in the book of condolences of the German Embassy.[123] And Franco's Catholic Spain sent its official condolences for the death of the Führer and the collapse of the regime[124] that it largely had to thank for its existence. But the intervention of the Soviets in Spain remained unsuccessful.

RUSSIA'S HELP FOR THE REPUBLIC

The Western democracies had decided on a policy of nonintervention in Spain while at an international conference and imposed a boycott on weapon supplies to the country that the Fascists took no notice of. But the democracies respected the agreement and even communist Russia had not supplied the Spanish Republic with any weapons at all in the first three months of the war. But at the beginning of October, the Soviet government declared it would annul its duties if the violations of the pact by other members were not prevented. "If there is an agreement we wish it to be adhered to. If the Committee . . . can guarantee that . . . . , then everything is fine. If the Committee cannot, then it should say so."[125]

The Legion Condor had been committing its heroic deeds for months in Spain before the first Soviet planes appeared. This is confirmed by the legionnaires themselves: "Almost no ground defense and no enemies in the air. We dropped our well-aimed bombs from a height of 800 meters and practice makes perfect."[126] (And when the first "sub-human Asians" then appeared, they were, of course, destroyed by the blond master race: "Let's give them a hammering, we thought, and dropped drum after drum of phosphorus and flares. . . . Two comrades have already been wounded, but they keep on firing. Let the drums roll! Right in their faces, again and again!"[127])

Help from the Soviet Union for the Spanish government—the first Russian ships with weapons arrived mid-October[128]—came at the last minute, at a time when the capital was already in danger. And by the end of November, the Russians, according to Spanish National sources, had delivered one hundred thousand guns, three billion cartridges, fifteen hundred machine guns, six thousand grenade launchers, three hundred bombers, forty-five thousand bombs, and seventy-five antiaircraft guns.[129]

The intervention of the Fascist states and the Soviet Union prolonged the war even more. But without the constant supplies from Germany and Italy, Russia would hardly have intervened. The Spanish people would have dealt with the rebels relatively quickly. "We are not demanding to be helped," said the republican head of government, "we are demanding that we not be punished for a rebellion having been stirred up against us."[130]

CONCERNING THE "CHRISTIAN" CRUSADE AGAINST THE "GODLESS REDS"

"The 'Great National Movement' was described by its leaders and the Church from the very first day as the 'Christian crusade against Bolshevism.' This 'Christian crusade' had the full support of the heathen Hitler and the atheist Mussolini. Some 150,000 hired Mohammedan Moroccans and a foreign legion of extremely questionable morals rounded off the holiness of this crusade."

—Charles Duff[131]

"As soon as it became clear that Franco could not win the Civil War immediately, the Vatican embarked on a vicious anti-Bolshevist campaign on the direct orders of the Pope. By doing this he supported Hitler's domestic and foreign policy plans; Hitler needed the specter of Bolshevism to push through his policies."

—Avro Manhattan[132]

The entire Fascist and cleric propaganda suggested to the whole world that the battle in Spain was between angels and demons, crusaders and infidels, Christians and "Reds." Cardinal Primate Goma y Tomás, who praised the raid on Abyssinia (which was carried out with the help of Madonnas and poison gas), as a "work of civilization,"[133] now informed the global public: "So on one side there are the defenders of those ideals born of the old tradition and history of Spain; on the other side there is a rag-tag horde. *Christ and the Antichrist are fighting on our land.*"[134] And the Catholic newspapers, which "only saw two large groups left in Spain, the Bolshevists, who wanted neither God nor ruler, and the right-wing parties, who are fighting under the battle cry: 'God, Fatherland, Authority,'"[135] spoke, just like the Fascists, only of the "Bolshevist regime" in Spain, of "Soviet Spain," the "Red rulers in Madrid," the "Red scourge," the "Red Spanish death regime,"[136] and so on.

This grotesque falsification of history, which was propagated by the Vatican press as well as by the Berlin Ministry of Propaganda and Mussolini, confused millions of brains—as other popular monochrome descriptions do today. And the unscrupulous agitation of the Catholic hierarchy certainly influenced the decision of nearly all the European countries and the United States not to support the Spanish government.

In reality, communism played no dominant role in Spain, least of all before the civil war, when Largo Caballero and his socialists bourgeoned powerfully. The manifesto of the People's Front was anything but Marxist: of the 473 members of parliament, there were only fifteen communists,[137] who were furthermore split into two small rival groups who opposed each other vigorously: they were the Moscow-influenced, Stalinist *Partido Comunista Española* and the more Trotsky-influenced *Partido Obrero de Unificación Marxista*. The republican cabinet had only one communist minister,[138] and the Communist Party of Spain had only ten thousand members.[139]

Even when their membership increased rapidly to five hundred thousand during the civil war,[140] the Spanish Republic, with a population of twenty-five million, was still not a communist state. "This government is neither communist," the minister of justice at the time, Manuel Irujo (who was, by the way, a Basque and a very good Catholic[141]), said to his Catholic interviewer Prince Friedrich of Loewenstein, "nor does this state have a communist structure. And as for me: you know I am no 'Marxist' or 'Red.' But I am a Christian, and I therefore believe that there can be no Christianity without social justice."[142]

And there were a lot of Catholics in Spain who believed that, too, and kept the faith with all the Basque Catholics. What led them to do this is shown in the letter written by a senior member of the clergy, Don Gallegos Rocaful, canon of Cordoba cathedral, to the Catholic *Schweizerische Republikanische Blätter*:

> There are also priests who, without having ceased to be such in the eyes of God and the Church, are still, *as constrained by their conscience, not on the side of the military revolution.* Please consider this statement to be an introduction to you. And at the same time observe what brought me to this position, in contrast, I know, to many of my colleagues and professional brethren. I have never been political. I have only ever been a pastor. As I love my profession, so I love the one in which it was founded, Jesus Christ, the savior of the world of which my poor Spain is also a part. When the violence broke out, there was only *one* question for me that would determine my continued position: *Who was the first* to use weapons, who violently attacked the legal order, even if was not an ideal one for us, who shed the first blood, thereby igniting this

terrible fire? It was *not the government*, who, even though it was not composed as we Catholics would have liked, did not create any difficulties for us: it was the military revolutionaries. . . . The government was planning the *distribution of large estate*, modest factory legislation with inspectorates, something you have had for a long time in Switzerland without having a reputation for being communists. *This* was the cause of the revolution. The will to help the poor and oppressed and found an independent peasantry in Spain *has always been choked in blood*. But it seems to me to be the will of Christ, who was always more on the side of the poor than the rich. I am a priest. So I am also on the side of the poor. And you must know that the entire Spanish Civil War is just a war between the poor and the rich, between the people and their feudal over-lords. There is no political meaning behind it, just social conflict.[143]

Just as the Spanish Republic was not communist, nor was it antireligious. "We found no signs of organized godless propaganda as it was being practiced in Soviet Russia" was the unanimous verdict of a delegation of English clergy who visited Barcelona, Valencia, and Madrid in January 1937 to form their own opinion of the position of the governing parties regarding religion. "Despite researching carefully we could find nothing regarding any satirical songs about God, Christ, the Holy Virgin and the Saints as could be observed in the godless movements of other countries. On the contrary, members of our delegation found Bibles being openly sold in street bookshops."[144]

But the Spanish Republic was not only not antireligious, it was also not anti-Christian either. The best proof of this is the complete religious freedom of the Protestant Church in the republican part throughout the entire war. At Easter 1937, for instance, the correspondent of the Swiss newspaper *Basler National-Zeitung* reported solemn services in all the Protestant churches in Madrid, which were packed to the rafters; the Bible society was distributing the New Testament as usual, and the people were expressing all their sympathy to it.[145] Furthermore, the Protestant priests stressed that "none of the Protestant churches had to cancel one single Sunday service for the entire duration of the Civil War and that there was finally *absolute religious freedom* for the Protestant Church, while the Spanish Monarchy and the Primo de Rivera dictatorship had always oppressed the Protestant religion."[146]

But practice of the Catholic religion was also allowed. No one prevented

Catholic services as long as there were no political sermons.[147] The Catholic prince of Loewenstein wrote in his report on his fact-finding mission in 1937 that two thousand masses were being read every day in Barcelona alone, in private houses, true, but with the express knowledge of the government.[148]

And the Catholic member of the French parliament, Raymond Laurent, who was definitely more to the right than to the left, previously the president of the city council of Paris who examined in depth the religious situation of the Catholics in republican Spain in the winter of 1938/39, talked of "unrestricted tolerance."[149]

The Basque Army, who were fighting on the government's side, were accompanied by one hundred Catholic clergy who had to celebrate the mass, administer the sacraments, and "educate the souls of the recruits in the Christian tradition."[150]

Finally, there were at least two bishops who refused to sign the pastoral letter from the Spanish episcopate of 1937 in which Catholics of all countries called for support of the rebels, two bishops who condemned the Franco regime to the end and fought courageously for the people and their legally elected government: the archbishop of Tarragona, Cardinal Vidal y Barraquer, and the bishop of Vitoria, Mateo Mugica. "All over the world, the Catholic press ignored the demands and accusations of these two bishops almost without exception. The truth was suppressed."[151]

So while there was neither a communist, antireligious, anti-Christian, nor even a basically anti-Catholic state in Spain, while the Anglican deacon of Canterbury Cathedral declared publicly, after his fact-finding trip, that the republican front for freedom, justice, and social order was closer to the intentions of Christ than the previous church system,[152] Catholic clergy all over the world, in beautiful association with the German and Italian Fascists, were defaming the Spanish Republic as communist and propagating the uprising and the three-year bloodbath as a *cruzada* against the "godless."

As the *Falange* general Yagüe spoke of a crusade on the first day of the putsch in Morocco,[153] and as Franco announced that the war against the republic (which he had just violated his oath to) was a holy war, a crusade of the Christian faith, and he himself was a fighter of Christ,[154] now the Spanish bishops, who had already demanded a "crusade" for the complete restoration of their "rights" in 1933 (p. 57), were now writing: "This war is not a civil war but a *crusade* against the global red revolution,"[155] "a *crusade* . . . insofar as it defends everything that is essential for religion."[156] "It is pitiful that it still has to be explained to the civilized world that this is no military *pronunciamento, no civil war*, no class struggle. Wise princes of the Church have now undertaken this educational work. It is clear and certain that this is . . . a purely defensive war[!] on our part" or, as Archbishop of Santiago de Compostela also revealed in his long pastoral letter, "*defense against a band of thieves*."[157] And Bishop Enrique Pla y Deniel of Salamanca immediately justified this "purely defensive war" morally—"with comprehensive erudition," as the organ of the German Jesuits guarantees.[158]

But in the rebel army's regulations, it stated: "Remember that you are called upon to reconquer for Christ the nation of his chosen that was wrested from him by others. If you dedicate yourself completely to this noble task and sacrifice your life for it, then praise the divine mercy that shines over the conscience with the sublime light of the *martyr's halo*. Your heroic courage, your readiness to be a martyr, leads to the ideal: For *God* and *Fatherland*!" And this is also exactly what Hitler's soldiers were fighting for; on whose stomachs the belt buckle proclaimed: "With God." "In your heart," it said in one of Franco's rebels' regulations, "you carry the fire of an apostle and your hands must be the instruments of the *Divine Omnipotence*."[159]

Antonio Ruiz Villaplana, a respected judge who was definitely not a communist, who performed his official duties in Burgos, the rebels' headquarters, during the civil war, reports in his book *This is Franco* that the Catholic Church was not only involved in all the military rallies but also actually conducted them, that they blessed the weapons and organized the Te Deums—which they also did in Germany during Hitler's war. "In this fight that has been unleashed," writes Villaplana, "the clergy have never forgotten their revenge. . . . The voice of the one who would be the shepherd and leader of the people calls out martial appeals like a trumpet of war: 'We cannot live together with the unholy Socialists. . . . War, blood and fire! There must be no ceasefire or pardon until victory for religion and order has been secured.'"[160]

According to the testimony of the pious Catholic minister of justice, Manuel Irujo, forty-eight of the Spanish bishops persisted with their "pro-fascist position."[161] And they were supported by the episcopates of the entire world.

In Austria, Cardinal Innitzer of Vienna and Prince-Archbishop Waitz of Salzburg, who later claimed, when Hitler was occupying their country, that the thousand-year longing of the Austrian people was finally being fulfilled (p. 131), already threw their lot in with the Fascists shortly after the uprising had started. Because, as Innitzer wrote, "godlessness raises its head against everything that is called religion, closeness to God."[162] Or, as Waitz knew: "Hell is currently on the loose. It seeks to carry its ruin to all peoples from its central point in Moscow."[163] Which is why both prelates ordered their clergy "to point out in appropriate fashion the great dangers from Bolshevism that also threaten the other countries of Europe."[164]

The dangers threatened by Hitler, which would eventually cost fifty-five million lives, were not affirmed by the bishops at all. On the contrary! They helped this criminal "with all means," as they acknowledged themselves.

On August 30, 1936, the German episcopate published a pastoral letter on the direct orders of Cardinal Secretary of State Pacelli, which states, with regard to Spain, "It is clear what task falls to our people and Fatherland. May our Führer, with God's help, bring about this monstrously difficult act of defense[!] in unshakable determination and the most loyal participation of all national comrades."[165] And on January 3, 1937, the German bishops, once again in regard to Spain, set to work on their faithful again: "Dear diocesans! The Führer and Reich Chancellor Adolf Hitler has seen the advance of Bolshevism from afar and set his thoughts and concerns on defending our German people and the Occident [West] from this monstrous danger. The German bishops consider it their duty to support the ruler of the German Reich in this defensive struggle *with all the means* at their disposal from the holy place."[166]

The Catholic hierarchy similarly made the most powerful propaganda for the Spanish Fascists all over the world, and even scored clear successes in Protestant countries, such as Great Britain and the United States.

In addition to this, there were even global relief efforts for Franco's poor Spaniards! In South America, where [in 1965] 33 percent of all Catholics live but 35–40 percent of the population are illiterate and 30 percent homeless,[167] which means that millions, to quote a Catholic relative of Adenauer, have "too little to live and too much to die,"[168] there were also "moving scenes" after an appeal from the archbishop of Buenos Aires:[169] "little old mothers donated their wedding rings, poor girls gave their last piece of jewelry inherited from their mothers. The entire Catholic people and *particularly the poorest classes* competed in this work of love."[170]

And it was all channeled to Spain, with Hitler's and Mussolini's material supplies, in order to continue the oppression of other poor people.

REPUBLICAN CRIMES AND THE CHURCH'S MARTYR LEGEND

> *"We need martyrs, otherwise we must be concerned about the Final Victory."*
>
> —*Deutscher Weg*, October 20, 1935

The Church's propaganda games at the time also included boasting with "martyrs."

Indeed, they lost significantly more priests in those three years than during the entire two hundred years of ancient Christian persecution, even though they have always grotesquely exaggerated the latter.[171] Although it was by no means 16,750 priests who died in Spain either, as the papal *Osservatore Romano* soon claimed,[172] a number that was even embarrassing to the Spanish cardinal primate, "because," as he said, "there were only 15,000 priests in all the areas under the Reds' control after the outbreak of the revolution altogether."[173] But nearly eight thousand Spanish clerics, including twelve bishops and 283 nuns, met their deaths at the hands of the republicans,[174] a monstrous figure. In addition, there were some extraordinary atrocities. In some cases, not only were nuns raped before their execution—as previously young "witches" sentenced to death by fire had been by clergy,[175] but priests were also burned alive,[176] as millions of "heretics" had been, admittedly, by the Inquisition; this does not excuse the terrible crimes of the republicans, but it was intended as a reminder that bloodlust and mass sadism had arrived in Spain long before then. A chairman of the Cheka was killed with a medieval choking collar, and the mother of two Jesuits was killed by the shaft of a crucifix being rammed down her gullet.[177]

Such acts of inhumanity, which spread, are much more deplorable than the burning down of churches and monasteries. In Madrid alone, fifty churches went up in flames on the night of July 19/20, 1936, that is, at the beginning of the putsch.[178] And after the first year of the civil war, a circular by the Spanish bishops numbered the churches and chapels destroyed at more than twenty thousand,[179] which is not, of course, all due to the republicans; it was possible only because, as a clergyman who fled to France said, "we had destroyed the church ourselves before."[180]

But nearly all the illegal killings carried out by the republicans happened at the beginning of the civil war,[181] when the position of the government, which in most places suddenly no longer had any police or troops at their disposal and even had prison inmates fighting for them, was still weak and the hate of the masses, which had been building up for a long time, spontaneously discharged. "As regrettable as it may be," said the then Catholic minster of justice of the republic, "it was not the fault of the State and at such times it is not possible to ask about the past of the people who are prepared to give their lives while the chosen representatives of calm and order become rebels. Of course there were many evil elements among the people we had to use, and a lot happened, which is deeply regrettable; but today there is only one authority in this country: the government, and only one power of decision about right and wrong, which lies with the courts and the Republic's Minister of Justice. Only yesterday, the political court of justice at Valencia, which consists purely of non-Catholics, acquitted nine priests who had been charged with fascist activities. They were innocent, so they were released . . . it will not be long before they are all free, I promise you. I take this so seriously on a personal level that I would rather resign than leave innocent people in prison."[182]

But no Catholic clergy were persecuted because of their faith—and this is what it is about here—none killed for religious reasons, as Roman propagandists all over the world would soon successfully suggest. "They are religious fighters," wrote the Jesuit Muckermann, "the like of which has only ever been seen in the Church. We see the martyrs' palm stretching up towards heaven on the field of honor where they have fallen."[183]

But Pope Pius XI did not even shy away from the claim, made in his global circular on March 19, 1937,[184] that the "communist rage of destruction" had "always in particular [tracked down] those" bishops, priests, men of the orders, and nuns "who had especially eagerly looked after the poor and the workers,"[185] which contradicts all the known facts from Spain. Why should its wretched peasants and workers have "always in particular" taken revenge on those who helped them?

"Never and nowhere in the whole world," said, by way of contrast, a higher Spanish clergyman during the civil war, "has a priest been shot by those to whom he revealed his love and sacrifice, never and nowhere in the whole world has a church been destroyed by a people that heard its human rights, as set out in the Gospels, defended from its pulpits. Where priests are at work who know that it is the sick man, not the healthy one, who needs a doctor, who leave ninety-nine sheep to look for the lost one and carry it back to the herd on their shoulders, *there are no priest murders, no storming of the monasteries, no church fires* . . . I have always loved the people and have therefore never been afraid. *Former Marxists minister to me today*, people who have never sought out a priest in their lives open their souls to me. *It is not the spirit of the religion that is being persecuted, but those who have not fulfilled it.*"[186]

According to José Bergamín, one of the best-known representatives of Spanish Catholic literature at the time, not one single priest or monk was murdered *before* the July uprising in Spain. Only when the clerics, as Bergamin describes, sided with the military and against the government on the orders of their superiors and sometimes even fought side by side with the Fascists, were they killed. But they died as Fascists or warmongers. "Not one of them," the Spanish Catholic stresses, "not one single one, suffered death for Christ. *They died for Franco.* You can make them nationalist heroes if you will, political victims, but not martyrs."[187]

But it was martyrs that Rome needed, even more urgently than its daily bread. And since in Spain, more than in any other country, Catholicism had lived on only in external attestations of devotion, in the pomp and splendor of ceremonies, as the result of centuries-old confessional unity and official protection, the Vatican in particular was delighted at the literally bloody interest that was suddenly being taken in the church. On September 14, 1936, Pius XI said in his summer residence at Castel Gandolfo: "On the one hand we must cry with most heartfelt, bitter sympathy. On the other, we must *rejoice* for the sake of the pride and the *sweet joy* that lifts Us. . . . This is a powerful show[!]

of Christian and priestly virtue, of heroic deeds and martyrdom. . . . How your expiation comes *just at the right time* for the sake of Providence, viewed by God as the expiation of faith, honor and glory."[188] So the eight thousand murdered Catholic clergy came "just at the right time" for the Holy Father! Because Rome always thinks in terms of the wider context. And ten thousand, one hundred thousand, or even more bodies, even if they are those of their own, may not only be irrelevant but even desirable.

("Religious" life always blooms in particular where a lot of people die, which is why the church is never uninterested in catastrophes.[189] The Spanish cardinal primate rejoiced: "On all fronts the national troops celebrated the sacrifice of the mass and thousands of young soldiers received confession and communion and when there was a ceasefire they prayed to the rosary together at camp. They stuck pious insignias on uniforms. Their enthusiasm for their faith," and so on.[190] Which is fatally reminiscent of the Jesuits' rejoicing during the First World War: "The whole country became a House of God. The sacraments were given at stations, in barracks, in taverns, under trees, in the bushes . . ." "Religious life is blooming amongst our troops in the most beautiful way." "The captains themselves were asking for camp services. . . . The rosary is being diligently prayed to. . . . A clergyman was veritably begging for rosaries as charitable gifts; he had already ordered so many but it had all been just a drop in the ocean" and so on, and so forth.[191])

And while they were screaming at the whole world about the republicans' crimes, hardly anyone mentioned their own.

THE CRIMES OF THE FRANCO REBELS

"How telling, and at the same time painful, for us Catholics, who have to watch the atrocities of this war of brothers with horror: the cause of Christianity is once again being fought for by the generals with machine guns; Christian brotherly love is demonstrated by mass executions; 'Love thy enemy' is being rewritten as 'They must be stuck like pigs!'"

—The Catholic *Entscheidung*, Lucerne[192]

The Marxists are rapacious animals, but we are Caballeros. Señor
Companys deserves to be stuck like a pig."
—Franco's General Gonzales Queipo de Llano[193]

The bishops and priests were being "murdered and martyred," wrote the Spanish archbishop of Santiago, de Compostela, "in larger numbers and with greater bloodthirst than Nero's henchmen."[194] But their own slaughterers were the "Caballeros"! "Christ's warriors"! "Instruments of the Divine Omnipotence"! And other such impudent phrases. Phrases that may be repeated . . . And Franco had risen with the most pious of intentions. For when he said, just after his coup, to a correspondent of the *News Chronicle*, that he would "liberate Spain from Marxism at any price," and the correspondent replied, "That would mean you having to have half of Spain shot," the general stressed: "I repeat—at any price!"[195]

So his "army of redeemers" murdered its way through the war with rather consistent intensity, even though this happened before drumhead courts martial later and courts martial at the end. But initially it carried out its liquidations without any trial. At this point, all possible opponents of the regime were shot, prisoners always randomly, which is why the new Italian ambassador Cantalupo started a mission with the request to stop the slaughter of prisoners.[196] Republican soldiers were often murdered in front of their wives and children, who were sometimes raped too[197]—"while victory celebrations and thanksgiving services painted the external picture."[198]

The rebels killed all the civil governors, all the generals and regimental commanders true to the government, and also the trade union functionaries that were left-wing and oriented to the People's Front, as well as the leading Freemasons on principle.[199] And where the advance was intended to be rapid, anyone at all who seemed politically suspect was eliminated.[200] There were even murders on the steps of the high altars of Badajoz,[201] and these were committed, as the Austrian Catholic paper *Österreichische Arbeiterzeitung* wrote, "in the name of Jesus Christ and the Holy Blessed Mother."[202] As in the Abyssinian War (p. 48 f.), Mary also played a major role with Franco's mercenaries. The defenders of Alcazar were Marian soldiers, including their general, Moscardo or, as Bishop Diaz y Gomara extolled, "Knights of the most blessed Virgin, the victor over the evil enemy!"[203] The Christian crusaders not only carried Madonnas in their processions[204] but also gave the Madonna of Pilar in Saragossa, where they set fire to the Protestant church,[205] the title of Generalissimus of the Spanish Army.[206] And at the same time, their priests cheered Hitler from their pulpits.[207]

But while they were purporting to fight for Christianity, they were not only setting Protestant churches on fire but also butchering Spanish Protestants as well.

In Granada, the two Protestant priests, Salvador Iniguez and Jose Garcia Fernandez, and the latter's wife, who did not want to leave her husband, were executed by Moroccans. In San Fernando, the priest Miguel Blanco was shot in the presence of his mother, who had been chained up, "to set the heretics an example."[208] The Protestant priest of Puerto-Real suffered the same fate.[209] Other Protestant clergy and teachers disappeared and were presumably murdered as well. The reformed community of Predajon, Provinz Logrono, thirty members strong, was massacred apart from six refugees. In Santa Amilia, the wife of a Protestant threshing machine driver had petroleum poured over her before she was set alight and beaten to death with an ax because she did not die from her burns.[210] This list could be continued.[211]

But it was not only Protestants who were killed by these "instruments of divine omnipotence": Catholic clergy who remained true to the republican government also died at their hands. There was even a plan that Basque priests should all be killed outright, all four hundred of them.[212]

What is proven beyond a doubt is that Franco had fourteen Catholic clerics who had stayed loyal to their communities shot after a summary trial in which they were not even allowed to defend themselves. They were buried as "common criminals."[213] And many hundreds of priests who also represented the cause of the people were persecuted by Franco.[214]

But the church propaganda made no mention of these clergy. Anyone who helped the government was a "red mob" and "a tool of Moscow,"[215] he belonged to that "handful of aberrated or Freemason-ridden Spanish Clerics," as a well-known German Catholic newspaper wrote, "who were not ashamed, as 'spokesmen for the Spanish Catholics,' to put their name to incendiary Marxist appeals."[216] It is also proven that Franco himself gave the order not to be presented with pleas for reprieve until executions had already been carried out.[217]

General Queipo de Llano's head of propaganda, Antonio Bahamonde, who would eventually flee the country in disgust, estimated the number of executions by the beginning of 1938 at 150,000 in Queipo de Llano's region alone; this, however, is exaggerated.[218]

Tellingly, the Franco government kept the civil war documents under lock and key[219]—as the curia does with the Inquisition archives. (And when the seventy-year-old French author Edmond Paris asked to view more recent documents at the Vatican, he was politely asked to come by again in one hundred years.[220])

There is as little doubt about the pope's role in the Spanish Civil War as there is about General Franco's.

FRANCO AND THE VATICAN

"I am the instrument of Providence."

—Francisco Franco[221]

The intense cooperation between Franco and the Vatican would be beyond doubt even if we did not know any statements made by the pope about the Spanish Civil War. Because what the Vatican desires is shown in the reactions of the episcopate, which is fully dependent on it. It could not have supported Mussolini, Hitler, Pavelić, or Franco without the pope's agreement.

There is, of course, that large circle in the Catholic Church for whom the pope is devoid of any guilt from the outset. These believers are convinced without any justification: "It is not the papacy, which is at the height of its mission and enjoys the highest reputation throughout the world, which is to blame. Those to blame are the leading Catholics in Spain."[222]

And there are those pious ones who draw conclusions with an honest look that would take one's breath away if one were not already long since immune to any shocking utterances they might make. The Catholic newspaper *Avvenire d'Italia*, for instance, commented on the interim continuation of Vatican diplomatic relations with the republican government: "This is the case because an attempt is being made to *prevent horrors* so that the whole world realizes that even if rivers of blood flow in Spain, not one drop will have been spilt because of any fault of the Holy See."[223] Incidentally, Hitler and Mussolini also nurtured relations with the Spanish Republic while their troops had been fighting against them for months.

And then there are those naïve souls who, as many Germans believed under Hitler, that "the Führer doesn't know." "If the Führer knew . . ." and the like; believed of the pope: "The Holy Father in Rome does not know that Catholicism in Spain has been a falsehood and a lie, that priests and monks, instead of evangelizing the people, occupied themselves with flattering the rich and dancing to their tune. His Holiness does not know that the people were going hungry. We Spanish Catholics all eagerly await the voice of the Holy Father in Rome. In these moments of agony that the Fatherland is going through, the voice of the representative of Christ on Earth will be that of the angels when the Messiah was born: 'Peace on Earth and good will to all men.'"[224]

Neither these naïve people nor the cynical hypocrites or a priori believers will be distracted from their belief or methods by any facts, however convincing they may be. It is a fact that the voice of the representative of Christ on earth did not preach "Peace on Earth" in the Spanish conflict. On the contrary; Pius XI, who at the same time as he concluded the concordat with Hitler's Germany propagated a crusade for the complete restoration of church rights in Spain (p. 57), not only knew months in advance what was planned there but was also the first to be informed of the beginning of the uprising by Franco.[225] And he quickly turned to the world at large in appeals and speeches to them to support the rebels.

As early as September 14, 1936, the pope, as the Berlin paper *Germania* put it, "raised a protest against the murderous Red Spanish regime in a solemn address.[226] Just a few days before, Hitler had demanded a fight against the Bolshevist threat at the Nuremberg Reich party conference. Now Pius XI called on the whole civilized world to fight against Bolshevism, which had "already proved its will to destroy every order from Russia to China, from Mexico to South America." The "fires of hatred and persecution" had been lit in Spain and, unless measures were taken immediately, would "be directed [against] all divine and human institutions." (Popes usually say "divine" and "God" when they mean Catholicism and their rule.) The pope then claimed, in an equally open and illogical manner: "Above all political considerations our blessing goes out in particular to those who have taken on the difficult and dangerous task of defending and restoring the rights and honor of God."[227]

And in all his following addresses,[228] Pius XI did not forget to incriminate and accuse the legal Spanish government directly or indirectly.

A few months later, the pope said in a speech that the Spanish Civil War was a "warning, more serious and threatening than all previous ones." "These are events that reveal and announce with shocking certainty and clarity what Europe and the whole world have to face if we do not resort to safeguards and remedies immediately and effectively."[229]

These safeguards and remedies were supplied by Hitler, Mussolini, and the "National" Spanish crusading army, spearheaded by the 150,000 Mohammedan Moors, who castrated their victims in accordance with an old Moorish battle custom, and the African legionnaires—their motto: "Down with intelligence!"[230]

That was the phalanx that fought for the Vatican, led by a man of which the French author Jean Cassou wrote, was "as criminal as Hitler, as hypocritical as Salazar and as simple as Pétain."[231] English author Charles Duff states: "Compared to the Spanish 'Caudillo,' the 'Führer' Hitler and the 'Duce' Mussolini are almost honorable men,"[232] which is true in Mussolini's case at least.

Francisco Hermenegildo Teodulo Franco y Bahamonde was said to be the youngest European general, extraordinarily brave as an officer but also emotionless to the point of cruelty. After becoming commandant of the Foreign Legion, he was a "glib opportunist" who always went with the flow and, after a while, came to believe in only one thing: violence and the ruthless elimination of his enemies.[233]

Charles Duff calls Franco a man "who publicly displays his Catholicism . . . , who has himself photographed kneeling before the altar in his private chapel and then chooses the best picture for propaganda purposes. Even if he is a sanctimonious Catholic, he still seriously believes he is a child of God that the Almighty has chosen to be 'Caudillo de todos las Españas'—the leader of all Spain."[234] He was also reinforced in this belief by his wife, an ardent Catholic who increasingly started to see him as the savior of Spain and the church, chosen by God,[235] and eventually he would say of himself: "I am the Instrument of Providence."[236]

Franco would not hesitate to defy the church when it seemed necessary. He even went so far as to ban the papal encyclical "With Burning Concern" in Spain because it criticized the totalitarianism that placed the state above the church.[237] And of course he had the courageous pastoral letter from the bishop of the Canary Islands, Antonio Pildain (which attacked the Franco regime in a unique way in 1946[238]) suppressed, and his security police search feverishly for every copy. But none of this diminishes his services to the Vatican in the slightest.

Franco, whose first deeds after assuming power included the construction of a concentration camp in Tetuán on July 19,[239] declared during the initial phase of the war that the Spanish state would "be set up according to the principles of Catholicism which are actually the principles of our Fatherland."[240] Consequently the entire civil war, which he, as the bishops, had presented as a holy war and crusade from the beginning, was also waged by him "under the sign of the cross."[241] And as he called himself a "warrior of Christ" and an "instrument of Providence," the nationalist Spaniards in general felt themselves "more as instruments of God than military putschists or reactionary conspirators."[242] This is also shown clearly in their regulations (p. 71).

In the summer of 1936 on Assumption Day, Franco replaced the republican flag with the flag of the monarchy, assisted by the cardinal of Seville, Illundaín. The little general kissed the flag many times, tears in his eyes, on the city hall balcony in front of a great gathering of people. And then the cardinal kissed it.[243]

By September 1936 religious education was made compulsory again in every school in Franco's Spain, the Madonnas and crucifixes appeared on the walls again, and pupils had prayers at the beginning and end of daily lessons and had to go to mass with their teachers on holidays.[244]

All the parties, including the Catholic CEDA, disappeared in national Spain apart from the Fascist *Falange* and the Carlists, since Franco represented the interests of Rome that could not be pushed through in parliament much more promisingly in military terms. The Vatican had also dissolved the Catholic parties under Mussolini and Hitler. It was the same bloody game.

How far the church's collaboration with the Caudillo went is attested by Cardinal Gomá's statement: "We are in complete agreement with the National government, which never takes a step without my advice, which it always follows."[245]

The first foreign flag to wave over Franco's headquarters was the papal one, and it was not long before Franco's banner was being flown over the Vatican.[246]

The Vatican Jesuit journal *Civiltà Cattolica* constantly propagated the civil war. "The army," it wrote on January 2, 1937, "took up a glorious stance, a hundred times blessed in the Fascist putsch."[247] And on November 20, 1937, the officious Vatican paper demanded: "At present . . . all honest citizens must, without consideration of any other differences of opinion, be agreed in the mutual intent to sweep away the new Barbarians, who have no fatherland and no God, come what may."[248]

Come what may! A sea of blood does not concern them as long as they retain their power. So in summer 1938, the pope bluntly rejected the request of the French and British governments to join a protest against the bombing of republican civilians.[249]

What did the pope care about the bombing of Spanish civilians! In the middle of the war, he thanked Franco for a telegram of homage, highly delighted that "we feel the ancestral spirit of Catholic Spain pulsating Your Excellency's message" and sent the rebel general "our apostolic blessing as a pledge of divine grace from our hearts."[250]

After the republic had been brought down with the help of the German and Italian Fascists, the recently appointed Pius XII congratulated Franco on April 1, 1939: "By raising our hearts to God, we celebrate with Your Excellency *this victory, which was so longed for by the Catholic Church*. We embrace the hope that your country *will resume the old Christian traditions* with renewed vigor after peace has been restored."[251] Franco expressed the great gratitude of the Spanish people and at the same time sent further telegrams to Mussolini and Hitler.[252] At the beginning of June 1939, the Franco regime committed itself to respecting the first four paragraphs of the concordat of 1851(!), which meant the clergy gaining the greatest influence once again. A few days later, Pius XII received 3,200 Spanish fascists, headed by Serrano Suner, Hitler's friend, and General Gambara, the commander of the Italian troops in the Spanish Civil War. Pope Pacelli bid his "loyal sons" welcome. They had, he said, afforded their mutual father great comfort because they had defended the faith and civilization and suffered a great deal for it.[253] The pope prophesied without shame that, with the rebuilding of Spain, "the glorious past of the Catholic Tradition should, as far as possible, even be exceeded."[254]

Freedom of speech, freedom of the press, and freedom of assembly were now banned again in Spain; literature, film, and radio were massively censored;

all parties apart from the Fascist *Falange* were banned, all non-Catholic religious faiths suppressed, and all Protestant churches and schools closed. Catholicism became the state religion; the remarkable thing here is that all the Bibles disappeared in the rural districts. The police confiscated one hundred thousand copies in Madrid. Bibles were simply taken at borders. In the last year before the civil war, the constantly increasing sales figure had reached 211,000 copies.[255]

"PEACE IN ORDER, HONOR AND WELL-BEING" —POPE PIUS XII[256]

Although around six hundred thousand had already died in the civil war,[257] the slaughter continued under Franco, whose "very noble Christian feelings" had already been admired by State Secretary Pacelli during the putsch.[258]

Military tribunals and execution commandos were constantly in action. Count Ciano estimated that there were 80 executions being carried out daily in Seville, 150 in Barcelona, and 200 to 250 in Madrid.[259] (For simplicity's sake, those executed were all described as communists.[260])

According to official statistics from the Spanish government, Franco had more than two hundred thousand republicans shot between the end of the civil war in 1939 and early 1942, in other words, at the time when he was beginning, at Pacelli's request, to restore "the old Christian traditions"[261]; this is a third of all the victims of the civil war!

Three years later, there were still more than 1.5 million political prisoners, doctors, lawyers, authors, Basque clergy, teachers, and day laborers in Spanish prisons—innocent people, many of whom were also murdered.[262] And three years after the end of the Second World War, there were still more than one hundred thousand political prisoners,[263] and torture, as Franco's authorities have admitted themselves, was still taking place.[264]

The methods of inquisition continued in Spain all the longer, since 30 percent of the staff of the director general of safety had been trained by experts of Himmler, with whom Franco had made a "Police Agreement" in 1940, that is, by German Gestapo members whom the general continued to employ as a "brain trust" even after the war.[265] His popularity among the people is supported by the fact that after the war he had to spend over 50 percent of his GDP on army and police to keep himself in power.[266] Social conditions were organized accordingly.

Franco, who had already had the support of the entire Spanish high finance behind him during the civil war, which meant that he could, for instance, order two million metric tons of oil from Texas at the time,[267] was a man, as the German ambassador General Wilhelm Faupel reported to Berlin, "to whom the questions of social legislation are personally alien," which is why the ambassador in national Spain recommended "the immediate announcement and execution of social reforms to alleviate the situation of the poorer and poorest among the population."[268] And quite a lot did indeed happen at the time. The spokesman of the British Catholic bishops, Prelate Henson, extolled from Valladolid that they ate no sweet dishes on Thursdays and only ate one course for their midday and evening meals on the first and fifteenth of each month. The money saved from this, along with returns from a special tax on tobacco and entertainment, was being used for the poor.[269] And in 1938, the rebels' minister of the interior declared the Feast of St. Joseph a national holiday. For this corresponded to the Catholic spirit in which they wanted to rule Spain. "The day should be a holiday for the working people in particular."[270] So the ruling classes selflessly sacrificed their desserts on Thursdays and even gave the people holidays as well. And Franco introduced the death penalty for strikes.[271]

Today [that is, in 1965], the social structure in Spain is approximately "the same as it was in 1936 or 1836,"[272] which means that there are still sixty families "who own more than two-thirds of all the valuable ground in Spain,"[273] that they "often live more opulently than the financial kings of the United States or the beef barons of Argentina,"[274] and that "the Church still continues to side against the poor and outcast if they call into question or threaten the privileges or interests of the ruling caste."[275] Exceptions among the clerics only prove the rule.

"Nowhere in Europe," writes the British parliamentarian Bob Edwards, "are wealth and power in so few hands. Nowhere in the world—apart from some countries in the Middle East—is wealth distributed so unevenly. Away from the popular holiday resorts and in the Spanish hinterland, a third of the population (ten million) live in dirt and misery and can hardly keep themselves physically alive. Their standard of living is indeed the lowest in Europe—in many rural areas it is as low as in Asia. . . . Without the help of the American dollar and the military Franco would soon vanish into the dust of history."[276]

But thanks to the dollars from the Protestant and democratic United States, the Spanish youth are now growing up Catholic and Fascist. And the youth can read the following in a "Grammar of the Spanish Language," which is recommended by the *Falange* and the church authorities (signed by Vicar General Dr. Manuel Rubio). "Copy the following for the purposes of writing practice: In history, Franco can only be compared to Christopher Columbus. . . . Our Spanish heroes have destroyed the Marxist mob of assassins, law-breakers and red incendiaries for all time."[277]

What would we read in German textbooks about Hitler today if he had won? The Vatican and the German episcopate wanted and worked toward this, as the next chapter proves.

3

THE VATICAN AND HITLER'S GERMANY

"The bishops, the successors to the Apostles and the representatives of the Holy See reaffirm with solemn determination their cooperation with the new Reich by means of a sworn oath placed in the hands of the highest state authorities."

—Franz von Papen[1]

NATIONAL SOCIALISM ASSUMES POWER

After the end of the First World War, the Vatican influenced German politics through the nuncio Eugenio Pacelli.[2] He had started his career in the diplomatic department of the curia in 1901 and lived in Munich and Berlin from 1917 to 1929 as, as Dorothy Thompson wrote, "the most well-informed diplomat in Germany." He became cardinal secretary of state in 1930 and pope, as Pius XII, in 1939.

The political instrument of the curia in Germany was the Centre Party, which had connections with well-known major industrialists from the Rhine, whose leader, Dr. Marx, made no important decision without consulting the papal nuncio. The influence of the cardinal on the Centre Party increased further when Prelate Kaas, professor of church history at the University of Bonn, became chairman of the party in 1928. Via him, Pacelli, who repeatedly spent his vacations with Kaas in Switzerland, steered the party more and more to the right. He sympathized with nationalist tendencies and circles out of fear of the increasing powers of democratic and socialist groups, especially as the Centre Party itself was losing influence.

It had already lost nearly half a million voters by 1928. And when, out of more than thirty-five million votes at the Reichstag elections in 1932, the National Socialists received 13.7 million, the social democrats and communists together received 13.2 million, and 5.7 million voted for the Centre Party, including the Bavarian People's Party, the Vatican saw itself—compare its behavior toward Mussolini—forced to bring Hitler to power out of fear of the left-wing parties.

The Catholic Franz von Papen

Franz von Papen helped them in this. Indeed, in many people's opinion, he became "Hitler's most important accomplice to power."[3]

The former Uhlan officer had been captured committing acts of sabotage during the First World War as a military attaché in Washington. After his expulsion, the British obtained documents through him with whose help the fleet of Admiral Graf Spee was to be lured into a trap by the Falkland Islands.[4] Furthermore, by doing this, von Papen had, as Hitler said, "sent about 5,000 agents to the gallows in the USA."[5] A similar mishap befell von Papen on the Turkish front not long after. After the war, he decided to become a politician. He joined the Centre Party, brought the Berlin Catholic newspaper *Germania*, of which he owned a large parcel of shares, under his influence, married the daughter of a Saar industrialist, and became Reich Chancellor on June 1, 1932, to the amazement of all. "Everyone," wrote the French ambassador François-Poncet, "whispered or laughed . . . , because von Papen was not taken seriously by his friends or his enemies. . . . Nobody who knew him would have thought he understood anything about politics."[6] "Not a head," said General von Schleicher, "but a hat."

So this Catholic cavalier abolished—a little outside the limits of the law—the Braun/Severing social democrat government on June 20, 1932, lifted the ban on the SA and SS by means of an agreement with Hitler,[7] and "then worked," as it says in the Catholic *Herder Lexicon*, "for Hitler's nomination."[8] "Because for all affirmations to the contrary it was he himself who took the initiative to associate with Hitler, who was already despairing as to whether he would ever gain power."[9]

On August 13, von Papen offered him the position of vice chancellor. On August 28, Goebbels noted a speech of von Papen's "which stems from our body of thought from A to Z."[10] On August 30, Göring became president of the Reichstag with the help of the Catholic Centre Party. On November 13, von Papen renewed his offer to Hitler. On November 17, von Papen requested resignation and recommended to Hindenburg that he should receive Hitler. On December 10, von Papen demanded Hitler's inclusion in the government at the Berlin gentlemen's club. And on January 4, 1933, they both met in the house of the Cologne banker and fellow Nazi party member Baron von Schröder, a friend of the major industrialists Kirdorf, Vögler, Thyssen, and Flick. At this notorious meeting, which was intended to remain top secret, von Papen promised Hitler, according to the well-founded opinion of many historians, the support of the pope while von Papen demanded in return the destruction of the Communist and Social Democratic Parties and the conclusion of a concordat. It is a fact that in this three-man debate, according to the statement made by Schröder at the Nuremberg trials, Hitler had spoken of the "removal of all Social Democrats, Communists and Jews from leading positions" and shortly afterward had concluded the concordat. "Von Papen and Hitler," said Schröder, "were basically in agreement, so that many points of friction were overcome and they could go forward together."[11]

Directly after the meeting, von Papen continued his journey through the Ruhr, and shortly after, the money was flowing once again into the Nazis' empty coffers.[12] A consortium of industrialists transferred one million reichsmarks to the SS alone.[13] The most urgent party debts, estimated at twenty million, which was probably exaggerated, were also paid off.[14] On January 9 von Papen spoke with the Reich president. On January 22, he conferred with Göring and other persons at von Ribbentrop's house. And on January 30, Hitler was appointed Reich Chancellor on von Papen's proposal. "Hindenburg only overcame his doubts because von Papen guaranteed that he himself, the Vice Chancellor, would be the real head of government."[15]

In an address on November 2, 1933, von Papen said, "As I supported paving the way to power for the young, fighting freedom movement when I assumed my position of Chancellor, as I was determined by a kind twist of fate on January 30 to place the hands of our Chancellor and Führer into the hand of the beloved Field Marshall, today I feel once again the duty to say to the German people and all those who have maintained their trust in me: Dear God has blessed Germany by giving it a leader in our times of deepest need."[16] And on November 9, von Papen avowed in a speech to the *Arbeitsgemeinschaft katholischer Deutscher* (Working Group of German Catholics) in Cologne: "Since January 30, when Providence determined me to make a *vital* contribution to the birth of the government of national rising, it was always in the back of my mind that the wonderful rebuilding work of the Chancellor and his great movement must not under any circumstances be endangered by a cultural break. . . . Because the *structural elements of National Socialism* are not only not alien to the Catholic view of life, they actually *correspond to it in almost all respects.*"[17]

In the same year, the Catholic von Papen concluded the concordat between Nazi Germany and the Vatican. In a secret communication from Rome to Hitler on July 2, 1933, the vice chancellor expressed the conviction "that the conclusion of this concordat must be deemed a great success of foreign policy for the government of national rising."[18] Indeed, von Papen had already made a contractual agreement with the Holy See in a secret additional protocol for the case of general compulsory military service in Germany! "I hope that this agreement will be pleasing to you," von Papen wrote to his most admired chancellor, Hitler.[19] On November 13, 1933, von Papen became a representative for the Saar and on July 26, 1934, an ambassador in Austria. Hitler assured him in the letter of appointment: "You have had my complete and unlimited confidence since our cooperation in the cabinet began, and will continue to have it."[20]

In Vienna, von Papen prepared the Nazi seizure of power. In the Nuremberg verdict, it says: "According to the evidence, there is no doubt that von Papen's main aim as an ambassador in Austria consisted in undermining the Schuschnigg regime and strengthening the Austrian Nazis in order to bring about the annexation."[21] Von Papen not only requested two hundred thousand marks per month for the "persecuted, silent National Socialist sufferers in Austria" but also asked for money in a memorandum to Hitler for the *Katholischer Freiheitsbund* [Catholic Alliance for Freedom] in Vienna in order to promote their "anti-Semitic work."[22] After Austria had been annexed, von Papen received the Golden Party Badge from Hitler "for loyal service," which he "accepted in ceremonious excitement and with all the appropriate demonstrations of gratitude."[23] And for his activity as German ambassador in Ankara (from 1939 to 1944), he was awarded the Knight's Cross to the War Merit Cross by Hitler.

But at the Nuremberg trials, the papal chamberlain Franz von Papen, against the objection of the Soviet member of the military court,[24] was acquitted. And Hitler's lackey, who accused the Germans of "lacking intelligence" and "lethargy of thought" because of their Führer cult in 1952,[25] was actually granted a pension by a German court ten years later.

THE ENABLING ACT

> *"What suffices for the Vatican must also suffice for the Centre Party. The presiding prelates in the Reichstag and Landtag factions cannot be holier than the Pope."*
>
> —Hans Bernd Gisevius[26]

After he took office, Hitler demanded an "Enabling Act" that would enable him to exercise dictatorship. He received the necessary two-thirds majority for this by illegally dissolving the Communist Party on the one hand and procuring the Centre Party votes on the other. As we know from Father Leiber, SJ, Pius XI praised Hitler, in a secret consistory on March 13, 1933—ten days before the Enabling Act was passed—for his banning of the Communist Party. And Cardinal Faulhaber, who had been received by the pope the day before, circulated his praise.[27]

The communists had been disabled, and the Catholics joined in. And after the Christian trade unions had also been won over, Centre and their leader Kaas, with the exception of one small group, committed to Hitler since he had guaranteed the conclusion of a concordat. Gisevius writes impressively under the title of "Schwarze Hintergründe" ("Dark Backgrounds"): "It is a pity that we have no photograph of the scene where the Reich Chancellor, listening carefully on the government bench, acknowledged the curial style of the Centre speaker with statesmanlike reserve. Only the uncanny glint in his eyes may, for fractions of a second, have given away the reaction these convoluted sentences may have caused within him. And then a papal prelate laying this capitulation at his feet! This must have been so much more important than any tumultuous applause in the Sportpalast or the Krone Circus."[28]

It is, of course, possible to suggest that Hitler's dictatorship had already begun before the Enabling Act was passed on March 23—with the Reichstag Fire Decree and the *Heimtücke-Verordnung* (Treachery Decree) (which gave powers to arrest anyone who was critical of the regime). But it was the Enabling Act or, as it was officially called, the "Law to Remedy the Distress of People and Reich," which sanctioned the dictatorship in full once and for all.

Theodor Heuß and Hitler

> *"Every pacifist, every communist was allowed to talk, including tact-less and tasteless foreigners—but the basic principles of the constitution obviously did not apply to this one man (Hitler), whose pure motives were not questioned."*
>
> —Theodor Heuß

It is well known that Theodor Heuß also agreed to the Enabling Act. The later German president had already dedicated the "not at all unlovable book" *Hitlers Weg* to Hitler a year before the seizure of power, in which Heuß, although he criticizes and satirizes several things about National Socialism, especially its race theories, also finds many things positive about it and above all spares Hitler conspicuously.

But that was not all. The "image of a Faust in the attic" is formed even in the view of the young Hitler. The "resilience" with which he overcame the failure of the 1923 Munich putsch was "admirable," and he was now commencing an "aston-ishing," even "great turn." "And no one can refuse to acknowledge the fortitude of the man, who . . . undertook and understood how to shape a new vessel from the shards." He also had "reason" to be "proud" of the development of this movement. His financing of the Nazi Party was "a fabulous achievement." But income from membership fees was "not merely a great organizational act." Hitler had "also set souls in motion and linked an enthusiasm ready for sacrifice and dedication to his appearances." In his book *Mein Kampf*, the "conqueror of men" talks in the sections on propaganda "with vivid fortitude." In his theories about people and state, there was to be recognized "the trusting intention to educate of a didactic presentation"; in the Nazi Party and their manifesto, "structural elements that are related" to Catholic social doctrine and the hierarchical construct of the Catholic Church. Although "the odd part [may be] wrong, even nonsense," "here is a will that wants to win and not beat about the bush." Yet Theodor Heuß certainly knew that "heads [would] roll." But Hitler himself is repeatedly defended or even praised. Again and again one encounters phrases such as "it is not necessary to reproach him for it"; "It cannot be doubted . . . that Hitler was acting in good faith"; "He is, of course, right in doing it"; "success proved him right"; and so on.[29]

Under Adenauer, Theodor Heuß was not only president for eight years, but he also received the German Booksellers' Peace Prize.

Adenauer, the Catholic

> *"You, young man, must learn how to despise people."*
> —Konrad Adenauer to a (fifty-five-year-old)
> member of the parliamentary council in 1949[30]

Dr. Konrad Adenauer was always up to date.

In October 1917, when he was mayor of Cologne, he assured that the city would be "a metropolis of the Rhineland *inseparably* united with the German Reich, always mindful of this . . . and always feel itself *as part of the German Fatherland.*"[31] And he finished his speech in front of the representative of the Prussian state government by turning fiercely against "the onslaught of the enemy and the enemy's lust for conquest" and saying, "How could we conclude this hour, which is so important for Cologne, more fittingly than with the *oath to Kaiser and Reich, aglow with burning gratitude*? Our call: long live His Majesty, our most gracious Emperor and King!"[32]

About sixteen months later, on February 1, 1919, Adenauer proclaimed: "Either we join *France*, directly or as a buffer state, or we become a *West German* republic, there is no third choice."[33]

But there was a third choice for him. On August 10, 1934, Konrad Adenauer wrote to the Nazi interior minister in Berlin: "I have always treated the Nazi Party very correctly and thereby repeatedly placed myself in opposition to ministerial instructions of the time and those opinions represented by the Centre faction of the Cologne City Council. For instance, I put the city's sporting facilities at the disposal of the Nazi Party for years, in contradiction to the regulation of the Prussian Interior Minister at the time and allowed it to fly the swastika flags on the city's masts at these places during its events. I refer to the relevant files of the City of Cologne and the testimony of the retired Assistant Billstein."

Adenauer repeated a long list proving his advocacy of a Nazi newspaper, Nazi civil servants, and his obligingness concerning Nazi events; he even stressed that he had expressly and openly declared in the winter of 1932/33 "that in my opinion *a party as big as the Nazi Party must have a leading role* in the government."[34]

THE CATHOLIC PARTIES DISSOLVED THEMSELVES ON CHURCH ORDERS

> *"Haven't you dissolved yourselves yet?"* . . . *"Hitler can steer the state ship well."*
>
> —Prelate Kaas's statements from the Vatican[35]

On March, the Centre leader from Baden (a federal state within the Weimar Republic), Monsignor Föhr, said that the cooperation of the Catholics was obligatory in the new Reich, and other Centre leaders expressed themselves similarly.[36] On June 29, the previous Centre chancellor, Brüning, admitted to the British ambassador in Berlin, Sir Horace Rumbold, that he had good reason to believe that the cardinal secretary of state was hostile to the Centre.[37] And on July 5, it dissolved itself on the orders of the curia. As did the Catholic Bavarian People's Party. And it was not only ex-chancellor Brüning, who was dismissed in May 1932 "100 m before the finishing line," who raged: "Pacelli envisions an authoritarian state and an authoritarian church run by the Vatican bureaucracy."[38] Many Catholics protested too. For this reason, the Vatican and

State Secretary Pacelli appeased them with a semiofficial statement. And to the surprise of many, Centre leader Kaas issued the following statement after a discussion with the pope and Pacelli: "Hitler can steer the state ship well. Before he became Chancellor I met him many times and was very impressed by his clear thoughts and his way of staring facts in the face but still remaining true to his noble ideals. . . . It does not matter who governs as long as order is maintained. The story of recent years in Germany has proved democratic parliamentarianism to be incapable."[39]

As the Vatican in Italy paved the way to dictatorship for Mussolini by elimi-nating the Catholic Party, it gave unlimited power to Hitler in Germany through von Papen, Kaas, and the dissolution of the Centre, the oldest Catholic party in Europe. In return, it expected the same cooperation from him as from Mussolini. This is what the papal nuncio in Berlin, Cesare Orsenigo, who "was openly exul-tant" about Hitler's seizure of power, "clearly signified."[40]

Hardly had Kaas secured the vote of his faction for the Enabling Act when he made off for Rome. Although he had not even informed his closest fellow party members about this; although he did have a private conversation with Hitler before leaving.[41] Kaas left Berlin on April 7, 1933. The next day, he went to Rome from Munich, along with von Papen[42]; on April 10, von Papen and Hermann Göring appeared at the Vatican, where they were received, as the press reported, with great honors, and Pius XI was very impressed by them.[43] The pope also noticed, writes von Papen, how happy he was to see a person at the head of the German government who fought uncompromisingly against com-munism and Russian nihilism in all its forms.[44] On April 20, Hitler's birthday, Kaas sent "sincere blessings and the guarantee of unerring cooperation."[45] Soon after, an astonished world was presented with a concordat.

THE CONCORDAT WITH HITLER'S GERMANY

"In terms of timing, content and official episcopal interpretation, the concordat abetted crimes and criminals, morally slandered any deter-mined opposition, gave the Nazi regime the legitimacy to portray itself as being 'a state power on the side of order' [Cardinal Pacelli on April

30, 1937] and committed the Catholic people to taking the path to a
mass grave in order to secure Hitler's dictatorship."

—Johannes Fleischer[46]

When the concordat was concluded between the Holy See and the German Reich on July 20, 1933, half a year after Hitler's seizure of power, no one, as a popular objection goes, could have recognized the character of his government or noticed their tendency for notorious crimes. But this objection does not hold up because there was no longer any doubt about the essence and method of this movement at the time.

A few facts should suffice to clarify this.

1. As far back as February 3, 1933, Hitler, in his first speech to the generals, demanded the reintroduction of general compulsory military service, the conquest of new living space in the east, and the Germanization of the areas thus conquered.[47]

2. On February 20, Göring said to leaders of German industry at the Palace of the President of the Reichstag: if they did not procure any funds to pay the SA, the Nazi leaders would no longer be able to hold them back from the "Night of the Long Knives"; the industrialists' villas would also burn then.[48] (Upon which Krupp von Bohlen expressed thanks and the industrialists made an election donation of three million.[49])

3. On February 28, the basic citizens' rights of the Weimar constitution "for the protection of the people and the state" were suspended "indefinitely": in other words, there was no longer any freedom of speech or the press, right of assembly, or postal privacy. Instead, arrests were made for the most trivial of reasons, and those arrested were refused the right to appear before a duly appointed judge.[50]

4. In the first weeks after January 30, leading men of the Weimar Republic such as the Prussian minister Severing, the president of the *Reichslandbund* [National Rural League] Hepp, the social democrat member of parliament Dr. Leber, and others were arrested, many by the SA and "Stahlhelm," whom Göring had mobilized as "auxiliary police" since February 22.

5. At the same time, the first concentration camps were being built for those the Nazis wanted eliminated quickly and without recourse to duly appointed courts; Hitler began to appreciate these immediately.

6. On March 3, Göring threatened at a voters' rally in Frankfurt am Main: "German citizens! My actions will not be weakened by legal objections and bureaucracy. I do not have to practice justice, just destroy and eradicate."[51] And the SA became more brutal than before in this month. Fifty-one people were killed and several hundred injured during the election campaign alone. More than thirty young people were in Berlin hospitals with stomach wounds.[52]

7. The first persecution of Jews had already started early that year. On April 1, the party leadership issued the following order: "Action committees must be organized in every local group and organizational unit of the Nazi Party immediately in order to execute, practically and punctually, the boycott of Jewish shops, goods, doctors and lawyers. . . . . The action committees must be driven on to the remotest farming villages in order to hit Jewish traders in rural areas in particular. It must be stressed at all times that this is a defense measure that has been forced upon us."[53] Acts of violence were already being committed at that time already.[54]

8. On May 2, all trade union buildings were occupied and trade union assets confiscated.

9. On July 14, a whole package of terrorist laws was introduced. Above all, the one-party system was legalized: "Section 1. The only political party in Germany is the Nazi Party. Section 2. Anyone who seeks to maintain the organizational cohesion of another political party or form a new political party will be punished with . . . imprisonment."[55] A further law passed on July 14 legalized the expulsion of political opponents or Jews.[56] Additionally, the "Reich Law for the Prevention of Hereditarily Diseased Offspring" was passed, which was later called by church circles "an assault on inalienable rights, on human dignity and freedom."[57]

This list could be extended. But it is sufficient to convince anyone that there could be no doubt about who they were dealing with when Hitler's vice chancellor von Papen and the cardinal secretary of state Pacelli signed the agreement that, in its first sentence, refers to "friendly relations" between the Holy See and the German Reich on July 20, 1933. The one-time "best-informed diplomat in Germany," who also, incidentally, repeatedly appeared at Nazi party rallies as a nuncio,[58] knew them well. He certainly did not see as clearly and far as the anticlerical Erich Ludendorff, who wrote to Hindenburg directly after January 30, 1933: "By naming Hitler Reich Chancellor you have put our holy German Fatherland into the hands of one of the greatest demagogues of all time. I solemnly prophesy to you that this disastrous man will drive our Reich into the abyss, bring incomprehensible misery to our nation and coming generations will curse you in your grave."[59]

No, Eugenio Pacelli did not see this far. But he could hope that Hitler would clear away several enemies of the church even more resolutely than Mussolini. Which is why they were certainly frequently in agreement with the acts of terror that they condemned so roundly later. Hitler's turn against the east was welcome because it was against the Bolshevists. His abolition of the basic democratic rights of freedom of the press, speech, and assembly corresponded to popes' ideas that go back centuries. And the arrest and killing of their communist, socialist, and liberal opponents did not disturb the church either. And it goes without saying that they did not feel for the Jews all too much, considering the Christian anti-Judaism that has been going on ruthlessly for nearly two thousand years.[60]

So for all these reasons, once again: they knew whom they were getting involved with. They knew that any rebellion against this government would be punished with imprisonment and the concentration camp. And Cardinal Secretary of State Pacelli did not neglect to acknowledge Hitler's government expressly in 1934: "If totality is to be understood as meaning that in everything that belongs to state responsibility in accordance with the purpose of the existence of the state, that the entirety of all citizens of the state without exception is subject to the state and the legal government that controls it, then it must undoubtedly be approved of."[61] They also certainly knew that Hitler had criticized religious disputes and the fight against ultramontanism in *Mein Kampf*, indeed, that he had even supported the significance of dogmas. He wrote: "The most pious Protestant could sit next to the most pious Catholic in the ranks of our movement."[62] And since the Weimar Republic, under socialists and democrats, had not achieved what Hitler was now guaranteeing, at least on paper—"a propagandistic chess move," he boasted later, that truly did him justice[63]—leading Catholic clerics and laypeople were soon trying to outbid each other with oaths of loyalty.

Although nearly two-thirds of the thirty-four articles of the concordat favored the church, it did not bother Hitler. Because at least the bishops, according to Article 16, had to swear an oath of loyalty and promise to respect the government and have it respected by the clergy. Article 27 gave the Nazis influence over the nomination of the Catholic army bishops and the Catholic military clergy. Article 30 provided for prayers to be said for the well-being of Hitler's Reich on all Sundays and holidays in all the churches in Germany after the main service.

But for Hitler, the concordat itself was more important than details. It made him socially acceptable, so to speak. His first agreement under international law was made with the pope. This gave the new state legality in front of the whole world. So the *Völkischer Beobachter*, Hitler's organ of government, rejoiced: "The signing of the Reich Concordat means that National Socialism has been acknowledged by the Catholic Church in Germany in the solemnest possible way. . . . This fact is a *massive, moral reinforcement* of the National Socialist government and its standing."[64] Hitler himself refused to debate details. "He was of the opinion," as it said in the minutes of the Reich government session on July 14, 1933, "that this could only be a great success. The Reich Concordat meant that Germany had been given a chance and an atmosphere of trust created, which would be significant in the urgent fight against international Jewry."[65]

According to these session minutes, Hitler saw three "great benefits" in concluding the concordat:

"1. that the Vatican negotiated at all, despite their stance, especially in Austria, that National Socialism was un-Christian and against the Church;

2. that the Vatican could be moved to establish a good relationship with this national German State. He, the Reich Chancellor, had until recently not thought it possible that the Church would be willing to commit the bishops to this State. The fact that this has now happened was undoubtedly an unreserved recognition of the current regime;

3. that the Concordat would mean the Church withdrawing from association and party life, which would mean, for instance, letting the Christian trade unions go; also something he, the Reich Chancellor, would not have thought possible just a few months ago. The dissolution of the Centre Party could also only be deemed final after the conclusion of the Concordat now that the Vatican had ordered the permanent removal of the priests from party politics.

The fact that the aim of an agreement with the Curia, an aim that had always been striven for by him, the Reich Chancellor, had been achieved so much sooner than he had thought on January 30 was such an indescribable success that any critical doubts had to fade away in its shadow."[66]

And how did the German Catholic princes of the church describe the concordat at the time? Well, they basically viewed it in the same way. Archbishop Gröber of Freiburg wrote in his *Handbuch der religiösen Gegenwartsfragen* (*Handbook of Current Religious Questions*) in 1937—incidentally, "with the recommendation of the entire German episcopate": "As far as the evaluation of the German Concordat is concerned, it was, from a domestic and foreign policy standpoint, the first far-reaching international agreement of the new Reich, which could be counted as a moral success for party and state, unlike the previous vain attempts made by the 'Weimar System' and had a joyful orientation of the loyal Catholics to the National Socialist State as a consequence."[67]

Cardinal Faulhaber, archbishop of Munich, emphasized the pope's support in particular. "Pope Pius XI," Faulhaber stated in a sermon in 1936, "was *the first foreign sovereign* to conclude a solemn treaty with the new Reich government, led by the desire 'to reinforce and promote the friendly relations that exist between the Holy See and the German Reich.'"[68]

But then the cardinal became even clearer. "In reality," he then added, "Pope Pius XI was *the best friend, and initially the only friend, of the new Reich*. Millions abroad initially took up a cautious and skeptical position regarding the new Reich and did not gain trust in the new German government until the Concordat was concluded.... The dictate of Versailles pronounced the Germans guilty in front of all the world; the Reich Concordat expressed the trust of the Pope in the German government and therefore raised its standing all over the world."[69]

Ten years later, let it be noted parenthetically, the role of the pope appears in a somewhat different light to a prelate of the cardinal, the Munich suffragan bishop Neuhäusler. Under the impressive headings (with the subdivisions, which were so popular with nearly all Catholic theologians and frequently extremely exaggeratedly exact, which were intended, by means of their visual impression, to lead the reader to infer reliability of the contents) "B. Centers of power of the Church resistance. 1. The Rock of Peter," the standard work on the Catholic Church struggle in the Third Reich: "The resistance against the anti-Christian National Socialism was at its most powerful on the Catholic side in the highest position of the Catholic Church, *on the Rock of Peter*. Admittedly, the Holy See did try to tame the evil spirits of National Socialism with a '*solemn accommodation*.'"[70]

So the best and initially only foreign friend of the Nazi Reich, as Cardinal Faulhaber expressed it in 1936, suddenly became, as his prelate expressed it in 1946, a tamer of evil spirits! This "tamer," as Leiber, Faulhaber, and von Papen attest, repeatedly praised Hitler for his anticommunist fight,[71] and Pius XI was also, let this be stressed again, in agreement with the introduction of compulsory military service by the Nazis already in 1933! The telling part of von Papen's letter to Hitler from Rome on July 2, 1933: "Finally we added a condition to this effect in the additional protocol . . . should Germany reintroduce general compulsory military service. This addition is valuable to me not so much because of the factual regulation as because of the fact that here the Holy See is already making a contractual agreement with us should general compulsory military service be reintroduced. I hope that this agreement is pleasing to you for this reason. It must, of course, be treated confidentially." Johannes Fleischer rightly comments: "The Vatican also showed itself here to be Hitler's ally, possibly disregarding international treaties in doing so."[72]

The curia wanted Germany to rearm under Hitler just as it did with the postwar West Germany under Adenauer. In my church history, *Abermals krähte der Hahn* (*And Again the Cock Crew*) I showed in my final chapter, which discusses the relationship of Pius XII to the federal republic, that it was Cardinal Frings of Cologne who, at the Catholic Day in Bonn on June 23, 1950, *was the first to demand the rearmament of Germany publicly*.[73]

ALL THE GERMAN BISHOPS CALLED FOR COOPERATION WITH HITLER IN 1933 BECAUSE THE VATICAN WANTED IT

Until then, they had had a strict ban on joining the Nazi Party.[74] Suddenly they were pleading in a united front for the party. Against the will of Rome? It shows an astonishing yet typical partiality (to avoid using a more negative word), when recently, in a clearly critical article about political Catholicism in 1933, they apparently in all seriousness believed in "the disapproval" of this development by Cardinal Secretary of State Pacelli by quoting him as follows—even with the qualification "according to Father Leiber": "Why did the German bishops have to accommodate the government so quickly?"[75]—while even the Catholic Walter Dirks talks of "Secretary of State Pacelli's very active involvement."[76] The Catholic *Allgemeine Rundschau* wrote quite openly in the middle of April that the bishops could not fight if Rome had decided on peace.[77] And a few days later, on April 24, Baron von Ritter, the Bavarian ambassador at the Vatican, reported that Kaas and Secretary of State Pacelli were in constant contact, there was no doubt about the position of the secretary of state and other prominent cardinals; they approved the "honest cooperation of the Catholics in promoting and guiding the national movement in Germany as part of the Christian world view. . . . I have also heard statements from the mouths of other prominent cardinals that were aiming in the same direction."[78]

It hardly needs saying that there was not too much sympathy for Hitler at the Vatican. For the Roman diplomats, he was no more than the "lesser of two evils" from whom they were hoping for the elimination of what they saw as the greater evil, communism. As is known, the curia was fundamentally wrong in this. Because today we know, to quote Dirks again, "that Nazism was an insane and criminal provincialism, a collective excess that lasted a dozen years before it could be choked, but communism is a system that has besmirched itself with crimes at times and that is still on trial today for the power it wields in many parts of the world, but at the same time is a movement of global significance, an epochal reality in whose destruction nobody is interested but in whose transformation we are all fervently interested—if only for the reason that its destruction would once again drag us all, or at least hundreds of millions of people, into catastrophe once again."[79]

In early 1933, the bishops confessed at their conferences in Fulda and Freising that they had "assumed a negative position through bans and warnings regarding the National Socialist movement in recent years." But now they believed, on the Vatican's orders, of course, which is self-explanatory considering the complete dependence of the Catholic episcopate, that they "trusted that the predetermined general bans and warnings no longer need to be considered necessary."[80]

At the end of April 1933, delegates of the high Catholic clergy held a conference with Hitler in Berlin. After he had revealed that he was himself a Catholic, he said: "I have been attacked for approaching the Jewish question. The Catholic Church has viewed the Jews as parasites for fifteen hundred years, putting them in ghettoes, etc.—they have recognized what the Jews are. . . . I am going back to the time of what was done for fifteen hundred years. I do not put race over religion but I see the parasites in the representatives of this race in state and church, and maybe I am doing Christianity the greatest service."[81] The meeting took place in absolute harmony. "The talks with Hitler," reported Bishop Berning, "were cordial and objective. He spoke with warmth and calm, with the occasional show of temperament. Not a single word against the Church, only recognition for the bishops."[82]

But he who recognizes the bishops is also recognized by them. They wrote in a mutual pastoral letter in June 1933: "If we compare our times with the past, we find above all that the German people reflect *on their own essence* even more than before to stress its values and strengths. *We German bishops are a long way from underestimating this national awakening, let alone preventing it.* . . . For this reason we German Catholics do not need *to readjust our attitude towards the people and the fatherland,* but at the most continue what we have previously viewed as our natural and Christian duty more consciously and with more emphasis. . . . For this reason it is in no way difficult for us Catholics to honor the new strong emphasis on authority in the German political system and willingly subjugate ourselves to it with that willingness that is characterized not only as a natural virtue but as a supernatural one, because we see a reflection of divine rule and participation in the eternal authority of God in every human authority (cf. Romans 13:1 ff.). . . . *And we Catholics must also welcome the aims that the new state authority is setting for the freedom of our people.* . . . If the new state authority continues to make such efforts both to break the chains that others have put upon us and to further the strength and recovery of its people, thereby rejuvenating our people and enabling them to start a new, grand mission, this is also entirely in accord with the path of the Catholic faith. . . . If then, according to the will of the state authority, the inner turmoil and dichotomy within our people should finally give way to unity and wholeness, then it will also find understanding helpers amongst us Catholics who are willing to make sacrifices." After the bishops had then also registered a series of reservations and made demands of the new Reich, they once again guaranteed expressly "that there [was] no concealed reservation as regards the new state." "We do not want to withhold the powers of the Church from the state *at any cost*. . . . Any cautious standing aside or even hostility from the Church towards the State would surely have a fateful effect on both *Church and State*."[83]

This pastoral letter, signed by all the German cardinals, archbishops, and bishops "on the anniversary of our redemption," is a rare testament to the "fight of the German episcopate." The Munich suffragan bishop Neuhäusler therefore proceeded in his *Kreuz und Hakenkreuz* (*Cross and Swastika*), a much-quoted Catholic standard work, in the following way when reproducing the important document. He suppressed all the bishops' expressions of support for the Nazis, which was the main tenor of the letter, without exception. This meant the immediate deletion of ten longer passages. Neuhäusler had sentences or smaller sections removed nine times without appropriately indicating this, and he even arbitrarily and repeatedly altered text that was in quotation marks. The pastoral word has, in this alleged document, been "altered to such an extent that it is almost unrecognizable"; the suffragan bishop's methods are "a slap in the face of historical truth."[84]

The collection published by the Catholic Herder publishing, *Zeugnis und Kampf des deutschen Episkopats, Gemeinsame Hirtenbriefe und Denkschriften* (*Attestations and Struggle of the German Episcopate, Mutual Pastoral Letters and Memoranda*), leaves out the pastoral letters from 1933 and 1934 entirely and only mentions some of them in commentaries.[85]

In an examination of postwar Catholic literature on the church struggle, Hans Müller reaches the following conclusion in 1961: "What is said or printed is so one-sided that referring to it as an objective report is out of the question.

Essential items are ignored and considerably less important ones described in full depth. The excuses that are presented are only really valid in the fewest of cases. The tendency to pass the entire blame to the National Socialists in order to be able to hide their own failure better after the event is evident in most of these books."[86]

The Bavarian bishops published a pastoral letter on May 5, 1933, to dispel the largely prevailing uncertainty, unrest, and worry of many souls and to contribute to "clarification and calm," "the return of inner peace": "Our current Reich government has set itself great and difficult tasks. . . . *No one can now step aside and grumble out of dejectedness and bitterness*; no one who is inwardly willing to cooperate may be put aside for reasons of bias and narrow-mindedness. This is why we bishops call upon our diocesans out of our deep love for our Fatherland . . . no longer to look back at the past, not to see what separates us, but to see what unites us. . . . *No one should withdraw from the great rebuilding work*."[87]

The bishops wrote regarding the referendum on November 12, 1933, after Germany's exit from the League of Nations, once again: "The Catholics express . . . their agreement with the far-seeing and energetic efforts of the Führer, to spare the German people the horrors of war and the cruelties of Bolshevism, to guarantee public order and create work for the unemployed."[88] What had been strictly prohibited until 1933 had, of course, long since been allowed: admission to churches for uniformed SA and SS men and the flying of swastikas on and in churches. At the Berlin Catholic Convention on June 25—Hitler had declined an invitation with regret—the papal nuncio was accompanied to the altar by the SA with swastika flags.[89] And when there was a thanksgiving service at the Berlin Hedwig Cathedral after the concordat was concluded, the instruction was: "The Catholic SA and SS men of Berlin will participate as one."[90] An SA band played church music on the *Opernplatz* square.[91]

Archbishop Gröber, who had implored the German Catholics on April 25 "not to reject the new state but must affirm it positively [*sic*] and cooperate in it unerringly,"[92] ordered in August: "Accordingly there is no obstacle to allowing the flags and insignia of the National Socialist German Workers' Party into the Catholic Church and letting them be raised in the nave."[93]

The cardinal of Breslau, who justifies the determined about-turn of the entire high German clergy toward the Nazi regime with the following shameless sentences: "It has been shown once again that our Church is not bound to any political system, any worldly form of government or any party constellation. The Church has higher goals, supernatural[!] tasks are incumbent upon it," protests expressly and very energetically "against assumptions that the Church may not be quite serious with its support for the newly created state order."[94]

Hitler thought of this intrepidly arguing cardinal on the evening of June 7, 1942, at Wolfsschanze, the Führer's then headquarters. He said, "he experienced how skillfully the Church, in particular the Catholic Church, understands how to present a harmless face to the bearer of political power and ingratiate itself during his first visit from Bishop Bertram after assuming power. For Bertram had so solemnly conveyed *humble greetings* from the Church in his speech that one could have believed, if one had not experienced it firsthand, that a National Socialist had never been expelled from the Church, persecuted or inhibited in his peace in death. The Church has always crept its way into power with such humble posturing and ingratiated itself with the German Emperors too, from Charlemagne onwards."[95] Hitler was right.

Bishop Vogt of Aachen promised him by telegraph on July 10 that he would cooperate joyfully on the building of the new Reich with his diocese.[96]

Bishop Berning of Osnabrück declared that the German bishops not only approved of the new state but also supported it with burning love and all their might.[97]

Archbishop Gröber of Freiburg said to rapturous applause at a Catholic Association meeting on October 9 that he was "completely backing the Reich government and the new Reich."[98]

Bishop Bornewasser of Trier put on a display of pathos in 1933: "We have entered the new Reich with our heads held high and with a firm step and are ready to serve it by using all the power of our bodies and souls."[99]

Suffragan bishop Burger even claimed: "The aims of the Reich government have been those of our Catholic Church for a long time."[100]

The vicar general of the bishopric of Berlin, Prelate Steinmann, who was deputizing for the sick Bishop Schreiber, summarized the faith of the German episcopate in the sentence: "Our Chancellor has been called by God."[101]

Cardinal Faulhaber of Munich, who had already served as a field bishop in the First World War, was an especially eager supporter of Hitler's party. His sympathies allegedly go a long way back. When people tried to put him in a negative light regarding the Hitler putsch on November 9, 1923, it was said that it "filled him with the greatest bitterness."[102] And the hostility to the Führer from abroad pained Faulhaber so much that he asked Cardinals Hayes of New York and Mundelein of Chicago to use all of their influence in their episcopal cities to desist from this "atrocious smear campaign."[103]

The bold cardinal hurried to reassure Hitler in a handwritten letter, "From our very soul: God keep our Reich Chancellor for our people."[104] "What the old parliaments and parties could not manage in sixty years," he said in thanks to Hitler after the conclusion of the Reich concordat, "has been realized by your statesmanlike farsightedness, unique in world history in six months. For Germany's standing in east and west and all over the world, this handshake with the papacy, the greatest moral force in world history, represents an exploit of immeasurable benefit."[105] In his Lent pastoral letter titled "Our Civic Conscience," Faulhaber announced, "So a ray of God's authority shines over all state thrones . . . it would be a crime against the civic conscience to overthrow an existing state form by revolution or coup."[106] The cardinal wrote to the Bavarian interior minister Adolf Wagner on June 12 that he had instructed the clergy to avoid anything in their sermons and private conversations that could damage the trust with the national government or the peaceful cooperation between church and state.[107]

And the book that appeared in 1934 with permission to print from the church (from Faulhaber's archiepiscopal ordinariate), *Wächter der Kirche, ein Buch vom deutschen Episkopat* (*Guardians of the Church, a Book from the German Episcopate*), guarantees—one can hardly believe one's eyes—that the end of the tensions between the church and National Socialism (in other words, Hitler's seizure of power) "had been wished for by no one more than the German bishops themselves."[108]

LEADING CATHOLIC THEOLOGIANS ALSO SUPPORTED HITLER

They even created a series of documents that, as the Aschendorff publishing house in Münster formulated on the back page of all these pamphlets, was "to serve the rebuilding of the Third Reich with the united powers of the National Socialist state and Catholic Christianity."

Michael Schmaus

> *"You must differentiate between such popular literature and an academic, theological interpretation."*
> —Michael Schmaus during a dispute on mixed marriage[109]

Schmaus recognized very precisely in the abovementioned Aschendorff series: "For I see the heaviest and most forceful protest against the intellectuality of the 19th and 20th centuries in the National Socialist movement," which Schmaus views positively, of course. He is enthusiastic about the "suppression of all damaging influences in literature, press, theatre, art and motion picture."[110] And while he roundly condemns liberalism, in complete agreement with the nineteenth-century papacy, he embraces "rushing blood and sustaining soil." "The principles of National Socialist intent and those of the Catholic imperatives," explains Schmaus, clearly not popularly but academically, "point in the same direction." And he gives credit to the "National Socialist vitality," stating that "in it the entire person comes to his rights, not just one side of the person, the mind."[111]

His educated interpretation of National Socialism did not harm Michael Schmaus in the Christian federal republic. He was called up to the *Bayerische Akademie der Wissenschaften* (Bavarian Academy of Sciences) in 1951 and became rector of the University of Munich. Sixteen Catholic fraternities, whose leaders once supported Hitler with equal enthusiasm, named Schmaus their "Honorary Philistine." Franco, Hitler's ally, awarded Schmaus the Knight Commander's Cross of the Spanish Order *Al merito civil*. And Hitler's collaborator Pius XII raised him to the status of papal house prelate in 1952.

Joseph Lortz

Joseph Lortz, as prominent as Schmaus and a party member since May 1, 1933, also spared no effort in making the turnaround of his church plausible. He complained of "an ignorance that can truly be called tragic [on the Catholic side] of the powerful positive forces, ideas and plans of National Socialism, as they have been set out authentically and been publicly available in Hitler's book *Mein Kampf* since 1925. We all have our own guilt to bear in this failure."[112] With respect to *Mein Kampf*, Lortz speaks of "stupendous assuredness," of "quite outstanding inner consistency," and he even used the formulation "truly great."[113] Theologian Lortz smittenly thanks Hitler for "the salvation of Germany, and thereby Europe, from the chaos of Bolshevism"; he announces the "discovery of *basic similarities* between National Socialism and Catholicism"; he writes: "In many crucial matters only Catholicism can fulfill National Socialism"; and he finally says "a big 'Yes' to him," and that because of a "double duty of conscience," because National Socialism is not only the legal force in Germany but "for the greater part Germany itself."[114]

A final, particularly considerable excerpt from Lortz's document. After counting liberalism as one of the deadly diseases of the time and one of the church's main enemies, he continues: "Compared to that, it is positively liberating that finally, in these modern times, there is a great force and shaper of life *outside* the Church that heralds it and penetrates well into real life, which Popes Gregory XVI, Pius IX and Leo XIII, in the 19th century, subjected to the arrogant mocking laughter of the so-called educated and progressive world that was fighting for 'culture,' taught or rejected: the overestimation of majority voting and its confusion with authority; the demand for unrestricted freedom of speech and the press, in other words, all the negative ideas that individualistic liberalism confused with the essence of freedom."[115] This theologian sees in such telling points complete agreement between the significant popes of the nineteenth century and the Nazi dictator or, as Lortz also writes, "the Catholic Adolf Hitler."[116] And Lortz is right.

Joseph Pieper

Joseph Pieper, the well-known theological author, said in a lecture on "Abuse of the Word and Power" to the German Research Foundation in 1964: "The journalistic word, once it has basically become a lie, is by its nature the prepared tool that waits for a ruler to take it into his hand and 'use' it for any purposes of power. But the more ground it gains, it creates from itself an atmosphere of epidemic predisposition and susceptibility to the rule of violence"[117]—Joseph Pieper spoke from experience. Thirty years previously, in 1934, he wrote a document proving the commonalities in Pius XI's *encyclica quadragesimo anno* and the social ideas of the Nazis. "The commonalities, which are very far-reaching and individually quite astonishing, between the illustrative guidelines of the encyclical and the socio-political goals and realizations of the National Socialist state, should therefore be clarified so emphatically so that the Catholic Christians outside the Nazi Party can come to see the bridge that binds the mind-set of Christian social teachings with National Socialist social politics, the centerpiece of domestic policy in the Third Reich."[118]

Karl Adam

Of course, not every prominent Catholic theologian chummed up so quickly. But the most famous one, Karl Adam, whose book *Das Wesen des Katholizismus* (*The Spirit of Catholicism*) was translated into all major languages, distanced Catholicism markedly from National Socialism as the speaker at the *Heilig-Jahrfeier* (Holy Year Celebration) in Stuttgart on January 21, 1934. Living religion, preached Adam at the time, "never [thrived] on the forces of national traditions," instead deriving its strongest impulses from an ultimate reality "beyond any national tradition." "A religion that did not want to find its highest value in an eternal reality of the beyond but in a perishable one, founded in this world—in the *myth of blood*, would have to sink into itself and cramp up with inner necessity."[119]

But gradually Karl Adam also saw the light, and in June 1940, at the peak of Hitler's glory, the intellectual stated the opposite of what he had supported just a few years previously, in Aachen: "The time is finally over in which National Socialism stood before us as just one of many political parties. Something *much deeper*, something totally new has arisen within it: a new way of seeing German reality, *of understanding it from its very basis, the peculiarity of blood and national traditions*, of distancing it from all alien nature and using *its own highest racial values* to construct a new Reich. Now this new Third Reich stands before us, full of burning will to live and passion, full of irrepressible force, full of creative fertility. We Catholics know our place as members of this Reich and see *our highest earthly task in our service to the Reich*. . . . *German blood* is and remains the substantial *bearer of our Christian reality*. . . . *For the sake of our conscience we will serve the new Reich with all our might, come what may*.[120]

And what came then! The year 1951—and the Great Federal Cross of Merit for Karl Adam. Awarded by President Heuß, who had also found such appreciative words for Hitler back in 1932 . . .

⸎

And it was not only the bishops and theologians: the Catholic German student-leaders also supported Hitler repeatedly. The leader of the Christian association, Forschbach, declared, on the occasion of the referendum and Reichstag elections in 1933: "Anyone who does not vote 'Yes' on November 12 is breaking his fraternity oath, because he his betraying his fatherland and his people in this hour of greatest danger."[121] The Catholic fraternity, who decreed a similar call for the election, had already declared in September: "We want the fraternity because we want the unity of the Catholic and German students under the National Socialist objective."[122]

The general secretary of the Journeymen's Association, Nattermann, wrote to Hitler that the Journeymen's Association saw in him not only the authority ordered from above but also the leader who had completed by political power what Adolf Kolping, the founder and leader of the Journeymen's Association, had wanted to bring about through intellectual transformation: to overcome liberalism and socialism.[123] And the general church president of the Catholic Young Men's Association, Monsignor Ludwig Wolker, guaranteed that his youth would be at the disposal of the National Socialist state with complete readiness and loyalty.[124]

And the Nazis themselves, incidentally, also plastered the advertising columns and houses with a poster depicting Hitler, the functionary Hermann Esser, and the papal nuncio surrounded by Swastika flags for the referendum on November 12. The text underneath read: "A solemn moment from the laying of the foundation stone for the *Haus der deutschen Kunst* [House of German Art]. The papal Nuncio Vasallo di Torregrossa is saying to the Führer: 'I did not understand you for a long time. But I made a great deal of effort to for a long time. Today I understand you.' And today every German Catholic understands Adolf Hitler and will be voting 'Yes' on November 12!"[125]

THE ALLEGED SCAPEGOAT: GERMAN "MILIEU CATHOLICISM"

The scapegoat was not discovered until thirty years later, by one of those Catholics who only criticize their church in order to be able to defend it even more convincingly—always the most fatal apologists.

When such an author opens a chapter with: "1933 and German Catholicism! Once again the dentist's drill is approaching—and once again the patient will flinch with a wild cry,"[126] his kitsch alone already makes him suspect. Carl Amery, in his paperback *Die Kapitulation oder Deutscher Katholizismus heute* (*Capitulation or German Catholicism Today*), blames the failure of the Catholic Church in 1933 not on the pope and the bishops, but on their believers. He calls this "Milieu Catholicism." This is quite reminiscent of Mr. von Papen, who put Hitler in power and then accused the Germans of "lacking intelligence" and "lethargy of thought." As compared to the "initial situation" of Catholicism "in 1933," claims Amery, "the significance of the bishops, the prelate Kaas, and even the Vatican in the 'arrangement' with the ruling powers is diminishing."[127] We hear, regarding the "initial situation," that German Catholicism was preserving "yesterday's ideal little world," its view of the church was in keeping, "of course, with the development of the German bourgeoisie in the 19th century," he stressed that there was "as good as no primary Christian virtue," and Amery finally writes: "In this small world, State and religious[!] authority ruled; the latter ensured with crook and dog, i.e., with the powers of its office and conformity in general, that the lambs not only remained in the pen of the doctrine but also in the pen of relative intellectual and spiritual safety. It was not the lamb's job to determine the pastures they were to graze on."[128] According to this, Milieu Catholicism is actually the result of the bishops' tutelage! Otherwise, what did the German bishops do *against* Milieu Catholicism? Amery's silence in this respect is deafening. He merely repeats what he cannot prove: "The capitulation did not primarily come about because of the bishops or the Centre Party prelates or the Monsignori, but the *juste milieu* of German Catholicism."[129] And then Amery reveals what he considers to be the ace up his sleeve: "Let us assume that Kaas had given in to Brüning, and the Centre leadership had stayed with the 'Left,' which would have fought to the bitter end. Let us assume the episcopate had stood up, with the volcanic force of the Prophets, not only for the rights of the Church but also the rights of all those who had been persecuted, wrongly imprisoned, chased through the streets, whipped, and treated with castor oil. Let us assume that the papal circular *With Burning Concern* had— with different contents, of course—already been released to German Catholic Christians in 1933. What would have been expected then? *The Milieu would still have capitulated."*[130]

Maybe. But if the milieu had capitulated but *not* the episcopate, then it would not need such a flimsy defense today. It is not about speculating on what would have happened but about determining what did happen. The church leadership supported criminals.

It was not the majority of the Catholics who turned to Hitler first, followed by the episcopate, then the curia. It was the curia that decided, after the experiment it tried with Mussolini had succeeded, to repeat it with Hitler. The German bishops obeyed and the believers had to follow them, which is even confirmed by the Catholic side. After all, the *Allgemeine Rundschau* wrote on April 19, 1933, as has already been said:[131] "The bishops cannot fight if Rome decided on peace." And Karl Bachem, the Centre Party's historian, declared resistance by the *bishops* after the new government had been recognized to be morally irre-sponsible and impossible. There is no choice for us, he admitted, but to follow the bishops' example.[132] And the analysis of the election results confirms that people in Catholic areas were still, in part, resisting the Nazis on March 5, 1933, while they had almost entirely gone over to them by the time of the November elections.[133] The folly of Amery's whitewash is also demonstrated if his claim that "Eugenio Pacelli, later Pope Pius XII, believed that he could prevent the worst using diplomatic methods"[134] is confronted with Pacelli's own words to Hitler's ambassador at the Vatican: the Holy See also approves the application of "external means of power against the Bolshevist threat."[135]

Now the Nazi-friendly maneuvering of the German episcopate is still widely considered to be a fleeting error, restricted to 1933, even to this day. Because were there not, shortly afterward, grievances, differences, disputes . . . in other words: What about the church struggle? There was surely that, even if there was no persecution of the church and most certainly no persecution of Christians.[136] But stressing the church struggle, with the pathos-tinged reference to the complaints the bishops made against the party and the government, the arrest of several thousand Catholics and even martyrs only disguises the contents, which are characterized by two fundamental facts:

1. With one exception, the protests of the high Catholic clergy only concerned Catholic interests.
2. Anyone who attacked the National Socialist state as a whole was not supported by the church, but attempts were often made to "convert" them to Nazism.

So as always with the church, it was only ever about maintaining their power. Anything else was met with indifference. No, worse than that, it was, apart from the killing of the mentally ill, positively in agreement with it. It was prepared to let millions of people die in order to survive itself. It drove the Germans toward—and in doing so, the British, French, Poles, Russians, and Americans against—Hitler and death even though he himself fought the church.

1. UNDER HITLER, THE GERMAN BISHOPS NEVER PROTESTED AGAINST HIM OR HIS SYSTEM

They never protested against the politics with which he brought calamity on half of the world. It did not matter to them. They supported it. No, their complaints were directed only against Hitler's *policies on religion*, his violations of the concordat. He had promised to respect the rights of the church but had no intention of keeping his promise. So the bishops fought back against the curtailing of church claims regarding youth education, the school system, the press; they fought back against the alignment of Catholic associations, against criticism of the Old Testament, the gospels, the clergy, against the confiscation of church property, the ban on processions, against the monk trials, although even the pope, after a series of trials, dissolved an entire province of the Franciscan order because of "debaucheries."[137] And sometimes the curia also, of course, used sharp language to criticize the violation of the concordat.

The Catholics' favorite showpiece is Pius XI's encyclical "With Burning Concern," dated March 4, 1937. But in reality, the pope addresses only Catholic Church issues and nothing else! In pages and pages of complaints, he interceded for true belief in God, true belief in Christ, belief in the church as the one and only true institution of salvation, the primate of the Roman bishop, the right to free religious activity (cf. Croatia!), Catholic youth education, and other similar things. But not a word against the concentration camps and the pogroms on Jews!

So in a long written communication from April 30, 1937, to the German ambassador at the Vatican, Secretary of State Pacelli was also able to describe the encyclical as "benevolent for all its candor" and state that it would be easy for the Holy See to prove with documentary evidence how it had, since the concordat was concluded, used every opportunity for "responsible agreement," "with patience that was felt by many to be excessive." But even Pacelli himself defended only the so-called rights of the Catholic Church in the communication, but he did not forget to praise the liquidation of the communists by the Nazis once again.

So all the complaints of the Catholica—this point can hardly be made expressly enough—concerned only the violation of *Catholic* interests.

What was the concern of the German episcopate on June 26, 1941, four days after Hitler's attack on the Soviet Union? In a mutual pastoral letter read out from every pulpit, they grumbled: "But we do not understand and are filled with great pain about the fact that some measures have been taken that deeply interfere in *Church life* without being founded *in the necessity of war*." These bishops were not concerned that millions upon millions would now have to die. Instead, they emphasized "the restrictions in the field of religious education, religious literature, exceptional pastoral care in spiritual exercises and retreats, services and Church holidays. We remember with sadness that so many mon-

asteries have been closed in recent months and reemployed for nonchurch purposes. We have heartfelt sympathy with the people of the Orders who have been
driven out of their monastic homes." They felt sorry only for themselves. These
bishops expressed no sorrow for the soldiers dying in foreign fields, the women,
children, and elderly who were being bombed and buried in their own homes.
Let alone any sign of protest! Instead, they reminded everyone of "holy duties
of conscience from which no one can free us and which we must fulfill even if
it costs us our lives: never, under any circumstances, must any man blaspheme
against God, hate his fellow man, never kill an innocent except in war or justified defense, never commit adultery, never lie. He must never deny his belief or
be led to leaving the Church by threats or promises."[138]

So this is what the bishops were concerned about after the German armies
had marched into Soviet Russia: not blaspheming, not committing adultery,
not lying, not denying one's belief, not leaving the church—and, yes, not killing,
"except in war." In war, they did (and still do) allow the mass slaughter of people,
including Catholics. They not only allowed it: they made it a duty! (And they
will make it a duty again!)

They were concerned only with maintaining their church interests and
nothing else, with one exception. The German bishops never condemned the
many thousands of judicial murders of their opponents, the elimination of liberals, democrats, and communists—which, of course, was what they wanted
anyway. These bishops never protested against Hitler's invasions of Austria,
Czechoslovakia, Poland, Denmark, Norway, Belgium, Holland, France,
Yugoslavia, or the Soviet Union, a war that they observed "with gratification."
They never protested against the pogroms on Jews, the destruction of more
than two hundred synagogues, the deportation and gassing of Jews, whom
their own church had been martyring and killing for fifteen hundred years.
They never protested against the system of Nazism at all. Not one pastoral
letter, as Cardinal Bertram stressed in 1936, criticized the state, the movement, or the Führer.[139] On the contrary; at that time, high clergymen such
as Cardinal Faulhaber of Munich, Cardinal Schulte of Cologne, and Bishop
Matthias Ehrenfried of Würzburg declared their complete readiness to
cooperate and regretted that they had been eliminated politically.[140] Indeed,
they admitted *in corpore* to supporting Hitler more the less resistance he

showed to them. In the "Pastoral letter of the German bishops concerning the struggle against Bolshevism" of December 24, 1936, it said: "Dear diocesans! The Church will be able to support the Third Reich all the more forcefully the more it enjoys that freedom in their own fields of law and labor that is guaranteed to them by God's law and the Reich Concordat." They did not wish to surrender "one iota" of the truths of their holy faith. But should they be bothered about a little humanity and ethics if only their self-serving wishes were respected? "But your bishops want to affirm equally fearlessly, and all *true* Catholics with them, their deep respect for state authority and, which is our affair, cooperate with the state in peace and trust."[141]

Again and again, year for year, the bishops sucked up to the brown criminals in this way. The church struggle did not stop them. They urged and complained, but at the same time sent the Catholics to Hitler and his generals—and to their doom. And afterward they pretended to have had nothing to do with it. Afterward, they filled the world with screams and grotesque propaganda tales. "*During* the Nazi regime," writes the Catholic Johannes Fleischer, "although they referred to the attacks that the Christian doctrine was exposed to by means of officially propagated neo-paganism, they affirmed at every given opportunity that these official attacks could not be 'in the Führer's interest,' that they undermined the 'Führer's rebuilding work,' that they should not be misguided by them out of 'loyalty to the Führer and the State' and that despite all this, in the 'globally significant historical defensive struggle against Bolshevism,' the Catholics could be counted on as the most loyal followers of the Führer and the state. *After* the collapse of the Nazi regime, however, they had allegedly been fighting against the 'entire totalitarian state' and were able, building on this historical lie, to place their irreplaceable services at the disposal of the *new* front against 'peace under enforced communist rule' as, one might say, 'old campaigners' for freedom and rights. Others could admit their guilt for their position towards the Third Reich—the Catholic leadership did not have to: *they* had always been against it."[142]

But anyone who had really been against it was deserted by them.

2. THE GERMAN CATHOLIC MARTYRS UNDER HITLER ARE WITNESSES AGAINST THE CHURCH

There have always been Catholics whose martyrdom has spoken against the church throughout history, even in ancient times. If, for example, the church *before* Constantine was proud of its executed pacifists, it no longer had any need for their martyrdom after 313. The Catholica, which had suddenly become friendly with the military, deleted the names of all the executed conscientious objectors from their calendars and replaced the real soldier martyrs with invented ones who were designed so that they could have only an uplifting effect on Christian soldiers.[143]

Under Hitler, too, Catholic conscientious objectors and opponents of the "state order" (Faulhaber) were completely undesirable to the church. But after the war, it *boasted* with them.

"At the time," the West German Catholic theologian Dr. Wilhelm Lenzen, who had once been in Dachau and whose vicar general in Aachen later banned him from taking part in the Easter antinuclear demonstrations, writes, "at the time, those men could say nothing else to priests and chaplains who had come into conflict with Nazi authorities but: 'You must also be careful!' No effective support for relatives, no help for those affected. . . . Those who showed courage and took a stance in those days, the 'careless ones' (Fr. Alfred Delp, SJ; Fr. Dr. Metzger; Fr. Rupert Mayer; Prelate Lichtenberg—to name just a few from dozens), are today used for glorious, kudos-charged Christian Martyrdom. No, at the time they had no effective support from those Church officials. Today, their truly glorious acts have been systematically reworked: those who were beaten down and murdered by a devilish, scandalous state power because of their own personal conscience are today presented as martyrs of the Church system."[144] And Father Alfred Delp, who was executed after July 20, 1944, as a member of the Kreisau Circle, affirmed: "German history will, in the future, have to write the bitter chapter about the failure of the churches."[145]

But the bishops themselves testified in all clarity that they also supported Hitler's fight against his domestic opponents. The Fulda Bishops' Conference of 1935 asserted in a "memorandum" to him: "The Catholic associations will always serve the German people and Fatherland in the National Socialist State with the courage to sacrifice and loyalty. We most strictly reject any subversive acts or positions from our members. . . . Anyone who would attempt to introduce anti-government trends into associations today . . . would strictly have to be removed from the associations. . . . The clergy ordered for the prisoners will . . . commit them to . . . recognizing state authority, thus contributing to the inner adjustment and improvement of the prisoners."[146]

So the bishops rejected any antigovernment act "most strictly"! And if that were not enough, they also wanted to make Hitler's opponents in prisons and concentration camps Nazi minions! The attitude of the high German clergy and their representatives to political opponents of the regime can be shown here pars pro toto by the little-known case of a Catholic clerk and his conviction by the Reich Military Court on December 16, 1940.[147]

This man had wanted to join the judicial service in 1935, but—in keeping with Catholic teaching—wanted only to acknowledge those laws that did not contradict it. He had doubts of conscience regarding activity in matters of divorce and hereditary health affairs and refused to swear the oath. He was taken into "protective custody" in 1937 and then examined in a psychiatric hospital for six weeks. When he was called up to the Wehrmacht in 1940, he emphasized that as a strict Catholic he recognized an absolute prerogative of the church above the people and the state. "He could," it said in the justification of the Reich military court verdict, "only swear the soldiers' oath to the extent that it did not contradict the teachings of Catholic beliefs and morals. He later expanded this statement to the effect that he considered the current war to be an unjust one and could therefore not exercise his military service to the full extent. Although he was ready to die for his people at any time, he would not himself be able to kill on orders, or if necessary without them. The accused persisted in this view despite thorough warnings and cautions even during the main proceedings."[148]

The view of the clerk that no Catholic should swear unquestioning obedience to Hitler or take part in this unjust war provoked "very drastically the indignation of a high member of the Catholic Wehrmacht clergy" at the Wehrmacht prison in Tegel. And a Father, summoned before Reich military court as an expert, said: "If the view of the accused were Catholic teaching I would lay down my vestment today."[149] The church abandoned him completely. It even testified against him. However, the prosecuting, non-Catholic, Nazi military court council conceded—and this is a unique disgrace of the episcopate that was collaborating with Hitler: "The view represented by the accused is undoubtedly Catholic teaching. There is no two ways about it. If the German bishops were really the religious fighters they portray themselves as being, they would be up before this court and not the accused. Their opportunism keeps them from that. The case of the accused is not yet concluded here: it will be revisited before the forum of the global public. But then there will be no cover-up, no silence, no avoidance. The facts will speak for themselves then."[150]

It is a fact that, according to Gordon Zahn's investigation, only seven Catholics refused military service in the entire Greater German Reich; six of them were killed, the seventh declared mentally ill.[151] It is a fact that a Catholic prison chaplain even refused communion to the Pallottine priest Franz Reinisch because he would not swear a military oath to Hitler.[152] It is a fact that the pope himself said to the Berlin correspondent of the *Osservatore Romano*, of the "millions of Catholics" in "the German armies": "They have sworn. They must be obedient."[153]

The pope and the German bishops demanded obedience to Hitler. As a consequence, there was no "Catholic resistance" at all. There was resistance from some individual Catholics. And it took place against the will of the church. The losses here were also minimal, compared to those of the Jehovah's Witnesses, whose small community suffered two thousand victims at the hands of the Nazi regime.[154] Furthermore, not one single German bishop became a martyr or was even interned in a concentration camp. Lower clergy sufficed for that purposes. And Orthodox bishops, who were deported to Dachau with the Catholics' help (p. 196)! Once again: not one German prince of the church even had a hair put out of place under Hitler, not even von Galen, who made himself a global epitome of the Catholic resistance fighter.

THE "LION OF MÜNSTER"

". . . to fight and die for Germany."

Bishop von Galen contributed to the abolition of the so-called Euthanasia program. On July 28, 1941, he filed a suit with the state prosecutor and the chief of police in Münster for the murder of mentally ill persons after around seventy thousand fell victim to "*Aktion Gnadentod*" ("Mercy Death"). Von Galen must be recognized for this action. Admittedly, others had also protested, in particular, Protestant theologians, among them Pastor von Bodelschwingh. Incidentally, these sparse church interventions brought Hitler, as the chief official of these crimes, Hefelmann, stated at the euthanasia trial in Limburg, to stop this action.[155]

Bishop von Galen also took steps against the arrest of clergy, monks, and nuns, the confiscation of church property, and the crackdown on religious institutions. But this was only in regard to Catholic affairs. Von Galen never protested against Nazi terror as such. On the contrary! On October 28, 1935, he stressed that it was not his job to grieve for past forms of government and criticize current state policy.[156] He sent an enthusiastic telegram to Baron von Fritsch, the commander in chief of the armed forces, regarding the occupation of the demilitarized zone of the Rhineland.[157] And above all, he never protested against the criminal war initiated by Hitler. On the contrary! The "Lion of Münster" defended his attacks with the claim that the antireligious politics of the Hitler regime was preventing Germany from victory! It could have a negative influence on the course of the war because it was undermining "internal national unity." The celebrated Catholic prince of the church guaranteed that "Christians will do their duty," German soldiers "want to fight and die for Germany," and similar such things.[158] Well, that was all Hitler was asking of them.

Let us also remember that all the pastoral letters in which the German bishops mutually declared that they would not withdraw the powers of the church from Nazism at any price, declared their respect for the authority of the Third Reich, accompanied the movement's work with the best blessings, reinforced trust in the Führer, called for loyal fulfillment of duty and brave persistence in war—let us remember that at the bottom of all these pastoral letters that supported a criminal, they were always bearing, among others, the signature of Clemens August Graf von Galen: the name of a resistance fighter?

The "Lion of Münster," as he himself admits, supported Hitler and the continuation of the war directly and indirectly, "again and again" and "most forcefully." And it was no other than von Galen who in 1938 authorized a lousy concoction, titled "Oath to the Flag" ("*Fahneneid*") to be written, which inflamed the Christian soldiers with the noblest of phrases to be unconditionally loyal to Hitler. "The Christian soldier obeys because he sees, in the command of every leading position in his unit, a radiation of that power that he has acknowledged and affirmed in the 'Oath to the Flag' he has sworn to the Führer of the German people and Commander in Chief of the Wehrmacht."[159] In every order from an officer or non-com there is still an aura of divine power! "If and insofar as a war is just," it continues in the opus authorized by von Galen, it "can never be subject to the judgment of an individual, least of all a soldier, so that he could make his willingness to sacrifice his life dependent on it. It is but the leaders who are to make decisions like this." Which means that von Galen, just like the entire German episcopate, incidentally, did not even concede soldiers a personal decision based on conscience. "To waver at such a decisive hour is not possible for a Christian, and it is certainly not possible for a Christian soldier who has sworn a holy oath of loyalty before God. He will see the war from the moral side as a struggle between right and wrong."[160]

Right and wrong. In the Second World War, the German Catholics fought for Hitler; the Polish and French Catholics, against Hitler. Only one side can have been on the "right" side. If it was the side of the Poles, French, British, and Americans, then it was not the German side. If the war on the German side was wrong, then the German bishops were wrong too. If Hitler was a criminal, then those who supported him who were in leading and influential positions for more than a full decade were criminals too.

In the middle of the war, the *Katholische Kirchenblatt für das nördliche Münsterland* (*Catholic Church Gazette for the Northern Münster Region*)— with episcopal approval from Münster, wrote: "It is always a matter of justice to defend one's fatherland when it has been attacked. It is a Christian's duty. Because the Savior said: 'Render unto Caesar what is Caesar's and unto God what is God's'!"[161] So we would be contravening the Savior's command if we were to desert our Fatherland when it was in need. So don't come to me with English Christianity, it has nothing to do with the divine Savior! And so what is happening to it now serves it right. God does not let himself be mocked. Sooner or later the hour of reckoning and retribution comes."[162]

When a fake sermon was distributed in which Bishop von Galen allegedly demanded the destruction of the godless Nazi regime, von Galen vehemently denied writing this sermon and emphasized that it was "in complete contradiction" to his views and position.[163] As late as summer 1945, von Galen demonstrated his fight against Hitler in a pastoral letter: "I said our soldiers would continue to do their duty. As long as there is a war they would use their weapons against armed opponents in the struggle for peace."[164]

This bishop, who had sanctioned the Nazi state, its murderous regiment, and its war crimes and committed soldiers to killing for Hitler, was later subjected to the beatification process. For the Austrian Catholic farmer and family man Franz Jägerstätter from St. Radegund, who was *executed* on August 9, 1943, because, for reasons of conscience, he had refused to do under any circumstances what Bishop von Galen had demanded from German soldiers under any circumstances, there still has not been any beatification process!

It is interesting that of all people it was Pius XII who drove forward the beatification and canonization processes of bishops, cardinals, and popes "as evidence that the Church can not only be holy in its limbs but also in its heads. This should, at the same time, be a definitive answer to articles, publications and books that only seek out holiness in monasteries and rectories and see people in the episcopal and apostolic sees who are so filled with earthly events that they simply have no time for holy matters."[165] One must—I emphasize, one must—read Breza to see what, for example, would have put the beatification process of the Milan cardinal Schuster, who was, as is well known, one of the most fascist-friendly princes of the church, in danger under Pius XII. Not his blessing of Italian troops before they invaded Abyssinia, but the appearance of dancers from the Folies Bergères, who, as the *Osservatore Romano* wrote, "wore three—yes, exactly three!—stamps as a costume." I repeat, one must read Breza to see that. Overall, his only subtly ironic book, which stems from the finest diplomatic pen, provides a shining insight into the curial life in the times of Pius XII.

The beatification process, which was conducted for Cardinal Clemens August Graf von Galen by the ordinariate in Münster in 1959, even raised protests from Catholics loyal to the church. Johannes Fleischer (unsuccessfully) tried to intervene at the episcopal ordinariate in Münster, then at the Congregation of Rites of the Holy See. With reference to the material he had supplied, which incriminated Cardinal von Galen "most seriously," Fleischer states:

1. "that Bishop von Galen and *all* the German bishops who ruled during the Nazi period falsified and disregarded fundamental principles of Catholic faith and moral doctrine regarding the most crucial questions in a downright blasphemous way and thereby betrayed Christ and his Holy Church";
2. "that Bishop von Galen and *all* the German bishops constantly violated their God-given official duties in the coarsest possible ways";
3. "that Bishop von Galen and *all* the German bishops led millions of Catholics, who trusted the episcopal announcements without hesitation, into the darkness of aberration, made them henchmen in the service of criminals and notorious Antichrists and thereby burdened themselves before God and Man with a monstrous blood guilt that has not been atoned for to this day.

But should the beatification process still be continued and even result in a beatification, then every discerning Catholic and the public who have been informed about the true contents by the articles named above must draw the conclusion that the Holy See not only approves the episcopal betrayal of Christ, his Church, his teachings, the office of bishop, and the perversion of the consciences of the trusting Catholic people by their bishops, but furthermore glorifies it as a positive example for every member of the *Corpus Christi Mysticum*.

However, there is no doubt that even the most enraged Church-hater could never damage the standing of the Church and Church doctrine with his attacks on the Church and its institutions as would be the case if Cardinal von Galen were to receive a beatification."[166] [He was finally beatified in 2005, PG]

⁓

Now the German bishops did not merely restrict themselves to supporting Hitler in 1933 and then—apart from many complaints relating to church policy—to silently accepting his dictatorship. True, almost half the world still believes this today, if one reads, for instance, in an otherwise correct article on the treatment of the church struggle in postwar literature, "that a considerable number of

German Catholics, among them, bishops and other high dignitaries, had for a long time been deceived by Hitler's diabolical tactics, and at least *supported the Führer during the first year*."[167] But this is contrary to the facts as set out in the following.

THE GERMAN (AND, AFTER 1938, ALSO THE AUSTRIAN) CATHOLIC BISHOPS SUPPORTED ONE OF THE GREATEST CRIMINALS IN WORLD HISTORY WITH INCREASING INTENSITY UNTIL THE FINAL YEARS OF THE SECOND WORLD WAR

> *"Apart from the mass killings of the mentally ill, the bishops went along with everything, absolutely everything."*
>
> —A. Miller[168]

Cardinal Faulhaber, who had already sympathized with Hitler so spontaneously in 1933, also *repeatedly* demanded "respect and obedience" of state authority in a pastoral letter in 1934 and extoled the "inestimable service" that the Nazi government had rendered to the people and to the church in many areas.[169]

The Bishop of Osnabrück, Wilhelm Berning, writes in a pastoral letter in 1934: "We *German Catholics*, who as loyal sons of our Holy Church support the preservation and maintenance of our religious and moral goods, are equally *loyal* sons of our *German State* who want to take a joyful and determined part in the construction and expansion of the new Reich. As German Catholics we have the *right* and the *duty* to do this."[170]

The bishop assures similar things repeatedly and describes personal sacrifices for the Nazi "national community" as "a duty inculcated in us by Christ."[171] Berning, who was appointed a member of the National Assembly on Göring's recommendation in 1933,[172] advised the concentration camp doctor at Auschwitz, Dr. Lucas, to "talk his way out of it" in 1944.[173]

The Freiburg archbishop Gröber, associate member of the SS, notes the loyalty to the state of Catholics through the centuries in a book he wrote in 1935.

Gröber even praises the Apostles' loyalty to the state,[174] even though we know virtually nothing about them that is historically certain.[175] But among the oldest Early Fathers whose writings we know, the author finds precious little in terms of patriotic testimonies, which is why he assumes, along with Carlyle, that love of the fatherland is always at its strongest when it is hardly ever mentioned.[176] Archbishop Gröber quotes from a Salian law: "Long live Christ, who loves the Franks."[177]

The state-supporting activity of Catholicism is stressed throughout the book—and Nietzsche defamed for being the good European! German soldiers did not go to war in the First World War with the *Zarathustra*. "What would our heroes have to learn from the *Zarathustra*? Enthusiasm for Emperor and Empire? In the first part they can read the chapter about the 'new tin gods,' in which they are taught the following about the state: "State? What is that? Now then, open your ears to me for I will now tell you my words about the death of the peoples. The State is the coldest of all cold monsters. . . . Yes, dying for many was invented which praises itself as life: truly heartening for all preachers of death.'"[178]

However, that was less likely to draw people into a slaughter that lasted four years and cost ten million lives than the advice of the Catholic Church on both sides.[179] Archbishop Gröber's reference to the "unanimous doctrine of Catholic moral theology" must have been so welcome to Hitler: "(Although) Catholic theologians have always differentiated between just and unjust war, and (but) have never left it to the discretion of the individual, with all his short-sightedness and moods, to even discuss what is and is not allowed (if only) in the event of war, but left the final decision to the respective legal authority."[180] That means, a Catholic comments, that "the 'Catholic theologians' assuage their boredom between the state-organized manslaughters playfully discussing the question: When is a war 'just' and when is it 'unjust'? They are filling weighty tomes with this question because the decision is 'morally, politically and technically so much more complicated' (the Jesuit Hirschmann), but as a precaution point more or less directly to the following: children, how stupid you are to take our moral theologizing so seriously! Because 'in the case of war,' when our 'decisions' should actually be acted upon, we withdraw quietly and secretly and leave the judgment on right or wrong to any criminal, only if he has been recommended by us—and that is always the case—as a 'legal authority' as 'God's servant for your good' (Hirschmann quoting Romans 13:4)."[181]

The Freiburg prelate, who recommends the patriotism to the Catholics of Nazi Germany to the Catholics, also closes very aptly, if not cynically, with a word from Leo XIII's encyclical *Sapientiae christianae*: "There is no better citizen in war[!] or peace than a Christian with a sense of duty."[182]

In 1935 the Fulda Bishops' Conference sent a memorandum to Hitler. "With you," it says, "Pope Pius XI has, as the first foreign ruler, shaken your hand in trust by means of the Reich Concordat, Pope Pius XI has praised you highly in the consistory before attentively listening to representatives of the other nations for being the first statesman to move away from Bolshevism along with him."[183]

And the bishops' protest was veritably moving: "It is untrue to say that the German bishops had never recognized the state, never agreed to cooperating in the renewal of the new state. . . . The bishops may do what they want—creating work through church construction, decreeing the Saar Rallies, recommending the winter relief organization, everything is suspected of being an expression of subversive views or hypocrisy. You, Reich Chancellor, once made a harrowing remark in one of your speeches: 'Whatever I do is misinterpreted. What am I supposed to do?' We bishops feel ourselves in the same situation."[184]

The bishop (and Prussian state councilor) Berning of Osnabrück went to visit the concentration camps in the Emsland in June 1936, which were extremely notorious even then. But Bishop Berning praised the "rebuilding work" of Himmler and his minions and did not hesitate to say: "This is where everyone must be taken who still doubts the rebuilding work of the Third Reich. What was previously neglected is being tackled here today."[185] And in the same year, Bishop Berning, as patron of the *Reichsverband für die katholischen Auslandsdeutschen* (Reich Federation for German Catholic Expatriates), demanded the return of the German colonies at a congress in Frankfurt.[186]

When Hitler occupied the demilitarized zone in March 1936, the church bells rang all across the Rhineland, the Catholics held thanksgiving services, and Cardinal Schulte of Cologne, who was allegedly much more skeptical to Nazism than many of his colleagues,[187] telegraphed the following to the commander in chief of the Wehrmacht: "In these memorable hours, since the Reich Wehrmacht has regained entry to the German Rhineland as protector of peace and order, I welcome those of our people appointed to bear arms, my soul moved."[188]

They could not escape their shock and emotion.

The bishops of Münster, Speyer, Mainz, and Trier expressed themselves with similar enthusiasm on the same occasion.[189]

On May 24, 1936, Bishop Rackl of Eichstätt preached that good Catholics have always been good patriots and Catholic soldiers have never been deserters. It was not, he assured, good Catholics who took part in the 1918 revolution, and good Catholics will never be on the side of revolutionaries, whatever may arise.[190]

When a Swiss Catholic called on children to pray for Hitler's death not long after, Cardinal Faulhaber spoke of a moment of madness from a crazy foreigner on June 7 and declared that everyone was witness to the fact that prayers are held for the Führer at the main service in all churches on Sundays and holidays. The cardinal was offended because the Catholics' loyalty to the state was being doubted and gave a "Christian answer" at once: he immediately rendered the Lord's Prayer with his faithful for Hitler's life![191]

On November 4, 1936, Faulhaber was received at the Obersalzberg and was once again impressed with Hitler during a three-hour talk. The Führer, he enthused, mastered diplomacy and etiquette better than any born sovereign.[192]

The bishops did emphatically stand up for their own rights in a pastoral letter in December 1936, but they also stood up for Hitler with equal force.

"The German bishops consider it their duty to *support* the ruler of the German Reich in this defensive struggle with *all means* . . .

The second weapon of the Church is the word. The word that announces the collapse of national economy and morality in Russia, the land of the godless. . . . The word that does not get stuck in criticism and lamentations and not always only sees the bad. The word that brings all divergent forces together in a *community of force* and *reinforces trust in the Führer*.

The third weapon of the Church is prayer, which . . . puts the heavenly legions on our side . . . which has the certainty of being heard . . . to maintain *loyalty until death* and to place a personality so full of character into the service of people and fatherland. *The Church will be able to support the Third Reich in the globally significant and unique defensive struggle against Bolshevism, which is unique significance in world history, all the more forcefully*, the more it . . . enjoys that freedom that is accorded to it by God's law and also by the Reich Concordat.

But now we observe the persistent mistrust with concern. . . . This has to dampen the *joy of cooperation* amongst the people. We observe with concern . . . *no help for the Führer's rebuilding work.* . . . We observe with concern . . . how in particular *the civil servants and employees in the movement that are true to the Church* . . . are being influenced.

We Catholics will be ready . . . to support the Führer in the defense against Bolshevism and his other tasks. But we must request. . . . We must demand . . .

We will not surrender one iota of the truths of our holy faith and always stand up for the inalienable rights of our holy Church. But your bishops want to affirm equally fearlessly, and all true Catholics with them, the veneration of state authority and, which is our affair, cooperate with the state in peace and trust. Even where we reject the interference to the rights of the Church, we want to respect the rights of the state on state territory and also see *the good and great in the* Führer's work.

And so your bishops conclude with a warning: *Do not let yourselves be talked into unease and dissatisfaction by dissatisfied people* who have always been a fruitful *breeding ground for Bolshevist tendencies*! Do not let yourselves be tricked or led astray *in your cooperation in your defense* against the deadly enemy! In this way, belief in the Christian doctrine and living in accordance with faith is at the same time a *service to the people and the Fatherland.*"[193]

So as one can see: it was only ever about the bishops' interests. And nothing else. Otherwise they were prepared to do virtually everything with the Nazis, even, as was soon to be shown, the most terrible war in history. As long as their church survived, armies and peoples could bleed to death.

In 1937, Archbishop Gröber published a *Handbuch der Religiösen Gegenwartsfragen* (*Handbook of Current Religious Questions*). In it, the Catholic Church leaders pledge

to Hitler their special loyalty and the joyful devotion of the Catholics to the National Socialist State;

they credit Hitler with the restoration of human dignity;

they celebrate the Third Reich as a state under the rule of law;

they praise it as a defender of European culture;

and they pledge themselves to the totalitarian regime.[194]

For the book not only expresses the opinion of the Freiburg archbishop and associate member of the SS. On its title page, it bears the note: "*Published with the recommendation of the entire German episcopate.*" "In this current, fateful hour in our nation's history, the leaders of the Church stand side by side with the men of the state. . . . Insofar as the state claims totality on the area it governs, if it . . . pulls in the reins more tightly in all areas of national life today, if it . . . goes further in the organization and control of the people's lives than in times of more peaceful development, then it is definitely right to do all of these things."[195]

Hitler's troops occupied Austria in early 1938.

The preparations had been made. Travel between Germany and Austria had already been de facto prevented by the end of May 1933 (i.e., allowed only for Reich citizens after the payment of a fee of one thousand reichsmarks).[196] Then Mr. von Papen was sent to Vienna as an ambassador, an "Austrian Legion" was founded in Southern Germany, intense propaganda took place via the Munich radio station, the Austrian federal chancellor Dollfuß was murdered in the chancellor's office, uprisings were organized in Styria and Carinthia, a German-Austrian friendship agreement was made in 1936 in which the "the German Reich government" recognized "the complete sovereignty of the Federal State of Austria,"[197] which was occupied two years later.

Cardinal Innitzer of Vienna, who had recommended subjugation in agreement with the Vatican Schuschnigg and declared, "The annexation is unavoidable," celebrated the invasion with ringing bells and swastika flags on the churches and charged his clergy to do the same. On March 12, he made them hold a thanksgiving service. And when he had an audience with Hitler on March 15, and the latter guaranteed him the preservation of church rights; all the Austrian bishops, apart from the Bishop of Linz, called on the people to vote for Hitler and concluded their call with "Heil Hitler."[198]

Cardinal Archbishop Innitzer, said Hitler himself, "spoke" to him at the time "with such a smiling face . . . as if he had never harmed the hair on the head of a single National Socialist during the entire Austrian *Systemzeit* [i.e., the pre-Nazi government from June 12, 1933, onward that had banned the Nazi Party]."[199] And Hitler's flight captain Bauer, who witnessed the scene, wrote: "The conclusion was just as cordial."[200]

On March 28, 1938, the Austrian press published a "Solemn Declaration" of the Austrian bishops to the referendum titled "Pledge of the Catholic Church to

Greater Germany. The Episcopate for National Socialism." In a foreword, Cardinal Innitzer and Prince-Archbishop Weitz of Salzburg first stressed that "the thousand-year longing of our people" was now being fulfilled and the Austrian bishops could decree "with all the less concern" their call to all the faithful, when the representative of the Führer announced the line of his policies, which were to be according to the motto: "Render unto God what is God's and unto Caesar what is Caesar's."[201]

What crimes Hitler's henchmen had already committed in the concentration camps and against the Jews! But as long as the bishops could receive "what is God's," they would not only go along with everything else, they would even support the regime with all their power.

They guaranteed in their "Solemn Declaration":

"We, the undersigned, the Bishops of the Austrian church provinces on the occasion of the great historical events in German Austria, declare the following from *utmost inner conviction* and *free will*:

We acknowledge *with joy* that the *National Socialist movement has done and continues to do outstanding things* for the German Reich and people in the fields of national and economic *rebuilding* and social policy, and specifically for the *poorest parts* of the people. We are also of the conviction that the actions of the National Socialist movement have *fought off the danger of the all-destructive, godless Bolshevism.*

The bishops will support this work for the future with their *best blessings* and will also make urgent appeals upon the faithful to this effect.

On the day of the referendum, it is, for us bishops, *a self-evident national duty to declare ourselves as Germans for the German Reich*, and we also expect *all faithful Christians* to know *what they owe their people*.[202]

This declaration was read out in all the Catholic churches in Austria.

A German historian who was traveling through Austria on the day of the invasion claims, with the intention of exonerating the Catholic Church: "The villages between Brenner and Innsbruck were deserted; pious Catholic people lived there who were hostile to Hitler."[203] If this is right, it proves only that in Austria, as in Germany, it was only the propaganda of the episcopate that won over the pious Catholics for Hitler. Because the Austrian prelates had previously publicly rejected Nazism, as had their German counterparts.

On April 6, Innitzer and some of his bishops were received by the pope and Secretary of State Pacelli. After his return from Rome, the cardinal instructed the Viennese clergy to fly German flags on the churches and let the bells ring on the evening before the referendum. On April 10, Innitzer entered a polling spot with the Hitler salute.[204] He had also started to close letters to Nazi functionaries with "Heil Hitler": after all, several German bishops had already been using this salute for years.[205] Incidentally, the German episcopate also let the bells ring with joy at the annexation of Austria.

When Hitler forced Czechoslovakia to surrender by threatening violence, also in 1938, the Fulda Bishops' Conference sent a congratulatory address to him and also ordered the bells to ring in celebration that coming Sunday.[206]

And on Hitler's fiftieth birthday, in the following year, the bishops ordered a celebratory peal of bells from every church in Germany. This is what it says in the official gazette for the Diocese of Bamberg:

For the Führer's birthday
(to be read on Whit Sunday after the sermon)

Next Thursday, April 20, the German people will celebrate the 50th birthday of our Führer and Reich Chancellor Adolf Hitler. To honor this day, our most reverent bishops have decided that there will be a celebratory peal of bells on the evening before April 20 after the bells for evening prayer. We want to express our congratulations already today on holy ground by saying a devout Lord's Prayer together for Führer and Fatherland: 'Our Father...'[207]

Swastika flags were put out on the churches in all the dioceses; special services were held everywhere.[208] The bishop of Mainz demanded prayer for the augmenter and protector of the Reich.[209] Cardinal Bertram sent Hitler a congratulatory telegram in the name of the episcopate.[210] And Cardinal Schulte declared at a rally on the day after Hitler's birthday: "We have once again solemnly affirmed our loyalty to the German Reich and its Führer on his 50th birthday. *This loyalty cannot be shaken by anything.* For it is based on the unchangeable principles of our holy faith."[211]

It is true—no crime that Hitler had already committed or was about to commit could shake their loyalty.

BISHOP VON GALEN AUTHORIZES THE "OATH TO THE FLAG" AS A PLEDGE OF ALLEGIANCE TO HITLER

Archbishop Gröber had already stated in 1935 that the Catholic theologians would never leave it to the discretion of the "individual with all his shortsightedness and moods to discuss what is and is not allowed in the event of war"; the final decision should be left to the respective legal authority."[212] The legal authority was Hitler.

And on November 8, at the time of the great pogrom on Jews (Kristallnacht!), Bishop von Galen authorized the abovementioned paltry booklet "Oath to the Flag," which now needs to be quoted from in detail. After the "will of the Führer" has been presented as the "will of the people" and the "necessity to do military service [as] a religious bond and duty," the "Oath to the Flag" is interpreted as follows:

> "I swear by God this sacred oath . . ."

Swearing by God means calling upon Him as a witness that one wants to tell the truth and keep one's promise, means *making Him a guarantor of the statement that is now to come*, putting oneself at the mercy of His revenge and retribution were one to involve Him in a lie or a violation of oath through the statement.

> ". . . that I will render to the Führer of the German Reich and people, Adolf Hitler, the Commander in Chief of the Wehrmacht. . . ."

With these words of the formulation of the oath are a personal relationship of loyalty to the highest commander of the army that had existed from the Great Elector to the collapse of the Nazi regime and was only interrupted by the times of the Weimar Republic, is restored and expressed here.

The Führer embodies the unity of the people and the Reich. He is the highest bearer of state power. A Christian German *is bound by conscience* to obey him as such *even without an oath*.

> "Let everyone be subject to the governing authorities, for there is no authority except that which God has established, the authorities that exist have been established by God. Consequently, whoever rebels against the authority is rebelling against what God has instituted."

This is what Paul writes in Romans 13. He wrote this, his *unreserved yes* to state authority, to Christians who tended to see in their state the expression of a power hostile to their faith.

With his statement, the apostle withdraws the right from individual Christians to make their obedience to state authority arbitrarily *dependent on conditions*. This point is mentioned here because one often falsely believes of Christians, especially Catholics, that their loyalty to the state is on shaky ground and they are only ready to obey based on any given situation.

If it is made easy for the German soldier to pledge such loyalty to his leader and Commander in Chief because he sees in him an example of truly soldierly essence and virtue, because he gives his loyalty to a man who sees the *sense of his life in terms of the augmentation of the greatness and honor of his people* and exemplifies his loyalty every day, then the Christian soldier will most certainly be able to make his vow in seriousness and joy of heart because his faith teaches him to recognize and acknowledge in the person of the ruler, beyond purely human abilities and achievements, *the glory and honor given to him by God.*

This means that also nowadays the truly Christian German soldier will also express *his reverent and loving devotion to the Führer* in the form of prayer.

> "... unconditional obedience ..."

The Christian soldier does not obey to save himself inconveniences but because he sees, in the command of *every* position of command in his unit, an aura of that power that he has *recognized and affirmed as having been given by God* in the oath he has sworn to the Führer of the German people and Commander in Chief of the Wehrmacht.

> "... and want to be willing, as a brave soldier, to sacrifice my life for this oath at any time."

Soldiering and military service should *not* provoke war, as pacifism would have one believe, but on the contrary be a powerful bulwark for peace.

But if the life and honor of people and Fatherland are in danger, an able man must be ready to defend these God-given goods *down to the last drop of blood.*

Christianity approves the moral legitimacy of just war. If and insofar as a war is just can *never* be decided by an individual, *least of all* a soldier, which means that he could make his willingness to sacrifice his life dependent *on that. It is but the leaders who make decisions like this, the leaders,* who are also solely responsible before God and their people.

Wavering at such a crucial hour is not possible *for a Christian* who has incorporated into his faith that the state authority has received its order from God; and it is absolutely impossible for a Christian soldier who has *committed himself to loyalty* in a *holy* oath taken before God. He will see it from a moral standpoint as a *struggle between right and wrong* and for himself as a test to prove his manliness.

> "What care I about cold and pain!
> In me burns an oath
> Blazing as a flame
> With sword and heart and hand.
> *Come what may*
> Germany, I am ready!"[213]

Come what may—von Galen authorized. And how did it end? Fifty-five million people were dead, and Bishop von Galen became a cardinal and was earmarked for beatification.

The behavior of the Catholic Church toward conscientious objectors under Hitler was, as already mentioned, clear. This is also shown in the memorandum titled "Conscientious Objection and Military Pastoral Care," by the *Weltfriedensbund Katholischer Kriegsgegner* (World Peace Federation of Catholic Opponents of War) sent by Dr. Josef Fleischer to the bishops: "The author had his defense bill on the table of his cell (in the Wehrmacht remand prison at Berlin-Tegel, 1940), in which the irreconcilability of the 'Oath to the Flag' and participation in Hitler's war with Catholic faith and moral teachings was very carefully explained and substantiated. But the vicar general and deputy army bishop *Werthmann*, who appeared in a uniform decorated with swastikas, refused to take part in any further discussions with the author, demanding instead that he swear the 'Oath to the Flag' to Hitler without any reservations, thereby swearing unconditional obedience to the Führer and participating in his war unreservedly. *In this context he noted that such 'elements' that made reservations in the matter should be eradicated and made a head shorter."*[214]

Hitler's Catholic vicar general was made a vicar general in the *Bundeswehr* in 1956.

THE GERMAN BISHOPS SUPPORTED HITLER EVEN MORE INTENSELY DURING THE WAR

"If our people had followed the bishops' words in 1939, countless of our comrades would not be in their graves today."

This is what Richard Jäger, who is vice president of the German Bundestag today [that is, in 1965], said at the fifth Allgäu Catholic Day in 1953.[215] And how was it really? The bishops, individually or unanimously, called upon the people "repeatedly" and "most urgently," as they put it themselves (p. 140 f.), to follow Hitler determinedly.

When Warsaw was bombed in the autumn of 1939 and masses of Polish Catholics were killed, the German Catholics, urged by their cardinals and bishops, prayed for the protection of the Nazi Reich. This is one prayer the clergy had to say on the instructions of Bishop von Galen: "Almighty, eternal God! We ask you to take our Fatherland into your firm protection: illuminate its leaders with the light of your wisdom, so that they recognize what truly serves the well-being of the people and do what is right in your power. Protect all the members of our Wehrmacht and keep them in your grace, strengthen those who fight."[216]

The Catholic chief of chaplains Franziskus-Justus Rarkowski, whom the papal nuncio Orsenigo, assisted by Bishops Preysing and von Galen, had solemnly blessed on February 20, 1938,[217] released a message at the time of the Polish campaign that was packed with more phrases than one of Dr. Goebbels's speeches. It is brimming with phrases such as "baptism of fire," "fight for its natural rights to life as willed by God[!]," "great and honorable task" and the like. "Your service is borne by a holy earnest, a great calling and duty . . . the glowing image of a true fighter, our Führer and Commander in Chief . . . into the shining joy and gratitude to almighty God, who has clearly blessed the engagement against Poland that has been forced upon us[!]"—and, as we must add, who had Catholic Poland destroyed in the most terrible way and then left to godless Bolshevism!—"the glorious rebirth of the Reich that we have been allowed to witness in the last six years."[218]

Of course, it was not only Rarkowski who instantly stood by Hitler but the entire German Catholic episcopate. "At this crucial hour," wrote the bishops in a mutual pastoral letter in September 1939, "we would encourage and exhort our Catholic soldiers to do their duty out of obedience to the Führer and be ready *to sacrifice their entire person.*" Now, could Hitler really ask more of people with whom he was fighting the church struggle? And, it has to be repeated, he did not want more than the sacrifice of the entire person or, as the bishops had already promised in 1936, "loyalty until death" (p. 128) or, as resistance fighter von Galen authorized, defense "down to the last drop of blood" (p. 135). "We appeal to the faithful to unite in heartfelt prayer so that God's providence may lead this war to a blessed success and peace for the Fatherland and the people."[219]

The "sacrifice of the entire person" was what the bishops demanded in 1939. And Mr. Richard Jäger lied like a trooper at an Allgäu Catholic Day: "If our people had followed the bishops' words in 1939, countless of our comrades would not be in their graves today."[220]

The bishops' words! Their mutual call to sacrifice the entire person out of obedience to the Führer was still not enough for them. Most of them spurred on their diocesans to support Hitler's war in their own pastoral letters. Archbishop Gröber invoked the blessing of the Almighty for the just cause of the German people.[221] Bishop Sproll of Rottenburg asked God to give strength and power to all those who had followed the Führer's call to win victory for the dear Fatherland or to die for it.[222] Bishop Rackl of Eichstätt promised that the priests would fulfill their duty to the Fatherland with greatest conscientiousness.[223]

After the defeat of Poland, the church gazettes, the *Passauer Bistumsblatt* (bishops' gazette from Passau), the *Klerusblatt* (clergy gazette), the newspapers of the Dioceses of Breslau, Hildesheim, and others celebrated the victory enthusiastically. There was talk of a holy struggle, everyone was exhorted to support the Wehrmacht out of religious conviction, to fight for the right of the German people to freedom and a just distribution of the necessary living space, and so on.[224] There was also, once again, a seven-day celebratory pealing of bells from all church towers to celebrate the victory. And in the following months of October and November, 214 Polish Catholic priests were executed by the Nazis.

After the unsuccessful assassination attempt on Hitler in November 1939, Cardinal Faulhaber held a solemn thanksgiving service in the Munich *Frauenkirche* and congratulated Hitler on his rescue along with all the Bavarian bishops.[225]

At the start of 1940, the Augsburg bishop Kumpfmüller affirmed that Christians were "always the best comrades." "A Christian stays true to the flag he has sworn loyalty to, come what may."[226]

At around the same time, Bishop Bornewasser of Trier appealed to the faithful to "devote [all their] inner and outer strength to serving the people." "We must make every sacrifice the situation demands of us."[227]

The Catholic military prayer and songbook, compiled by the Wehrmacht field bishop in 1940, also brought the Virgin Mary into intimate connection with Hitler's battles: "O bless us in dispute, Mary, our Queen, Blessed One, Mary, our Queen! You reign in the glory of victory, give us victory in our dispute! In life a laurel wreath, in death beatitude! In the thunder of the cannon, Mary, our Queen, give us the crowns of victory . . . !"[228]

Furthermore, the Catholic military prayer and songbook, approved by the bishops, instructed the German soldiers: "Military service is a service of honor. The army has a lot to be thanked for in terms of making Germany great. It is a school of bravery, the birthplace of great heroes, a theater of honor and glory! . . . Keep to the motto: 'With God for Führer, People and Fatherland!'" . . . Let us pray! . . . Let us be a heroic breed. . . . Bless in particular our Führer and Commander in Chief of the Wehrmacht in all the tasks that are set before him. Let us all see a holy task in our sacrifice for People and Fatherland under his leadership . . . " and so on, and so forth.[229]

Cardinal Bertram sent Hitler the "warmest wishes" in the name of the episcopate for his birthday on April 20, 1940.[230] And after the quick defeat of France, the bishops praised the Wehrmacht exuberantly, and once again they let the church bells ring and the flags fly for a week.[231] On November 8, 1940, Bishop Berning called upon the faithful to pray for a German victory.[232] On February 8, 1941, Archbishop Gröber pleaded once again for the necessary "living space."[233] And the pastoral letter that Bishop Kaller of Ermland published in January 1941 was so enthusiastic that it even earned the applause of the extremely anticlerical police chief Heydrich.[234] After the German invasion of the Soviet Union, Chief of Chaplains Rarkowski, of whom even some Catholics admitted that his pastoral letters "abounded . . . with National Socialist support for the war,"[235] sent a pastoral letter to the Catholic Wehrmacht members in which it said: "As so often in history, Germany has once again become the *savior and champion of Europe*. . . . Many European states . . . know that the war against Russia *is a European crusade*. . . . This strong and binding experience of your campaign in the east will make you conscious of how unspeakably great our luck is to be German."[236]

But Rarkowski was in no way an "outsider," as many Catholics often claim today. The entire German-Austrian episcopate behaved the same way.

Archbishop Jäger of Paderborn spoke of a fight to protect Christendom; Bishop Kumpfmüller of Augsburg compared the Bolshevist threat with that from the Turks in previous centuries; Bishop Rackl of Eichstätt declared Hitler's invasion to be a crusade and a holy war; and even Bishop von Galen repeated his hope for a German victory.[237]

The Bavarian Catholic bishops wrote in a pastoral letter in 1941: "We lived through similar times in the World War and therefore know from hard and bitter experience *how necessary and important* it is that in such a situation *everyone fulfills his duty completely, willingly and loyally*, maintains calm prudence and firm trust in God and *does not start to hesitate and complain*. For this reason we address you, dear diocesans, in fatherly love and concern, with *a word of exhortation, which should encourage you to use all your power to serve the Fatherland and your beloved home with conscientious fulfillment of duty and serious professional ethos*. . . . We saw with joy and pride what great things unity can achieve in the first years of the World War, but we also had to witness at its end how disunity can destroy all great things again. We want to be united in love and the service of the Fatherland and to form a unique community of work and sacrifice to protect our homeland."[238]

And all the German bishops encouraged the faithful in a pastoral letter on June 26, 1941: "In fulfilling the difficult duties of these times, in the hard visitations that will come over you in the wake of the war, may you be strengthened by the *comforting certainty* that you are not only serving the Fatherland in this but also *following the holy will of God.*"[239]

So according to them, Hitler's Russian campaign was the holy will of God!

And on December 10, 1941, all the Catholic bishops of Germany affirmed once again: "We are with our soldiers in prayer and remember the dead who have given their lives for their people with grateful love. We have *repeatedly*, and again in the summer pastoral letter, insistently called upon our believers to *fulfill their duty with loyalty, to stand firm courageously*, work in willingness to sacrifice and fight *with all their might* in the service of our people in the most serious times of war. We follow the fight against the power of Bolshevism, about which we German bishops warned German Catholics in several pastoral letters written between 1921 and 1936 and called for vigilance, as is known to the Reich government, *with gratification.*"[240] No commentary is necessary here.

And still in 1942 and 1943, the bishops stood by one of the greatest criminals in world history in this unmistakable way.[241] Then, however, they did become more cautious, even though the odd one, such as the Austrian prince-bishop Ferdinand von Seckau, was still babbling about "great times" and "heroic deeds" as late as 1944,[242] or Archbishop Kolb of Bamberg, after whom there is a street named in Bamberg today, wrote on January 31, 1944: "When armies of soldiers fight, then an army of prayers must stand behind the front." Yes, even at the beginning of the sixth year of the war, the spiritual leader of Bamberg was encouraging the Catholics to take the yoke of war bravely upon themselves: "It is precisely because the world is so in need that the Lord God needs people who can take this need upon themselves with composure. . . . Christ expects us to take on the suffering obediently as He did and carry the cross bravely." And Kolb demands "*burning prayer* for our beloved people and Fatherland in this hour of extreme tensions."[243]

Archbishop Jäger of Paderborn, who even expressed sympathy for the Nazi expletive "subhumans" with reference to Slavs and did not shy away from the lie, in a pastoral letter in February 1942, that the Russians had almost degenerated into animals because of their hostility to God and their hate of Christ,[244] exhorted the Catholics to make their contribution in the fight against Germany's greatest enemies, liberalism and individualism on the one hand and collectivism on the other, as late as January 1945.[245] (In 1957, Jäger demanded the fulfillment of the "ideals of the crusades . . . in a modern form"[246]; in 1965, he became cardinal.)

But the Catholic chief of chaplains Rarkowski still spurred Hitler's troops on in 1945, calling upon them to go "forward, Christian soldiers, on the way to victory!"[247] The Catholic moral theologian Angermair called this a *"private* conviction."[248] Millions of soldiers and civilians died for this "private" conviction. But is the church bothered about this?

And what one of their so-called moral theologians dismissed as a "private" conviction *after the war* was praised by all the German and Austrian bishops *during the war* as the "holy will of God"!

But scarcely was Hitler dead than they went over to his enemies. The same bishops who had been raising their influential voices for at least a full decade since 1933 in support of a man an American senator had once mildly described as an international bandit—the same bishops who, despite all the differences in religious terms, had always called upon their faithful to give their allegiance, unerring cooperation, and unconditional fulfillment of duty in Hitler's war— were now declaring to the British and Americans that they had always condemned Nazism. One glaring example is Cardinal Faulhaber.

THE FLEXIBLE CARDINAL FAULHABER (OR, HOW TO SURVIVE FOR TWO THOUSAND YEARS)

> *"Cardinal Faulhaber was, so to speak, a duke in the great levy of German Catholics who repeatedly campaigned unflinchingly against Hitler and his cohorts."*
>
> —Suffragan Bishop Johann Neuhäusler[249]
>
> *"There is something uncanny about people's short memories. They can no longer remember after hardly three years. This book may remind such people with short memories about the reality of the past years."*
>
> —Cardinal Faulhaber[250]

The great prince of the church, after whom streets and squares are named in Germany today, who once defamed the Weimar Republic as a product of "perjury and high treason"[251] but guaranteed in a handwritten letter to Hitler in 1933 that this came from the bottom of his heart: "God preserve our Reich Chancellor for our people" (p. 107); who instructed the Bavarian Catholics in a pastoral letter in 1934: "The Church's moral doctrine will benefit the state order as education for simplicity and loyalty to duty, a sense of community and spirit of sacrifice. On the other hand, our state authority has removed coarse negative developments in books and bathing, film and theater and other areas of public life and . . . also done the moral life of the people an inestimable service."[252] Cardinal Faulhaber, who gave his declaration, along with all the German bishops, on the referendum on March 29, 1936, in order to disperse any doubts of conscience among the Catholics, which had admittedly been a possibility, and "open up the path to a determined 'Yes'": "we give the Fatherland our vote, but that does not mean agreement to things that we would consider unconscionable. This declaration will suffice for all Catholics to vote 'Yes' with a clear conscience and the awareness of standing up before the whole world for the honor, freedom and safety of our German Fatherland in doing so"[253]—upon which, three years before the outbreak of the Second World War, Hitler received almost 44.5 million of the 45 million votes cast, as opposed to 17.25 million on March 5, 1933. Cardinal Faulhaber, who celebrated a thanksgiving service after the failed assassination attempt on Hitler in November 1939 and, directly after Stauffenberg's assassination attempt on July 20, 1944(!), congratulated Hitler on his rescue both personally and in the name of his bishops and had a Te Deum sung in the Munich *Frauenkirche*.[254] Hardly ten months later, on May 12, 1945, this same Faulhaber cursed the Hitler regime in front of American journalists in the most vehement way and concluded: "Nazism must not be revived."[255] Indeed, he did not hesitate to claim "after the end of the most terrible of all wars" with all the Bavarian bishops: "The German bishops, as you know, made serious warnings about the false doctrines and aberrations of National Socialism right from the very beginning and repeatedly pointed out . . ."[256]

Cardinal Faulhaber, who had already served Germany under Kaiser Wilhelm as deputy field provost and then actual field provost of the Bavarian army from 1914 to 1917; who called the character of Western democracy a "moral of the devil" and celebrated German soldiers as "protectors and avengers of the divine world order" in 1915.[257] Cardinal Faulhaber, who said in 1915: "It is my conviction that this campaign will become the textbook example of a just war in terms of war ethics[!],"[258] (while the Archbishop of Cambrai wrote in a pastoral letter in the same year: "The French soldiers feel with more or less clarity but firmly and resolvedly that they are the soldiers of Christ and Mary, the defenders of the faith; and to die French means to die a Christian. Long live Christ, who loves the French!").[259] Cardinal Faulhaber, who had a document published in 1936, on his twenty-fifth anniversary of becoming a bishop, in which twenty-four of the roughly one hundred pages were dedicated to the time when he was a soldier, in which not only every promotion from private upward was carefully registered but also with which gun pattern the later prince of the church was trained. He states here, among other things: "Service in the King's dress was *a school for life*."[260] Cardinal Faulhaber, who, in 1941, with all of his bishops, warned in a pastoral letter: "We have already lived through a time like this *in the World War* and therefore know from hard and bitter experience *how necessary and important* it is that in such a situation *everyone fulfills his duty completely, willingly and loyally* . . ." (p. 139). Cardinal Faulhaber, who, although standing up, along with the Bavarian bishops, for church rights as usual on August 17, 1941—"Dear diocesans, pray that crucifixes are not removed from schools!" or, as it says, in part almost in the style of that author whose novels, according to the *Herder Lexicon*, corresponds to the average taste of those modest spirits longing for happiness: "There is a painfully restrained woe shivering through the entire Catholic people that the *penitential processions* were no longer allowed to be held" and similar such things—in this communication, Cardinal Faulhaber also did not even consider publishing a single syllable against the war for which he had only recently called so urgently. On the contrary, he was thrilled about the Wehrmacht high command because it had issued "extraordinarily joyful and pious instructions" regarding the funerals of the war dead, which reached their climax in the demand: "For each, a cross with a name and further details or a great, mutual cross" on a mass grave, let us add. "We, and most surely the entire German people, would like to thank the Wehrmacht for this sensitive Christian care from the bottom of our hearts"[261]; Cardinal Faulhaber, who in 1941 also agreed to deliver the church bells in order to enable the continuation of the war and the Nazis' victory, as his "Declaration from the Pulpit on Taking Down the Bells" testifies: "But we also wish to make this sacrifice for our dear Fatherland since it has become necessary for a favorable outcome of to the war."[262] This same Faulhaber, along with the entire Bavarian episcopate, spoke of the "most terrible of all wars" and complained to American correspondents in May 1945 about the Nazis relentlessly disseminating propaganda for *militarism*![263]

And Faulhaber's prelate, Johann Neuhäusler, wrote under the bold headline in 1946: "3. The unanimous Bavarian Episcopate. a) clear language from the first year onward." And under that headline: "The resistance also seen here was already powerful in May 1933."[264]

But this is still not enough! What is, in a way, the worst of all is that matter that is treated in all detail by the supplement to Official Gazette no. 20 of the Archdiocese of Munich and Freising from November 15, 1934: "A sermon against the hatred of Jews and race hatred attributed to Cardinal Faulhaber."

What had happened?

In August 1934, the journal of the German Social Democratic Party in Prague, the *Sozialdemokrat*, published a sermon of Faulhaber's *against* the hatred of Jews and race hatred, which he had, of course, never held. How would Faulhaber have summoned up the courage to protest publicly against Hitler's pogroms against the Jews, even if he had been against them, which is definitely doubtful? Because in his Advent sermons of 1933, he had said expressly that today's rejection of the Jews must not be applied to the books of pre-Christian Jewry, which could only suggest that the rejection of contemporary Jews is allowed. At the time, the cardinal, like Paul, did not let "the hour of mercy" not "strike [for the Jews until] the end of days!"[265] So the cardinal complained and made his corrections to all parties. He telegraphed or wrote to the Reich Ministry of the Interior, the Reich Ministry of Public Enlightenment and Propaganda, the Bavarian Political Police, the Bavarian State Chancellery, the German embassy in Prague, numerous domestic and foreign newspapers, and even to private persons—the great confessor avowed to the whole world that he had never preached against race hatred and the hatred of Jews, not one single sentence.[266] "Faulhaber sermon against race hatred never read. Please withdraw false announcement," the archiepiscopal secretariat telegraphed to the *Basle Nationalzeitung*, for instance.[267] Faulhaber himself addressed the Nazi minister of the interior on November 9, 1934: "But it is urgent that the sale of such a disgraceful inflammatory article, based on a Marxist forgery, be banned by law and the public are informed as soon as possible about this shameless lie, and I ask for this most seriously and urgently."[268] So at the end of 1934, Faulhaber called his alleged advocacy *of* the Jews and *against* race hatred a Marxist forgery, a shameless lie, or, as he also says in this context, "insane claims."

But still not enough.

When, in their need, the Jewish World Conference (which was taking place in Geneva), to use the cardinal's language, "seized the alleged sermons for Jewry" because they obviously believed that a Catholic bishop could have stood up against Hitler's persecution of the Jews out of charity or simply for the sake of justice, Faulhaber wrote in a communication to the Jewish World Conference, as his official gazette put it, a "determined protest against his name being named at a conference that was demanding a trade boycott of Germany."[269]

So Faulhaber's sermon *against* race hatred was forged. But what was not forged was that sermon from 1936 in which the cardinal praised Pope Pius XI as the best and, initially, the only friend of the Nazi Reich, a sermon that he kindly left for us in his own official gazette. But in this sermon, there is the following, almost certainly unique statement from a Catholic prince of the church: "The personally most spiteful untruth about the Holy Father Pius XI," states Faulhaber in defense of the first foreign friend of Nazi Germany, "was presented to the German people in a German newspaper on the first day of this year: the Pope is a half-Jew, his mother was a Dutch Jew. I see my listeners rise up in horror. This lie is especially suited to surrendering the Pope's standing in Germany to mockery."[270]

Surely not! Should the cardinal not have been aware that what had his Catholic listeners rise up in such horror and seemed a reason for him himself to surrender the pope to mockery most definitely applied to his Lord Jesus Christ, who was a "full Jew"! Or, even when applying the Catholic belief that Jesus was of supranational origin on account of his father, still half-Jewish, so that Jesus is accordingly exactly what the *Deutsche Volksschöpfung* in Düsseldorf claimed the Holy Father to be on January 1, 1936: the son of a Jewess. What a shameful and ridiculous spectacle!

But, as Cardinal Faulhaber had, under Hitler, forbidden the Jewish World Conference in Geneva even to mention his name and informed them angrily that he had "defended the Old Testament script of Israel but not given an opinion on today's Jewish question,"[271] in early 1946 there was to be read in the German newspapers of the appearance and explanation of Cardinal Faulhaber before the Anglo-

American Palestine Commission (which was meeting in Rome at the time), because he had been standing up for the Jews since 1933 and had been severely persecuted in the Third Reich!

So the highly honored cardinal survived both the Emperor and Hitler, one of the "most upstanding bishops," as Carl Amery tells us, "certainly willing to risk arrest and a martyr's death,"[272] a "leading figure in the German episcopate," as it says in the Catholic *Herder Lexicon*, "of great receptiveness to the times and *powerful confession of belief.*" Indeed, no one can deny this, neither the position regarding the Führer nor the receptiveness to the times, nor the powerful confession of belief: before Hitler against, under Hitler in favor, after Hitler against—and if the cardinal had lived long into the era of Adenauer, he would certainly have told us once again, in his commemorative publication on his fiftieth anniversary as a bishop, with which gun pattern he had been trained. . . . Of course, the other German bishops reacted similarly. Archbishop Gröber, for example, who had previously called upon the Catholics to cooperate unswervingly in the new Reich, who very quickly allowed the Nazi flags and insignias to be "displayed on the nave," and published a book in 1935 in which he glorified the Catholics' patriotism and loyalty to the state ("Long live Christ who loves the Franks"!), and defamed Nietzsche for being a good European (p. 126 f.); Archbishop Gröber, who declared in 1935: "The Catholic theologians have never left it to the discretion of the individual, with all his shortsightedness and moods to discuss what is and is not allowed in the event of war, but left the final decision to the respective legal authority"[273]—Hitler and the bishops were the legal authority; Archbishop Gröber, who did everything to strengthen the regime (p. 129), who was an associate member of the SS and one of the Nazi-friendliest bishops of all, was already not ashamed to write, in a pastoral letter in the summer of 1945 already, that "gray old men were tormented mercilessly or sadistically beaten to death in the concentration camps only because they had *character* and did not want to sacrifice *their own loyalty of conviction to the insanity of the Third Reich.*"[274] In a second pastoral letter dated September 21, 1945, it says: "And how not only our soldiers, but the entire German people . . . were lied to regarding the causes, prospects and aims of the war." (Yes, lied to by whom?) And: "Was it not we who hoped for redemption and a new freedom for us and our church, for our people and Fatherland through the downfall of the Third Reich?"[275] And Archbishop Gröber did not hesitate to declare: "We ask the world to read the words of the Holy Father Pius XII in his address of July 2 of this year, in which *the German bishops in particular received high praise on account of their loyalty and courage* because they never neglected to raise their voices courageously and earnestly, not even in the final years of the war."[276]

They certainly did. For Hitler and his war!

PRELATE NEUHÄUSLER'S RÉSUMÉ

But Johann Neuhäusler reveals to us, at the conclusion of this standard work on the Catholic Church struggle: "The fight is at an end, the World War with its thousands of different murder weapons, the battle of cultures with its attack on God, Christ and Church, with its deification, enslavement and destruction of human beings. Corpses and ruins cover the field."[277]

To which the following should be added: 1. The "battle of cultures with its attack on God, Christ and Church" was not only fought by Soviet Russia, which was attacked by the curia, but also by the Nazi Reich with whom it was allied.

2. The "deification of man" was also driven by the high German clergy to such an extent that Hitler figured in an opus authorized by von Galen in 1938 as an "example of truly soldierly essence and loyalty," as a "glowing example" in a Christmas 1942 pastoral letter by the chief of chaplains, while all Catholic German bishops saw "an aura of divine rule and a share of the eternal authority of God" in every human authority, and therefore also in Hitler's, in 1933.

3. The "human enslavement and destruction of man" in the concentration camps, in the massacres of the Jews and in the war, was never condemned by the German episcopate; on the contrary:

4. They *committed* the Catholics to participating in the "World War with its thousands of different kinds of murder weapons" and pursued their application "*with gratification.*"

Prelate Neuhäusler kept these small incidentals from his readers. But he did not forget to tell them the most important thing in the last bold headline: "D. The cross stands!"[278]

THE GERMAN CATHOLIC PRESS ALSO INTERCEDED FOR HITLER'S WAR

> *"There is an unwritten law for the Catholic newspapers and publishers that only what suits the people governing at the particular time and their way of thinking is allowed to be printed. Not God's command, not the truth matters, but the personal opinion and the mere "wish of the persons ruling at the time."*
>
> —Father Heinrich Bremer, SJ[279]

It goes without saying that the Catholic public in Germany and Austria eventually stood behind Hitler completely by the end.

The Catholic newspapers, insofar as the Nazis had not confiscated them, called for support of the war as they had *already done in the First World War*.[280] So in 1941, the following appeared in the *Klerusblatt* (clergy gazette): "We experience today our people seeking to find their way back to all the values[!] that once made them so great and powerful that it offered protection and order not only to the Germans but also to the entire Occident [West] as the Holy Empire."[281] Bishop von Galen's gazette wrote at the time: "God has allowed the sword of vengeance against England to be placed in our hands. We are the executors of his just, divine will."[282] And in the church newspaper of the Archdiocese of Cologne, the following appeared at roughly the same time: "There are only few men ... and one of these great men is indisputably the man celebrating his 52nd birthday today—Adolf Hitler. Today we promise him that we will put all our powers at his disposal so that our people will assume the place in the world that it deserves."[283]

Whole volumes could be filled with such outpourings. The American academic Gordon C. Zahn, according to an investigation of "The German Catholic Press and Hitler's Wars" that appeared in 1961, encountered, in the "representative group of journals" that he had read, "not one single example of even hidden opposition to the war." On the contrary, the "Catholic press [was] full" of "calls to support the war," they "dedicated page after page to fiery calls to be 'patriotic' and exhortations to 'duty.'" "The overall impression for the reader," the American sociologist writes—in a decidedly Catholic journal, incidentally—"is of extremely nationalistic support for the war," a résumé that the author completes with the following: "The tone of the hypernationalistic enthusiasm in all the papers we read for this study does not give the reader the impression it was forced."[284]

And nor was it. The writers, of whom, as Zahn notes, "many, if not the most, were clergy,"[285] followed their bishop superiors, and these followed the pope.

In order to mention it at least, the representatives of the German Protestants were by no means behind the Catholics at that time. In fact, they rather exceeded them in terms of eagerness to collaborate and enthusiasm for the war, as shall be shown in the conclusion to this chapter.

A BRIEF SIDELONG GLANCE AT THE GERMAN PROTESTANT CHURCH IN HITLER'S REICH

"The individual church authorities bore witness in a plethora of rallies and calls, that they were cooperating in the great work of unity and stressed their unity with the great events in the political life of Germany."

—theologian Karl Kupisch[286]

The Catholic bishops of Germany had fought Nazism with a united front until 1933; but theological circles of the Protestant Church sympathized with him before that time, such as the *Arbeitsgemeinschaft nationalistischer Pfarrer* (Working Group of Nationalist Priests), which had been in existence since 1931. But after Hitler seized power, the pro-Nazi calls of the Protestant church leaders thundered out one after the next.

The Protestant federation demanded for the March 1933 elections: "Protestant Christians, recognize the seriousness and promise *of this election outcome.* . . . Support the men of this current government to give them the opportunity to do creative work. Be mindful of your responsibility: this is about Germany's salvation!"[287]

After the elections, the *Allgemeine Evangelisch-Lutherische Kirchenzeitung* (Lutheran Protestant newspaper) wrote: "There was no room for standing in the wings for the Church here—action was necessary . . . and it becomes clear to us every day: we are consciously witnesses to a great, unfolding history. . . . But for all the joy about domestic changes, we must not forget for a single day that liberation of foreign policy must also be fought for!"[288] On April 25, 1933, the so-called Group of Three (Kapler, Marahrens, Hesse) declared, as representatives of the German Protestant Church committee and thereby of all the Protestant churches of Germany, at a rally: "We say a grateful yes to this turning point in history. God has sent it to us. To Him be the glory!"[289]

The Protestant military district priest Ludwig Müller introduced himself in an appeal one day later: "I set about my work with the trust of God and awareness of my responsibility to God. The aim is the fulfillment of the German Protestant longing that has been in existence since the times of the Reformation."[290]

The two latter appeals were expressly affirmed, in the name of the *Jungreformatorischen Bewegung* (Young Reformists' Movement), among others, by today's regional bishop, Lilje.[291]

The regional bishop of Thuringia, Reichardt, wrote on October 25, 1933: "A great duty of gratitude to God and Adolf Hitler drives us to stand solemnly and unanimously behind the man who has been sent to our people and the world to overcome the powers of darkness. We therefore call upon our congregations to stand behind the Führer, in the same spirit as us, as a united people of brothers."[292]

A renowned Protestant university theologian can also be quoted here as one example among many. "Anyone," says this exegete of the New Testament in 1935, "for whom the New Testament has improved awareness of God's will and path in history and the ultimate realities of the world will recognize in the Third Reich more than one of the characteristics that are set out in Pauline state theology. . . . The Church must say yes to this state, a *yes from the New Testament* to the historical mission and purpose of the Third Reich, as Paul said yes to the God-granted office of the Roman Empire." The theologian, who fights against liberalism, Bolshevism, Jewish capital, and all "utopians"(!); who extols the basic Nazi principles of blood and soil, race and people, honor and heroism, and the swastika, even at the expense of theology; who calls Hitler a powerful personality; who mentions that Horst Wessel was the son of a military clergyman; and who orders German theology students to march "properly in line in the SA,"[293] has, of course, a professorship here in today's Germany again [that is, in 1965].

During the occupation of the demilitarized zone of the Rhineland in March 1936, the Reich's ecclesiastical committee telegraphed to Hitler: "Deeply affected by the earnest of the hour and the firm determination of the Führer, who is acting from his responsibility to God, the German Protestant Church stands ready *joyfully to the last mission* for the honor and lives of the German people." The Protestant priests' associations took this announcement of loyalty to the Führer "completely to heart."[294]

On November 20, 1936, the Protestant regional bishops vowed: "Along with the Reich's Ecclesiastical Committee we stand behind the Führer in the German people's fight for life against Bolshevism. . . . We will untiringly call upon our congregations to commit fully their Christian powers in this struggle in the certainty that this is *the most valuable service* to the German people."[295]

On September 30, 1938, eleven months before the war started, the Protestant Church leaders telegraphed: "Thanks be to God, who has kept an honorable peace for us through the Führer. Along with our liberated brothers we invoke God's blessing for the promising work of peace. Hail to the Führer!"[296]

But the Protestant Church leaders were also there right away when it comes to the work of war—"in war and peace," as Pope Leo XIII also wrote. On September 2, 1939, at the beginning of the Second World War, they affirmed: "The German Protestant Church has always had a loyal bond with the fate of the German People. It has added unconquerable forces from the word of God to the weapons of steel. . . . So now, too, we unite with our people in the intercession for Führer and Reich."[297]

The national leader of the Protestant priests' associations made an appeal on September 8, 1939: "Greater Germany is calling to service. It is calling everyone, old and young, man and woman—and it is calling us too. Some for service out in the field, others at home as servants to the one who said: 'Come to me all you who are tired and oppressed and I will restore you.'"[298]

After the successful invasion of Poland, the German Protestant Church leaders thanked God and Hitler in their pulpit declaration at the harvest festival in 1939. "And we combine the thanks to God with the thanks to all those who have brought about such a mighty change in just a few weeks: the Führer and his generals, our brave soldiers on land, water and in the air. . . . We praise You above, You controller of battles, and beg you to continue to stand firm with us."[299]

After the invasion of the Soviet Union, Hitler received a long, enthusiastic telegram on June 30, 1941, that started with the words: "The Clergy Consultative Council [*Vertrauensrat*] of the German Protestant Church, assembled for the first time since the beginning of the crucial battle in the east, guarantees you once again, my Führer, the unchanging loyalty and willingness of all Protestant Christians in the Reich in these enrapturingly moving times. . . . The German people and with it all its Christian members thank you for this deed."[300]

But the leaders of the Protestant Church also showed support for Hitler much later—indeed, they even joined in the call for "total war," such as the president of the Lutheran world convent, Marahrens, who demanded "ruthless determination" from the pastors on July 20, 1943. "We must make everyone aware, everywhere: we are in a war that demands our complete commitment and this war must be waged with unerring devotion, free of all sentimentality." Just a few lines later, the high Protestant Church leader shamelessly refers to Luke 9:62, where it states: "No man, having put his hand to the plough, and looking back, is fit for the kingdom of God."[301]

Bishop Hanns Lilje, who had supported Hitler since 1933, and who played down the Nazis' crimes on a trip to America in 1938 and answered the critical question from a reporter with: "What is there for the Church to protest against?"[302] and in the third year of the war published a document with the telling title "*Der Krieg als geistige Leistung*" ("War as an Intellectual Performance"). In this, Lilje writes: "Or where is the *delicacy* of life appreciated more than in war?" "'With God!' must not only be on the soldiers' belt buckles but in their hearts and consciences too. This sacrifice can only be legitimized in the name of God." And since this includes Jesus, Lilje concludes his commentary on Hitler's war as follows: "These words of Jesus apply in a much deeper sense than everyday bourgeois wisdom can possibly know: 'He who loves his life loses it.'"[303]

Bishop Lilje still propagates the gospels in his own way today [that is, in 1965], just as he did under Hitler. In a television interview in 1962, he made it clear that Christians in East Germany not only had a passive right to resistance but also an active one. But the supporter of the Nazi regime did not want to "advise anyone to hastily reach for a gun at the moment."[304]

But like Lilje, most of the current crusade ideologists had served, as submissive minions of Hitler's, an Eastern European policy that led to the deaths of fifty-five million people while the Christian pacifists of the time still fight militarism today.

Because there were, of course, Protestants who were not only immune to National Socialism but also publicly testified to it. Remember the Confessing Church, men such as Karl Immer, Paul Schneider, Regional Bishop Wurm, and Martin Niemöller, who, although initially welcoming the Nazis' seizure of power, quickly distanced themselves from them. Niemöller's letters to Hitler's ministers must be read so that their intrepidness can be honored. Tellingly, he is also strictly opposed to the federal republic's policies today.

But even a member of the Confessing Church, Hans Asmussen, admits the cowardly attitude even of this group relatively openly. While Asmussen was a witness to many of Goerdeler's talks with the highest eastern front army leaders, in which "the question of when it was time to strike out against Hitler was being openly aired," he says it was "hard to say" when the Confessing Church "learned to see the state as its enemy because it could not be said openly and we often kept our opinions amongst ourselves."[305] Because, as Asmussen himself stresses, there were "only *very* few people one could talk with openly."[306]

Even a bishop who saw himself affiliated with the Confessing Church stated at the beginning of the war on the basis of the twenty-third psalm, that God also had a "table prepared opposite our enemies" for the Germans through Adolf Hitler.[307]

And even the chairman of the first "Provisional Leadership" of the Confessing Church, the then regional bishop of Hanover, declared in a report: "We would like to repeat expressly at this juncture what we have publicly and solemnly declared countless times[!] since the dawn of our National Socialist State: that we are prepared to support this state with loyalty and willingness to sacrifice."[308]

This was the same, as we have seen, that the Catholic bishops of Germany declared, in closest cooperation with the pope, of course. We will see in the next chapter how Pius XII comported himself during the war.

THE VATICAN AND THE SECOND WORLD WAR

"The Pope's hands dripped with blood."
—Italian parliamentarian Laura Diaz[1]

"In all the wars of the recent past, it [the Catholic Church] has strengthened the soldiers of all[!] armies in their sense of duty."
—*Herderkorrespondenz*, February 1952

WHAT DID PACELLI WANT?

"Under the leadership of this Pope it now looks so gloomy in the Catholic Church that it only remains to say with resignation, as an honest Catholic: The situation is hopeless!"
— Johannes Fleischer[2]

As the Catholic Church had disputes with Hitler, there were also, albeit more rarely, differences of opinion with Mussolini. But for all the differences, all the complaints of the bishops and even the Vatican, Popes Pius XI and XII held on firmly to the alliance with the Fascists, who had, after all, come to power with curial help.

This significant fact must be stressed again, especially the way Monsignor Pacelli served as a pacemaker for Hitler. Eugenio Pacelli, who had lived in Germany for thirteen years, admired the "great characteristics of this people."

So he surrounded himself with Germans when he became pope. He was advised by Kaas, the former chairman of the German Centre Party, and also by the German Jesuit Hentrich. He had a German private secretary, the Jesuit Leiber, and a German confessional father, the Jesuit Bea. The German Father Bruno Wüstenberg had a significant official position in the secretariat of state. Even the nun Pasqualina Lehnert, who was especially close to the pope and was called "the Popess" or the "*virgo potens*" by frivolous tongues, who had already served him at the uncanonical age of twenty-three—in the German nunciatures with the dispensation of Benedict XV, in the Vatican palaces with the dispensation of Pius XI, and finally in the papal suite, to which she took other sisters, "since the suite was very large," with the dispensation of Pope Pacelli himself—came from Bavaria.[3] And not only were the pope's two splendid Persian cats called "Peter" and "Mieze," but the canaries and "other birds, of which there were many in the papal chambers" also had mostly German names.[4] The author Pallenberg, when visiting the Vatican, found that the *pontifex maximus* was living "on a German island," and the Italian Vatican ambassador di Custoza spoke of the "Pope of the Germans," who was often directly called the "German Pope."[5]

Of course Pius XII did not have any particular sympathy for the anticlerical Hitler. That does not need to be stressed at all. But he appreciated Hitler's destruction of the liberals, socialists, and communists in Germany. And he expected him to destroy Bolshevism in general. For Pacelli, National Socialism was, as already noted above, no more than "the lesser of two evils" with which he hoped the greater evil would be eliminated. There is no doubt about this. Pacelli, like most curia cardinals molded by diplomatic rather than emotional considerations, was a cold calculator who thought in terms of greater contexts throughout his life and whose soft spot for Germany and fear of communism determined his politics.

When Cardinal Döpfner claimed, on the twenty-fifth anniversary of Pacelli's coronation, "the view that Pius XII saw National Socialism as an ally in the fight against communism and deemed it to that extent as the lesser of two evils is historically untenable,"[6] he was deceiving his audience more than he was himself. Even the papal private secretary Robert Leiber admitted that the pope saw Hitler's unconditional surrender as "a misfortune." "Regarding the two systems, National Socialism and Bolshevism, Pius XII considered Bolshevism the more dangerous one to the global consequences and with a view to the future. The military, politicians, and statesmen of the Allies, who had been visiting the Pope in large numbers since June 1944, can confirm this. He always pointed out that now, when National Socialism was reaching its conclusion, the more difficult task, the confrontation with the world of Bolshevism was yet to be mastered. He was, however, misunderstood."[7]

What did Pacelli want? A mutual European and American "crusade" against the Soviet Union. As far back as April 30, 1937, he wrote Hitler's ambassador at the Vatican, Diego von Bergen, that the Holy See "[does] not [dismiss] the great significance that the formation of internally healthy and viable political fronts of defense against the danger atheist Bolshevism possesses." The Holy See, affirmed Pacelli, was also fighting Bolshevism but with different means. But he did approve of the use of "external means of power against the Bolshevist threat"; indeed, he saw "a crucial mission and task" in this.[8]

THE GERMAN INVASION OF CZECHOSLOVAKIA

> *"Henlein summarized his view to the Führer as follows: 'So we must always demand so much that we cannot be satisfied.' This view was affirmed by the Führer."*[9]

When Eugenio Pacelli mounted the papal throne in March 1939, Hitler's troops entered Czechoslovakia. Pacelli, who had already played into Hitler's hands when he was nuncio in Berlin, cardinal secretary of state in 1932/33, and, when Austria was annexed, ignored the new act of violence completely. Not even "urgent efforts," as the German ambassador to the Vatican telegraphed from Rome on March 25, were able to "move the Pope to join the protests of the democratic states against the annexation of Bohemia and Moravia to the Reich." On the contrary: he rejected "this request most determinedly."[10] He declared instead—and this was one of his first statements as pope—that he wished to inform everyone "how highly he estimated Germany and that he was willing to do a great deal for Germany."[11]

After von Bergen had passed on Hitler's congratulations on the papal election, he was soon allowed to appear. "The Pope stressed during the audience, during which I expressed the congratulations once again, that I was the first ambassador he was receiving; he put great value on asking me personally to express his heartfelt thanks to the Führer and Reich Chancellor; he combined with this his sincerest wishes for the prosperity of the German people that he had come to appreciate and love more and more from his years of contact while he was employed in Munich and Berlin. The Pope then added his 'great wish for peace between Church and State'; he had said this to me frequently as Secretary of State but today he would like to confirm it expressly as Pope."[12]

Four days after his election, on March 6, 1939, Pius XII also wrote Hitler ("Honorable Sir!") and, unshaken by what was already his seven-year rule of terror, prayed for "the protection of heaven and the blessing of Almighty God with the best wishes."[13] The basic tenor of the letter, Ambassador von Bergen comments, was "considerably friendlier than that in Pius XI's communications to the previous Reich president. . . . What is particularly remarkable here is the desire for agreement that was also expressed at this juncture. The German text was clearly formulated in the Pope's style; according to reliable sources he expressly reserved the processing of German questions for himself."[14] And von Bergen noted on March 17: "Pope told me the Führer was the first head of state he told about being elected Pope; he also broke previous protocol etiquette by not only, as usual, signing communications composed in Latin but also a version in German that was to be understood as not merely a translation. He also wanted to make known his German-friendly views and his wish for peace."[15]

Even Prelate Alberto Giovannetti, the pope's apologist, concedes that the letter goes beyond a purely protocol form. "In its scope and the feelings that are expressed, it is unparalleled among the official communications sent from the Vatican at the time."[16] And only a few weeks later, Pius XII communicated with Hitler again. He sent him a handwritten message on the occasion of his fiftieth birthday that was very well received.[17]

On April 25, 1939, ten days after the German invasion of Czechoslovakia, the pope said, according to eyewitness reports, to around 160 Germans who were visiting Rome whom he was receiving: "We have always loved Germany, where We have had the privilege of spending many years of Our life, and *We love it even more now*. We are glad about the greatness, the upturn and the welfare of Germany and it would be wrong to claim that We do not want a thriving, great and powerful Germany. But for this very reason we also want the rights of God and the Church always to be acknowledged, for every greatness is all the more secure the more these rights are guaranteed and taken as a foundation for development."[18]

Of course Pacelli also always condemned the Nazis' hostility to the church. When the relationship was especially troubled in summer 1937, the German ambassador to the Vatican reported on July 7 that, above all, the mood of the secretary of state was "more agitated than ever." No wonder. Precisely because he approved so wholeheartedly of Hitler's anti-Bolshevist policies, his anticlericalism must have been all the more awkward for him. But just two weeks later, von Bergen wired to Berlin that the declarations made by the cardinal secretary of state on July 16 were astonishingly contrary to the position of the pope. "Pacelli received me with a marked amiability and assured me emphatically[!] during the talk that relations with us would be made normal and friendly once again as soon as possible; this applied especially to him, who had lived in Germany for thirteen years and had always been extremely sympathetic to the German people. He would always have been prepared to talk to prominent persons such as Foreign Minister and Minister President Göring."[19] And so Cardinal Secretary of State Pacelli distanced himself clearly from his predecessor Pius XI, whose anger about Nazi church policy occasionally got the better of him.

In April 7, 1938, Cardinal Pacelli also "repeatedly and forcefully stated the requirement for a compromise between the Vatican and the Reich and went so far as to declare that he, Pacelli, was ready to come to Berlin for negotiations" to the Danzig senate president Greiser.[20]

So it was only logical that Pacelli's coronation was welcomed in Germany. Even Giovannetti wrote: "Even the National Socialist press spoke appreciatively of him."[21] Count Ciano determined on June 13, 1939, "that the position of the Reich towards the Church is improving." And even Chief of Police Himmler admitted to Ciano "that he understood the Pope's tact and cleverness. Himmler's journal *Das Schwarze Korps* [*The Black Corps*] has not attacked the Church since this Pope took up office."[22]

Actually, they knew well what Pacelli was to be thanked for. The little-known statement from Austrian president Wilhelm Miklas, who was in office until 1938, should be quoted in this context: "The Church authorities are also to blame. Pacelli was Nuncio in Germany at the time when the system of violence was introduced. The Pope was in Poland at the time of Pilsudski. Pacelli was pushing in this direction. Now we see the result of this system."[23]

The Vatican had already been working on the destruction of the "Hussite Republic," in which well over one million Catholics left the church between 1918 and 1930, before Hitler by supporting the separatist movement of the Slovakian Catholics, in particular, the Slovakian People's Party. This was a conservative and Catholic party with an anti-Semitic hue that was led first by the prelate Hlinka and, since 1938, by the clergyman Tiso. Soon after becoming prime minister of Slovakia; the latter, a former Catholic professor of theology, demanded absolute autonomy, even though he had, only shortly before, sworn an oath of allegiance to the president of the Czechoslovakian Republic. Now removed from office, Tiso fled to Berlin on an airplane supplied by the Austrian Catholic Seyß-Inquart, made Slovakia independent in alliance with Hitler and the Vatican in March 1939, and became state president in October.

In April 1939 the pope was one of the first to acknowledge the new Slovakian state and awarded Tiso the rank of papal chamberlain and the title of monsignor.[24] The Catholic bishops of the country had a pastoral letter read out in all the churches on October 24 in which they blessed the Fascist Tiso regime.[25] "Catholicism and National Socialism," said Monsignor Tiso, "have a great deal in common and work hand in hand to improve the world."[26] And Tiso's deputy, Prime Minister Tuka, who, as Keitel attests, idolized Hitler,[27] said in August 1940 that the Slovakian state system would be a synthesis of German National Socialism and Roman Catholicism.[28] And so the Hlinka Guard was created in the style of the Hitler Youth: a German-style fatigue duty was introduced; freedom of speech, press, and assembly were suspended, much as in Franco's Catholic Spain; all other parties were banned; and Orthodox, Protestants, and Jews were put under severe pressure.

Prelate Tiso was an outspoken anti-Semite. Because he was pressed on this point by some Catholics, he said on August 28, 1942: "As far as the Jewish question is concerned, some inquire as to whether our methods are Christian and humane. To them I would ask this: Is it Christian for the Slovaks to want to liberate themselves from their eternal enemies, the Jews?"[29] The Catholic bishop Ján Vojtassák, the leading representative of the high church hierarchy in Slovakia, even denounced the Jews and, on March 25, 1942, said at a meeting of the Slovakian State Council, whose deputy chairman he was: "We have continued the expulsion of the Jews. We have increased the total."[30] And indeed, the bishop, who was receiving an annual income of three to four million korunas, used the Fascist race laws to gain ownership of Jewish possessions in Betlanovce and Baldovce.[31]

According to a publication of the Czechoslovakian Foreign Ministry that appeared in London in 1941, 90 percent of all Slovakian Catholic clergy prayed for Hitler.[32] The papal chamberlain Tiso sent a legion to the eastern front and repeatedly visited and encouraged his legionnaires. He called for the war to continue right up to the end and made this assurance on September 27, 1944: "Slovakia will stand by the Axis powers right until the final victory."[33] And the Catholic bishops Ján Vojtassák and Michal Buzalka blessed Tiso's troops before they set out on the campaign against Catholic Poland and the Soviet Union.[34]

Tiso fled to Germany in 1945, but the Allies handed him over; he was tried in Czechoslovakia and convicted of war crimes. The pope did everything to try to rehabilitate him morally. In the *Catholic Encyclopedia*, published by the Vatican with the full approval of Pius XII, it says: "Tiso was a model priest who led an unblemished life. He dedicated himself to politics because he *saw himself forced to do so by necessity*; because only the clergy have defended the rights of the Slovakian people since the beginning of this century. This is why everyone loved him like a father. Slovakia made great progress under the Tiso government, in cultural, economic and social terms, and also proved its *national independence*." Finally, Tiso himself is quoted: "I die a martyr. . . . I also die a defender of Christian civilization against communism."[35]

Tiso also died a rebel against the Czechoslovakian state, a war criminal and a rabid anti-Semite, and in general as a man who, in alliance with the pope, supported a system in whose concentration camps millions of people perished.

In Czechia, too, the high Catholic clergy collaborated with the Nazis. The governor of Prague, Frank, wrote to Hitler's headquarters as late as July 5, 1944, saying that he, Frank, would rely on the higher dignitaries of the Czech Catholic Church.[36]

Two years previously, on June 10, 1942, the Czech village of Lidice was burned to the ground on Frank's order as "retribution" for the shooting of the "Reich Protector" Heydrich; 184 men and 7 women were shot on the spot, and 203 women and 104 children were deported to a concentration camp. Of them, 153 women and 16 children returned.[37] The high clergy in the Czechia would work with the initiator of this crime even two years later.

When the Czech bishops asked for permission to have a peal of bells organized and a requiem read for SS leader Heydrich, Hitler said to the pious men that it would have been better "if they had prayed in good time for the Deputy Reich Protector to be kept alive."[38]

DANZIG

"Splett was appointed Bishop of Danzig one year before the war broke out. He was very strict to the Poles and removed the Polish priests from all the parishes and Church authorities wherever he could. During the war he went the whole hog and used the Gestapo. After the war he was sentenced to life imprisonment."

—Tadeusz Breza[39]

The Vatican had accommodated Hitler even before Danzig was annexed to Germany, the event that initiated the invasion of Poland. Because the pope, at the insistence of the Nazi Party, removed the bishop of Danzig, O'Rourke, a count of Irish origin, whom the Nazis accused of "Polonizing" the Danzig church. Additionally, the pope changed the project of the city's Polish church communities that he had previously approved. O'Rourke was replaced by one of his priests, Dr. Maria Splett, which led to the beginning of close cooperation with the party. In a pastoral letter dated September 4, 1939, Splett gratefully welcomed the return of Danzig to the German Reich, made possible by the invasion of Poland, and asked God Almighty to bless the "Führer."[40]

On September 15, Splett issued the following order in a circular to all the pastoral offices and chaplaincies in his diocese: "The presbyteries and churches must all fly flags and the bells must be rung during the Führer's visit, which is expected soon. The individual presbyteries will be informed about the time of the ringing at an appropriate time by the local party authorities by telephone."[41]

At the Nazis' suggestion, the curia also transferred the church administration of the Polish dioceses of Gniezno, Poznań, and Chełmno to the bordering German dioceses. So the bishop of Danzig became the apostolic administrator of Chełmno.

Splett now also undertook everything to suppress Polish identity, in accordance with the Germans' wishes, in church matters. The bishop decreed on May 17, 1940: "All objects with Polish inscriptions and emblems [prayer cards and the like] and other Polish inscriptions and paintings must be removed from the churches immediately [by Monday, May 20, cr., at 12:00 noon]. But flags, etc., may not be stored secretly in the presbyteries or private houses. Polish inscriptions and emblems must be removed from flags, monuments, etc., immediately."[42] Splett issued a reminder of this decree in a circular on October 15, writing: "Should, in individual cases, Church employees have been charged with executing this order, I commit all priests and clergy to convincing themselves personally that said order has actually been executed."[43]

The bishop ordered the following on May 25, 1940: "The Polish language is banned in confession, effective immediately, both from the penitent and the confessional father."[44]

The pope himself advocated a return of Danzig to the German Reich in the summer of 1939.[45] Sir Percy Loraine, the British Ambassador in Rome, telegraphed to Lord Halifax on July 7, 1939: "As regards the Vatican and Danzig, Mr. Helfand thinks that the Vatican has already worked out concrete proposals and probably communicated them to Berlin and Warsaw: Poland should not only admit that Danzig is a German city but also that it should be returned to the Reich."[46] And Colonel Beck reports in his memoirs: "Towards the end of August the Pope addressed us again and declared to us that the cession of Pomerania and Danzig could keep the peace."[47]

THE GERMAN INVASION OF POLAND

> *"The Vatican is one of those mainly responsible for the tragedy of my country. I recognized too late that we were conducting foreign policy in the interests of the Catholic Church."*
>
> —Polish foreign minister Jósef Beck[48]

When Austria was occupied, Göring, as Hitler's representative, gave the Czech ambassador Mastny his "word of honor" that this purely "family matter" would not disrupt the desired improvement of relations with Czechoslovakia.[49] Poland kept quiet during the conflict with Czechoslovakia because Hitler had concluded a nonaggression and friendship pact with it in 1934. And when he waged war on Poland, the pact with Russia was beneficial to him.

Pius XII had already found out about the planned attack on Poland from his Berlin nuncio in the middle of August 1939.[50] Hitler asked the pope not to condemn the attack at the time and to win over the Polish Catholics to take part in a crusade against the Soviets.[51]

Now the Vatican had been longing for nothing more than the destruction of communism and the Soviet Union for twenty years, and this was connected to the curia's second-greatest wish, the subjugation of the Orthodox Church to Roman Catholicism. But Poland was a purely Catholic land, steadfastly faithful to the Vatican for centuries, and was also ruled by a Catholic dictator who had close connections to the pope. Nonetheless, Pius XII still decided to sacrifice Poland. But he stipulated three conditions.[52]

1. Hitler must try everything to achieve a compromise with Poland and the Western powers beforehand.
2. Should the invasion take place, he must only cause Poland a minimum of physical and moral damage and not have the Polish Catholics persecuted for their resistance; all church interests must be preserved.
3. The Vatican negotiations with Germany regarding an invasion of Russia must never become known.

Hitler promised everything.

And the Catholic chief of chaplains, Rarkowski, spurred the German soldiers on: "Each of you knows what is at stake in these tempestuous days for our people, and everyone can see before them in this operation the glowing example of a true fighter, our Führer and Commander in Chief, the first and bravest soldier of the Greater German Reich."[53] When France and Britain joined the war after the invasion of Poland, despite all papal efforts, Pius XII was so affected by the start of the Second World War that there was concern about his health for several days. The pope even suffered a nervous breakdown in November.[54] But he kept his promise. Just as with the German invasions of Austria and Czechoslovakia, he also kept silent now and did not waste a word on condemning Hitler's Poland campaign. Even when Britain and France insisted that the pope declare Germany to be the aggressor, he refused, referring to the alleged traditionally neutral position of the Vatican, "which avoids direct intervention in international affairs."[55]

Instead, Pius XII protested all the more energetically against the conclusion of the Hitler-Stalin Pact via his nuncio in Germany, the *Osservatore Romano*, and Vatican Radio. And when the Soviets swept into Poland and occupied it on September 17, 1939, the Vatican interventions were almost endless.

The pope also protested against the Russian invasion of Finland.[56] He was able to protest when he wanted! And the *Osservatore Romano* incessantly castigated "Russia's aggressive intentions," "the most cynical aggression of modern times," and accused the Russian government of not only "proceeding according to the law of the jungle but also publicly defending it."[57] And indeed, the Soviets did not leave out any rigorous measures. Church schools, theological seminars, and monasteries were closed, chapels were confiscated, churches were heavily taxed, clergy members were exiled, and Christian teachers were replaced by communists at public schools.[58]

(Before, however, there had already been, especially in the areas ceded to Poland from Russia after the First World War, comprehensive religious persecutions under the guidance of Catholic bishops. Because in these areas there were seven to eight million White Russians and Ukrainians, about half of whom were members of the Russian Orthodox Church. Despite the Poles' solemn promises to the great powers that the rights of these minorities would be respected, attempts were soon made to convert them. With the Vatican's approval, more than one thousand Orthodox priests were incarcerated and whole villages depopulated in massacres. A document published in 1931 in the United States reads: "Most of the Orthodox churches were plundered by Polish soldiers and used as stables or even latrines."[59] Vatican visitors incessantly traveled to the country at the time to convince themselves the mission was being continued.)

But the religious persecution in Poland by Hitler's units was so obvious that even the Vatican repeatedly expressed its disapproval. These protests were essential for the pope, who, for the sake of the Catholic world, kept up the appearance of strict neutrality for the entire war. On the one hand, they served to camouflage his pro-Fascist policies, and on the other, he sought to win concessions from Hitler's government in church matters. The Nazis' anticlericalism in Germany had impaired cooperation between Pius XII and Hitler just as little as the excesses in Poland had. Nuncio Orsenigo—a diplomat, as Monsignor Giovannetti praised, "of great political sagacity"[60]—did protest, it is true, but he also congratulated Hitler on behalf of the pope on his survival of the Munich assassination attempt.

THE POPE'S "EFFORTS TO MAKE PEACE" AND ITALY'S ENTRY INTO THE WAR

"All those not seeking to further themselves with lies but want to stick to the truth instead know that We remained strictly impartial to all war-waging parties in the last conflict. We have even testified to this frequently in word and deed and united all the nations in love." "All those who fight with weapons and are divided by disputes are Our beloved sons in Our eyes."

—Pius XII, July 7, 1952[61]

"It is certain that only the malignant can deny that the Popes in both World Wars urged for peace in many statements, implored nations to stop this 'fratricide' and make sure material help was provided for the countless suffering people by the papal relief organization without distinction of their nationality. But what did the complete impartiality of the Popes look like in practice? It consisted of Popes who had their

bishops on either side call for . . . mutual destruction of the Catholics
and not being biased in this respect for or against either party, in strict
'neutrality.' But it is simply unfathomable how such an "impartiality"
can be paralleled to the behavior of a father 'who loves all his children
with the same affinity,' and can be characterized as an upright effort
'to unite all nations in love.'"

—Johannes Fleischer[62]

Anyone who reads the book by the Vatican chronicler Alberto Giovannetti, *The Vatican and the War*, will quickly notice that the word *peace* plays an even greater part in it than in Heinrich Böll's satire "Christmas Not Just Once a Year."

Initially, Pius XII himself chastises in an epigraph (as early as June 13, 1943), "the folly of the accusations that the Pope wanted war" and "did nothing for peace" and prophesied that anyone who "always tries to use deceitful words to push the blame for the blood that . . . has been shed onto the papacy" would be shamed. The affirmation of Monsignor Bruno Wüstenberg, one of Pacelli's German employees, in the first sentence of the foreword, was that not one single pope in history has ever, in all probability, striven for peace with more dedication than Pius XII. And then it is the turn of Giovannetti himself. Although this report is, as he writes right at the beginning, "only a few rays of light"—"for the uninterrupted hard work for peace, whose untiring champion the Pope was from the start of the war to its end, has not yet been portrayed to the extent it deserves to be"[63]—the figure of Pius XII soon becomes ever lighter, ever brighter, ever more sublime. One incantation of peace follows another, peace is the predominant word, either in the mouth of the author or in that of the oft-quoted pope, who, as he said himself on June 13, 1943, "had uninterruptedly called and urged: peace, peace, peace!" whose last publicly uttered word is said to have been "Peace,"[64] and who in general was such a tremendous pacifist that Cardinal Tardini was able to credit him with peace being the word that passed his lips most.

The style of these Pacelli sermons should be examined more closely. "Lonely on deserted paths," said Pius XII in an audience granted to the Roman patriciate on January 8, 1940, for instance, "in the shadow of vague hopes, peace wanders aimlessly in fear, and the traces of its steps are being followed in the Old and

New Worlds by people seeking it who are its friends, seeking it with concern and in deep thought about the question of how they can bring it back to the people in a just, solid and lasting way," and so on.[65] Or one day later in an address to the ladies of the Roman Caritas: "Threatened by a new deluge, a fearful humanity searches longingly for the return of the dove that will herald the rainbow of peace. But the winged messenger will only bring peace for all, for individuals and nations, if it can once again pick the greening branch of the olive tree on earth, the tree that gives soothing anointing oil but also requires the sun of love for growth and fertility."[66]

This typical Pacelli tone is judged as little here as is Giovannetti's astonishing claim: "Rarely has the word of the Church achieved such masterful heights in the face of the most difficult problems of the modern world."[67] But what do addresses and mere calls for peace prove? What do they prove when they come from the mouth of a pope who, in 1939, answered the question of the duty of obedience to Hitler that the "Führer" is the legal ruler of the Germans and anyone who refuses obedience to him is a sinner?[68] What do they prove when they come from the mouth of a pope who, on November 8, 1939, gave the French bishops the right to take all measures to defend their country?[69] And who, on August 6, 1940, expressed his admiration to the German bishops for the German Catholics who were fighting "loyally and to the death" for their "national comrades"?[70] So what do such speeches prove when they come from the mouth of a man who, during a cruel six-year war, preached "Peace! Peace!" with the monotony of an automaton *but at the same time, through his bishops, committed millions and millions of Catholics to serving in the war and thereby killing other Catholics (and non-Catholics) until the fronts collapsed*? Because it was easier for him, as it was for his predecessors, to violate the commandments of the biblical Jesus than those of Hitler and other potentates. Is there any thinking person who can still take the peace sermons of a pope like this seriously? This mockery of humanity and this affront to reason?

It is, though, obvious that Pius XII was energetically petitioning for a kind of "peace," but not global peace. France's and Britain's entries into the war shocked the "Pope of the Germans," particularly as he himself had created the preconditions for it with his support of Hitler in 1933 with the annexation of Austria and the invasion of Czechoslovakia. So after the Poland campaign, as became known in the Nuremberg trials in particular, he made intense efforts to establish a compromise peace between the Allies and Germany, if only in the attempt to unite the West against Communist Russia.

At Christmas 1939, he unmistakably expressed his fears: "How, after a war, can an economy, exhausted and sucked dry, raise the means for economic and social reconstruction if difficulties from all sides increase to the extreme, and if the forces and temptations of disorder that are lying in wait make an effort to use them in the hope of giving Christian Europe the fatal blow?"[71] Giovannetti states correctly: "The reference to the godless and subversive communism was clear enough."[72] But the pope became even clearer one day after he read out his Christmas message, on December 25, 1939, when he exclaimed at a reception of the College of Cardinals: "Let us end this fratricidal war and concentrate our efforts against the mutual enemy, atheism!"[73] Shortly after, on December 31, Pius XII gave thanks in a private audience granted to the German representative Menshausen for the New Year wishes he had been conveyed and asked to "return my best wishes to the Führer, the entire Reich government and the 'dear German people.'" He also said that "His great affinity for and love of Germany continued *undiminished* and maybe he loved it—if that were even possible— *even more* in today's difficult times."[74] What Pius XII had said after the occupation of Czechoslovakia, that he "now loved [Germany] even more," he was now repeating using almost the same words after Hitler had conquered Poland and thereby expanded his reach of power even farther eastward.

Again, a few more days later, on January 4, 1940, Mussolini wrote to Hitler in full agreement with these papal "peace efforts": "Our two revolutions will not achieve their goals until we have destroyed Moscow Bolshevism. . . . The solution to your living space problem is in Russia, and only in Russia."[75]

The negotiations with the aim of a mutual fight against the Soviet Union in which the pope also tried to persuade the United States to take part took place at the end of 1939 and the beginning of 1940. But on June 10, 1940, Italy declared war on France and Britain. Pius XII, who would have preferred nothing more than a European "crusade" against Russia, had urgently wanted to prevent Italy from joining the conflict. But the Duce was able to answer a handwritten letter from the pope saying: "The history of the Church—and you, Holy Father, also tell me so—has never accepted the formula 'Peace for peace's sake,' of peace at any price, peace without justice, i.e., a peace that could, under the given circumstances, put the current and future fate of the Italian people in irretrievable jeopardy." Furthermore, the Duce was comforted by "the thought that God will protect the armed forces of a pious people whatever happens—and Italians are a pious people."[76]

The Italian episcopate immediately spoke of a holy war when war was declared and sent Mussolini and the king a message of greeting. The *New York Times* correspondent at the Vatican, who inquired about the position of the curia regarding these clerical war demonstrations, received an answer from the Vatican state secretariat that the Holy See was responsible for all Catholics; "but the Italian clergy and the Italian Catholics have special duties to Italy and will fulfill these honorably as always."[77] And the Vatican Jesuits' journal *Civiltà Cattolica* called on all Italians "to seal the loyal performance of their duties with their blood."[78] But the pope continued to profess impartiality and proclaim peace.

THE GERMAN INVASION OF NORWAY AND THE OCCUPATION OF THE NETHERLANDS, BELGIUM, AND FRANCE

When Hitler invaded weak, Protestant Norway in April 1940 and Pius XII was urged from many sides to condemn the latest aggression, he covered himself in silence as he had on previous occasions. He just suggested via the *Osservatore Romano* that there were 2,619 Catholics living in Norway but thirty million in Germany.[79]

And, incidentally, the pope never condemned Mussolini's wars of aggression, neither the Italian invasion of Abyssinia nor those of Albania or Greece. After all, these raids would not only strengthen his Fascist ally but also open up those countries for the Catholic mission. Alberto Giovannetti, however, concludes that Pius XII's wish not to make the living conditions of the Italian people even more difficult (let it be added that they had already been difficult enough in the pope's own country, of all places, for a long time) "occasionally had to advise him against making formal condemnations that would of necessity have led to an open dispute between State and Church."[80] Because for the church, humanitarian motives, as their history since the fourth century proves, play an infinitely smaller part than their relationships with states, especially powerful ones on whom it is dependent. But the pope "never" neglected to "raise a firm and clear protest regarding the Church-hostile position of the Fascists at all times."[81] And indeed, when this was the case, he intervened in Italy, in Germany, and wherever Catholic interests were harmed. But he still supported the anticommunist policies of the Axis powers as well as he could. And just as Nazi Germany welcomed his appointment for this reason, the Italian undersecretary of state Buffarini Guidi also said with full conviction: "This is the Pope we need."[82]

After the occupation of the Netherlands, Belgium, and France, Pius XII, although mildly regretting the occupation of these states against the will of their sovereigns in personal letters to the queen of the Netherlands and the king of Belgium, nonetheless suggested, as the German embassy at the Vatican reported, that he "wanted to preempt any appeal by King Leopold and avoid having to respond." He stressed here that "the telegrams were not intended as a dig against Germany."[83] And when the French and British governments asked the pope for an express condemnation of the aggression, he refused,[84] as he had in previous cases. "Incidentally," Saul Friedländer wrote sarcastically, "the Pope's wisdom increases with every German victory."[85]

Because on May 27, von Bergen communicated the opinion being expressed in the Vatican to the foreign ministry that it would be best if France made an independent peace treaty and left it to Britain to fight on alone.[86] On May 29, von Bergen telegraphed to Berlin: "According to my strictly confidential information, the view in the Pope's Secretariat of State is that it was a good idea for Belgium to surrender and France should do the same as quickly as possible."[87] The ambassador repeated on June 8: "The Vatican remains of the opinion that France should follow the example of Belgium."[88]

On June 10, 1940, just a few hours before Italy entered the war, the papal nuncio Orsenigo, at the foreign office, "very cordially expressed his joy about the German victories" to the leader of the Political Department, Woermann. "He seemed to be longing for Italy to join the war and jokingly said he hoped Germany would invade Paris via Versailles."[89] After the rapid defeat of France, the nuncio conveyed his enthusiastic congratulations at Wilhelmstraße on

July 11, combined with the hope "that we would finally get rid of people like Churchill, Duff Cooper, Eden, etc."[90]

And the pope instructed the German episcopate to hold thanksgiving services for the Führer in all churches.[91]

Just as the Catholic hierarchy supported Hitler after his invasion of Austria and Czechoslovakia, they also did so, initially at least, in the occupied West. In a common pastoral letter dated October 7, 1940, the Belgian bishops demanded recognition of the authority of the German occupying powers and called for obedience[92]; there had been, after all, especially in Belgium for many years already, a subversive political movement with strongly Fascist overtones, "Christus Rex,"[93] founded by *Katholische Aktion* [the lay movement of the Catholic Church].

When, before the German invasion, nearly all the diplomats left Brussels, the papal nuncio Monsignor Micara remained in the city. He had already said, days previously, that he would not desert his post "whatever may happen."[94] After the occupation, he was immediately granted freedom of movement in Belgium again, and when the German general von Falkenhausen invited the few remaining diplomats to a breakfast, he gave the papal nuncio "his special attention."[95]

The Paris nuncio Valerio Valeri had already been charged by the Vatican in July 1940 with lending support to the government of Pétain, the French marshal allied with Hitler. Pétain had had contact with Berlin for a long time, in particular with Göring, and was an ambassador in Franco's Spain from 1939 to 1940. The pope gave him and his helpers his blessing and guaranteed the new French ambassador to the Vatican that the church would warmheartedly support "the work of moral rebirth" in France.[96] On July 9, 1940, the official organ of the curia praised Hitler's ally as "the good Marshal who embodies the best traditions of his nation more than anyone else," and praised his salvation of France. The *Osservatore Romano* closed with the prophesy of "a new, shining day, not only for France but for Europe and the world."[97]

Even when Pétain's authorities gathered seven thousand Spanish refugees who had fled from Franco, including several thousand Basque Catholics and Catholic clergy, and put them in a concentration camp, the pope did not raise a single word of protest.[98]

The leading Catholic newspaper in France, *La Croix*, which was prosecuted after the liberation because of its collaboration politics, called on the people every day to cooperate with Pétain and Hitler, demanded the merciless elimination of the resistance movement, and praised Pétain's course for being "astonishingly in accord with the instructions of the Holy See."[99] After all, Pétain had annulled all the laws restricting the power of the church in the Third Republic and regulated social questions in accordance with the papal encyclicals and Fascist ideology. Compare the document written by the Catholic Pieper (p. 109 f.) in this regard. The position of the pope at that time also becomes clear in the letter written by the French curia cardinal Tisserant on June 11, 1940, to Cardinal Archbishop Suhard of Paris. "Our superiors," it says in the document, "do not want to understand the nature of true conflict, and they doggedly persist in fooling themselves that this is a war like those that took place in olden times. But the fascist ideology and that of Hitler have transformed the consciences of young people, and all those under the age of 35 are willing to do any kind of wrongdoing for the purpose their Führer orders them. I have persistently been asking the Holy Father since the beginning of December to issue an encyclical about the duty of each individual to heed the call of their consciences, because that is the crucial point of Christianity, while Islam, which, thanks to the son of the Muslim woman Hess, served as an example to Hitler's theories, has replaced individual conscience by the duty to obey the orders of the Prophet and his successors blindly. I fear that history will have to reproach the Holy See for pursuing a policy of convenience for itself and not much more. This is extremely sad, especially when one has lived under Pius XI. And everyone relies on the fact that, after Rome has been declared an open city, no one will have to suffer because of the Curia; this is a disgrace."[100]

CLOSER AFFILIATION TO THE VICTORIOUS FÜHRER

After Poland had been overrun in nineteen days, Denmark and Norway occupied in two months, and Holland, Belgium, and France subjugated in six weeks, many circles all over the world considered victory for Hitler's Germany to be certain. In the autumn of 1940, the pope and his secretary of state held long talks in Rome with three German bishops,[101] who then reported at the annual Fulda Bishops' Conference. The prelates promised to prompt stronger support by the Catholic people for victorious Germany and its great chancellor.[102] They decided to hold their meetings in the capital of the Reich, in Berlin, from now on to demonstrate their closer alliance with it. And they agreed on the publishing of a new official organ of the German Catholics by the Wehrmacht chief of chaplains under the title of *Der neue Wille* (*The New Will*). The journal called on everyone to fight for Hitler.[103]

And all this was happening although, at roughly the same time, the German security police were putting two hundred Polish Catholic clergy in concentration camps. But when Orsenigo talked of this at the foreign office on December 11, 1940, he told von Weizsäcker that "he believed that a fairly large room with a chapel-like character was being set up in Dachau for these clergy." You would not believe your eyes: "The Nuncio mentioned this happily."[104]

The Holy Father himself was also clearly happy at the time when, at the New Year audience, he asked the German ambassador to convey "his sincere thanks" for Hitler's congratulations. He responded to them "most cordially for the Führer, the government and the entire German people. He mentioned in particular the Reich's Foreign Minister, whose visit the previous year he looked back on with fondness."[105] (A few years later he was hanged as a criminal.)

And when the Vatican registered the killing of seven hundred Catholic clergy in Oranienburg, Dachau, Buchenwald, and Auschwitz, and the fact that there were another three thousand Catholic priests in concentration camps, an official representative of Pius XII communicated on his "direct order" "that the Pope would be most delighted if it were possible to organize, following the guest performance of the Berlin State Opera in Rome, a concert of the State Orchestra at the Vatican, during which the last scene of the musical drama *Parsifal* could be performed in the form of a concert."[106]

While his clergy were bleeding to death at the hands of concentration camp henchmen, Christ's representative was feasting on Hitler's favorite music; of all ensembles, he invited the Berlin State Orchestra to the Vatican. But should he really care about a few hundred, or even one thousand, massacred clerics if he could, with God's and Mr. Hitler's help, defeat the evil Bolshevists and fetch the Orthodox Church home?

THE GERMAN INVASION OF THE SOVIET UNION

"We follow the fight against the power of Bolshevism with gratification."
    —the German Catholic bishops on December 10, 1941[107]

"A victory over Bolshevism would be as important as a triumph of the teachings of Jesus over those of the unbelievers."
    —the German Catholic bishops in 1942[108]

The centuries-old, extremely instructive history of the relations between Russia and the Vatican must be passed over here. It has recently [that is, in 1965, PG] been published, for the first time in summary, in the three-volume work *Rußland und das Papsttum* (*Russia and the Papacy*) by the Berlin Slavist Eduard Winter with academic meticulousness, but also made easily understandable to the nonspecialist.[109]

Hitler had been warned urgently against the attack on Russia: by the German ambassador in Moscow, Graf von der Schulenburg, by the German military attaché in Moscow, General Köstring, and by several high members of the military. But in the night of June 22, at 2:00 a.m., Ribbentrop ordered the Soviet ambassador, Dekanosov, to appear at 4:00 a.m., and, when the latter offered him his hand unknowingly, he brusquely revealed to him that on account of the Soviet threat "appropriate countermeasures in military terms [had been] taken."[110] At the same time, in violation of the pact, German, Finnish, Hungarian, and Romanian troops invaded the Soviet Union from Finland to the Black Sea.

The papal nuncio in Berlin had been informed of the planned invasion in a private talk with Ribbentrop on the evening of June 20. In this way, the most ardent wish of the Catholic hierarchy, which had been preaching and writing untiringly against communism all over the world for two decades, was fulfilled.

Let us remember in this context that the Eucharist Congress held its conference in Budapest a year before the Second World War started. This congress was (which was announced not only in a speech by the papal legate Eugenio Pacelli urgently stressing the "danger of Bolshevism") clearly an international demonstration of the Catholic Church against communism—as was the Eucharist Congress in Munich in 1960.

The enthusiasm of the Catholic episcopate for Hitler and the campaign against Russia was enormous in most countries. In America, the "radio priest," the Jesuit father Coughlin, who had more than twenty million listeners and was well known for his anti-Semitism, stated on July 7, 1941: "Germany's war is a war for Christianity."[111] The high American clergy tried to influence Roosevelt's government, and this went so far that some representatives of the Catholic Church, including Bishop Duffy of Buffalo, threatened to call upon the Catholics in the American army to refuse orders if the United States formed an alliance with Soviet Russia.[112] On July 24, 1941, the bishops of France also demanded obedience to Pétain in order to help Hitler.[113] And of course, the clergy in Italy and Spain with a vengeance also conducted a massive anti-Soviet campaign, as did those in South America.

Naturally, nobody would expect the pope to even pretend to condemn the attack on Russia. A week later, on June 29, the Feast Day of the Apostles Peter and Paul, Pius XII did not lack "rays of hope," as he put it in a radio address, "that raise the heart to great, holy expectations: magnanimous courage for defending the foundations of Christian culture and optimistic hopes for their triumph."[114] By which the pope, as Embassy Counselor Menshausen wrote to Berlin by way of explanation, wanted to express his hope "that the great sacrifices this war demands would not be in vain and would lead to victory over Bolshevism according to the will of Providence."[115]

The secretary of the *congregatio de propaganda fide* (Congregation for the Dissemination of Faith), Archbishop Constantini, put it more clearly than Pius XII but "certainly not without the approval of the Holy See"[116] at a festival service at the beginning of August: "Yesterday on Spanish soil, and now today in Bolshevist Russia, in that vast land where Satan seems to have found his representatives and best collaborators in the heads of the republics, brave soldiers from our Fatherland too are fighting the greatest battle. We wish from all our hearts that this battle will bring us final victory and the downfall of Bolshevism, that ideology aimed at negation and subversion." At the end, Archbishop Constantini called for God's blessing on the Italian and German warriors who were "defending the ideal of our freedom against the red barbarism at this crucial hour."[117]

Admittedly, the curia did not propagate a crusade against the Soviets either, from which they refrained, as the Jesuit Gundlach, formerly professor at the Pontifical Gregorian University, revealed, "in view of the intellectual faultiness of unity in the West"[118] (which was intended to mean the faultiness of intellectual unity in the West). Since so many Christian countries were fighting alongside the "atheist" Soviet Union, Pius XII was not able to describe the Nazi Germany invasion as a crusade. And church policy under Hitler also forced him to be a little reserved, since the news "constantly arriving" at Rome in this regard constituted, as the German Vatican embassy wrote to Wilhelmstraße on September 12, 1941, "overwhelming evidence."[119] So the great pope of peace remained silent. But he also remained silent when, in October 1941, the American president Roosevelt asked him to protest against the mass shootings of hostages by Germans.[120] (In Yugoslavia, for instance, one hundred Serbs were shot for every German soldier that was killed, on the orders of the military commander.[121]) And Pius XII also remained silent on the destruction of almost two thousand churches and more than five hundred synagogues, as well as on the murder of numerous clergy during the war in the east. After all, the Vatican now wanted, just like in the other areas occupied by Hitler, to see Catholicism spread in Orthodox Russia as well.

There was a special priests' seminar in Rome, which had been set up a considerable time before: the Collegium Russicum, where clergy were being taught Russian, Ukrainian, and other Slavonic languages and clerics were being trained for missionary activities in the Soviet Union. There was also a special agreement on this between the Vatican and Hitler's government, which was even openly admitted in the foreword of an anthology of papal messages that appeared in 1945 in Paris.[122] The general of the Jesuits, Count Ledochowski (1866–1942, superior general since 1915), had already conferred with representatives of the German secret service with a view to cooperation between the Jesuits and the SS and Gestapo in 1940.[123]

A year before Hitler's attack on Russia already, Jesuit graduates from the Collegium Russicum, called "an institution for training Vatican agents" by the Catholic bishop Dr. Michael Buzalka in 1951, crossed the Soviet border in disguise and using false names in order to spy for the Vatican.[124] The plans of the Holy See were also mentioned in an OKW (Wehrmacht High Command) circular from August 14, 1941. The curia, it says in the document, had been trying to overthrow the communist regime since 1919. "A group of Vatican officials, disguised as cattle traders, engineers, etc." had been "particularly [active] in the Ukraine." The Vatican intended "to send as many priests as possible to the Russian-occupied territories in order to prepare the ground for further plans of Vatican policy regarding Russia."[125] On November 8, 1941, the OKW instructed all commanders in chief of the German armies in the east "to facilitate the missionary activities of the Catholic priests in the occupied territories . . . [by taking into consideration] the agreement with the Vatican."[126]

(Incidentally, today's Bundestag president [that is, in 1965, PG], Senior Consistory Councilor Eugen Gerstenmaier, was the person in charge of the eastern countries on the Protestant side. Although he sympathized with Hitler's opponents when the latter faced defeat, he sympathized with him before. This is enough to be considered a resistance fighter in today's Germany. The Protestant theologian Gerstenmaier not only published the small book *Die Kirche und die Schöpfung* (*The Church and Creation*), in which he stood up for "Blood and Soil," for the dictatorship, "its necessity and its right," and even for the "eradication of inferior life" in 1938,[127] but he also visited the Balkans, as proved by foreign office documents found in Poland, in cooperation with the foreign office during the war, in order to mobilize the Orthodox churches of Bulgaria, Romania, Yugoslavia, and Greece for the Nazis' anti-Bolshevist fight. "Like Dibelius and the Vatican, Gerstenmaier is expecting a large harvest after Hitler's invasion of the Soviet Empire."[128])

The counselor at the German embassy at the Vatican, Fritz Menshausen, concluded on September 12, 1941, that Pius XII was "on the side of the Axis powers in his heart."[129] At the same time, the undersecretary of state at the foreign office, Luther, came to this conclusion in a longer memorandum: "Since the beginning of the war, the current Pope based his political plans on the victory of the Axis powers."[130] And a leader of the German secret service, SS *Oberführer* Schellenberg, wrote the following to Wilhelmstraße in a five-page report on a discussion with the pope: "The Pope will do everything in his power to secure a German victory. His aim is the destruction of Russia."[131]

This intention of Pacelli's cannot be disputed with plausible reasons. He had already, as secretary of state, affirmed to the German ambassador to the

Vatican that the Holy See "also" approved the application of "external means of power against the Bolshevist threat." Back in 1937, Eugenio Pacelli had already seen these means, which would include war, as "a crucial mission and task."[132]

Another item that is characteristic of his position to Hitler's Russian campaign is a small diplomatic intermezzo. After the German dictator had met with the Caudillo in Hendaye on October 23, 1940, the pope was told that Hitler had told Franco that Pius XII was an enemy of the Führer. Upon hearing this, the nuncios in Madrid and Vichy declared in a discussion with the Spanish ambassador in virtually the same way, that is, clearly according to orders: "Should such words have been said or if they even corresponded to the views of the Führer, then the Pope regretted this. Pius XII had feelings of friendship towards the Reich. He wished the Führer nothing more fervently than a victory over Bolshevism. After a decisive defeat of Soviet Russia, the moment might have come where peace would be declared. The Pope would regret it if, especially after what the Führer and the Third Reich have achieved, such incorrect ideas concerning his feelings should prevail here in Germany."[133] And when Franco had Pius XII informed that the information he had received was incorrect, the pope replied that he "was filled with joy at this communication because he continued to hold not only the warmest sympathy for Germany, but also admiration for the great personality traits of the Führer."[134]

PAPAL POLICY IN THE FINAL YEARS OF THE WAR

But when the collapse of Germany came ever closer, the Vatican set its sights more and more on America, where they, despite cautious contacts with the Eastern world, are still set, as is known.

The American press noted the turnabout of curia policy very precisely. And so the *New York Herald Tribune* wrote in the summer of 1944 that the pope did not doubt that the Allies would win and was therefore very interested in the conditions of peace. "In the past, the Vatican fought against the forces of revolution by cooperating with the Mussolinis, Francos and Pétains. . . . But today, the Vatican seems to have undertaken a significant change of its policy in the hope of achieving the same goals with the help of the Anglo-Saxon countries."[135]

But Pius XII still supported the Axis powers even after the first major German defeats—even more intensely, in fact, and for two reasons in particular.

The Fascists feared a fiasco and embraced the pope more closely, as the repositioning of the ambassadorial posts shows. Because in February 1943, Mussolini appointed his son-in-law, the former foreign minister Count Ciano, as Italy's ambassador at the Holy See. And in July von Bergen, who had been German ambassador to the Vatican since 1920, was replaced by secretary of state von Weizsäcker, Ribbentrop's closest assistant.

But while the Fascists feared collapse, the curia feared that communism would constantly gain ground. Pius XII, who had never condemned Hitler's numerous aggressions, now untiringly raised his voice to warn about the danger from the east, which meant he was doing the same as Joseph Goebbels in Berlin, but only for reasons of "pastoral care," of course. The pope strived for the United States and Great Britain to separate from the Soviets and conclude a peace compromise between Hitler's Germany and the Allies.[136]

"The fact is," wrote von Weizsäcker on August 4, 1943, "that the Church feels uneasy today because communism is and remains its archenemy, in terms of both domestic and foreign policy."[137] At almost the same time, the German embassy in Paris observed "an increased tendency in Vatican circles . . . for leading the Axis powers and the Anglo-Americans towards rapprochement in order to fight Bolshevism."[138] On September 23, von Weizsäcker telegraphed what Cardinal Secretary of State Maglione had observed to Ribbentrop: that "the fate of Europe depended on Germany's victorious resistance on the Russian front. The German army was the only possible bastion, *baluardo*, against Bolshevism. If this were to break, it would be the end of European culture."[139] On October 7, von Weizsäcker wired: "There is no need to mention any anti-Bolshevist statements. I get to hear them every day. . . . As a matter of fact, anti-Bolshevism is the most secure component of Vatican foreign policy. Anything that serves the fight against Bolshevism is welcome to the Curia."[140]

The pope himself, in answer to an Italian journalist's question of what he thought of the German people in the fall of 1943: "It is a great people that is bleeding not only for its friends but also its current enemies in the fight against Bolshevism. I cannot believe the Eastern front will collapse."[141] And at the end of the year, Pius XII declared to a German liaison officer "with impressive inner agitation": "We expressly authorize you to tell everyone that We have always taken the German people to Our heart and We are more concerned about the German people, which is currently so beleaguered, than about all other nations."[142]

The pope wanted to avoid the destruction of the Nazi Reich by Russian troops at any price out of concern for communist influence in Europe.

His fear was soon shared by the American and British governments, who had allied themselves with the Soviet Union only under the necessity of pressure, whose social and economic principles they utterly condemned, while the Nazis' economy had even been cofinanced by the United States. In October 1944, Florida senator Claude Pepper said that one of those who had helped Hitler to power was John Foster Dulles, "because it was Dulles's company and the Schroeder Bank that had provided Hitler with the money he needed to embark on his career as an international bandit."[143] Banker and party member Baron Schroeder was not only in constant contact with Hitler's economic advisor Keppler but also with an American banking group that was being legally advised by John Foster Dulles. According to American newspaper reports, Dulles also took part in what was, as von Papen later wrote, "that discussion that was now part of history" in Schroeder's house, in which, as one may assume, von Papen guaranteed Hitler the support of the pope. The *New York Times* reported on Dulles's visit to Cologne in January 1933 and mentioned it again on November 11, 1944. But both articles have allegedly disappeared from American libraries.[144] And the former American ambassador in Berlin, Dodd, notes in his diary that the American banks represented by Dulles had already guaranteed Germany bonds to the value of one billion dollars at the end of 1933.[145]

There were constant negotiations in the Vatican regarding a special peace agreement from the fall of 1942 to 1944. In a letter on January 5, 1943, Pius XII urged President Roosevelt to bring a rapid end to the war and offered his cooperation, which undoubtedly meant help for Germany.

Roosevelt sent a personal ambassador as well as Cardinal Spellman, an especially enterprising prince of the church, who traveled in Europe and Africa for half a year but above all conferred at the Vatican for quite some time with the German foreign minister, among others. But Roosevelt was not prepared to negotiate peace unless Hitler resigned. And the pope finally informed Hitler that all negotiations would otherwise be useless. He would be performing a "great deed" if he made way for a government that could make peace with the Allies in order to prevent Germany from being occupied by the Red Army.[146]

The fact that Vatican circles and maybe even Pius XII himself had contact with German resistance groups and members of the group that tried to assassinate Hitler on July 20, 1944, is not proof against the line of curia policy outlined here. Pacelli would have wanted Hitler eliminated by the end, but not Germany under any circumstances, which Pacelli, as he admitted in conversation, wanted preserved "as a powerful moral force," but "not in its current form."[147]

But no result was achieved, especially as Roosevelt's repeated efforts to bridge the divide between Moscow and the Vatican failed because of the pope's persistent rejection, as did the equally many attempts to reach an agreement Stalin made in 1942 and 1943. Even when Washington and London supported the Russian efforts together and Stalin sent a personal letter to Pius XII, he permitted no negotiations with the Soviet Union, despite even some curia cardinals supporting it.[148]

THE TURNABOUT OF THE CATHOLIC CHURCH AFTER GERMANY'S DEFEAT

In view of the impending catastrophe and the increasing enmity toward Hitler's Germany, the high clergy also gradually changed its position, at least externally. In 1943, the Belgian episcopate complained about the removal of church bells by the Germans and the forcing of miners to work on Sundays. The Dutch church also took a stance against Nazi excesses. In Hungary, Cardinal Seredi even claimed that Fascism was in contradiction to Christianity. But in fact, the *episcopate and the curia* were both on the side of the Axis powers, while a considerable number of members of the *lower clergy* in all the occupied countries were actively taking part in resistance against the German occupants and often paying with their lives for doing so.[149]

But after the invasion, the bishops in the west also became firm supporters of the Anglo-American occupation—and the bishops in the east approached the communists.

The French episcopate, who—unlike many of the lower clergy—supported Pétain to the last, immediately went over to de Gaulle.

The archbishop of Paris, Cardinal Suhard, who expressed the wish in the summer of 1943, as the envoy von Krug reported from Paris on August 18, "to seek the Pope's audience in order to tell him that the German army and church were the only possible columns in place to protect Europe from communism. Therefore, everything had to be done in order to help the German army in the East to win,"[150] this cardinal, who celebrated a service in the presence of Pétain in Notre-Dame Cathedral still several months later, celebrated a service at the same place in the presence of de Gaulle in the summer of 1944.[151]

On June 16, 1943, Cardinal Gerlier, in the Vatican's opinion a member of the "moderate" wing of the high French clergy, also said in regard to Pétain that "in one of the most tragic hours in our history Providence sent us a leader that we are glad and proud to rally around. We ask God to bless our Marshal and accept us as his fellow fighters, especially those whose task is so difficult. The Church continues to trust the Marshal and pays him loving admiration."[152]

But when Pétain's opponents triumphed over him, he was also finished as far as the church was concerned. On behalf of the prisoner, the French lawyer Jacques Isorni asked in vain for an audience with Pius XII. On the last day of his stay in Rome, Isorni sent the following handwritten letter to the Vatican:

Holy Father,

Kneeling beseechingly at the feet of Your Holiness, I wish to tell you that I, as a defender of the Marshal of France, Philipp Pétain, came to Rome with the order to hand over a personal message to Your Holiness. A message from the famous old man who can only make contact with his environment via his legal counsel on account of the harsh imprisonment in which the injustice of humanity is keeping him.

I have been trying to fulfill this order, which to me is the most imperative of tasks, for the ten days I have spent in Rome—in vain.

At the age of 93, on the threshold of death, Marshal Pétain, the prisoner, wishes me to take him back a blessing or even a word of sympathy from Your Holiness from Rome. His ordeal—as he said to me—would be easier to bear, because the victor of Verdun is suffering desperately. Because it has been impossible for me, despite everything that I have undertaken, to reach Your Holiness, I wish, before I leave Rome, and since I only have today, to turn to you directly in order to be granted an audience. This audience would allow me to tell Your Holiness that the man who was the head of the French State and protector of the Church, is more than ever Your respectful and loyal son who begs the fatherly blessing of Christ's representative in his days of pain.

I am, Holy Father, Your Holiness's very obedient and humble son:

Pétain's lawyer added to the communication of his letter:

"I was not granted the honor of a reply. Of all the French who were seeking an audience I was the only one who was not received. I was sadly surprised. The bronze portal that had opened wide in front of the French head of state's ambassadors remained closed before the prisoner's envoy. The Marshall remains a condemned man even at that place where Christ's representative prays for all sufferers—whoever they may be."[153]

France would definitely have held it against the pope if he had expressed any sympathy for the imprisoned Nazi collaborator. So he now coldly refused to bless the old Catholic man, close to death, whose "work of moral rebirth" under Hitler he had so warmly supported (p. 172). But apart from this, Pius XII was siding with the Fascists to the very end.

Jacques Isorni.

THE PROTECTOR AND SHIELD OF THE FASCISTS TO THE VERY END

Not only had the pope, on the occasion of the destruction caused by the German V rockets, called upon Londoners via the archbishop of Westminster in August 1944 to display "the Christian feelings of clemency, sympathy and grace" to their enemies,[154] he also stood up for Nazis at the Nuremberg trials. And a not-inconsiderable number of seriously incriminated Germans were given, along with Italian, Czechoslovakian, Yugoslavian, and other war criminals, permanent or temporary asylum in the Vatican.

So according to Scheinmann, the clergyman Dragonovic, who was a lieutenant colonel on the Fascist side and who is alleged to have been guilty of the murder of sixty thousand people, disappeared there—and was made a professor at the German Catholic Seminary.[155]

And remains of the "Blue Division," the Spanish Fascists who had been fighting on the eastern front, reached South America via the Vatican.

Even many SS leaders escaped in this way. Including Adolf Eichmann. He fled, as Joel Brand, one of the witnesses in the Eichmann trial testified, with the help of a certain curia father, Benedetti, who had connections with Odessa, an SS underground organization. The question as to whether other high-ranking Nazis had fled in this manner was answered by Joel Brand as follows: "Yes, very many SS generals made their way to Egypt in this way. And don't forget Bormann."[156]

Anyone who knows not only the relationship between the Vatican and Fascism but also the history of Christian anti-Semitism[157] will not be surprised by this. It has already been noted that the pope never condemned the Nazi pogroms on Jews. Even when the Jews were gathered together and deported before his eyes, so to speak, he did not protest. This is attested to by the German ambassador at the Holy See, Ernst von Weizsäcker, in a letter sent by courier to the foreign office on October 28, 1943: "Despite, by all accounts, being assailed[!] from various sides, the Pope *could not be moved into making a demonstrative statement against the deportation of Jews from Rome*. Although he has to reckon with this position being held against him by our opponents and being used for propaganda purposes against Catholicism by Protestant circles in the Anglo-Saxon countries, he *has done everything, even in this delicate question, not to strain the relationship with the German government and the authorities situated in Rome*."[158] In this context, there is a letter from the last German mayor of Dresden, Dr. Hans Nieland, which is of interest. In the letter, which was handed over to the Institute of Post-War German History in Tübingen only recently, it says: "In the fall of 1944, Prince Friedrich Christian, Duke of Saxony and Margrave of Meißen, came to me. It concerns the head of the House of Wettin, who lived in my neighborhood. We had good relations with each other. Friedrich Christian made the following, completely surprising statement to me: He was, as I well knew, on intimate terms with the Vatican. I think that the Margrave was a papal Chamberlain. The Pope was ready to support an honorable peace for Germany if it was ready to remove the ban on the Jesuit Order and stop the persecution of Catholic priests and members of the orders. *But the Pope had no objections to the German policy on Jews* and the handling of the Freemason question. I should communicate this matter to the Führer and let him, the Margrave, know of his decision."[159]

And one of the greatest criminals of the century, Ante Pavelić, whose horror regime, which is still widely unknown today, is described in the next chapter, was also protected and blessed right to the end by Pius XII.

5

THE VATICAN AND THE CROATIAN ATROCITIES

"Hate and sadism in the form of the most diverse kinds of torture were widespread and cannot be compared even with the atrocities committed in darkest medieval times."

—Edmond Paris[1]

The Orthodox idea of the Ustaša leader and Poglavnik (State leader) of Croatia, Ante Pavelić, is reminiscent of the bloodiest religious wars: 'A third must become Catholics, a third must leave the country and a third must die!' The last item on this agenda was carried out. When leading Ustaša men claimed that a million Orthodox Serbs (including infants, children, women and elderly) were slaughtered, this is, in my opinion, a vainglorious[!] exaggeration. On the basis of the reports I have received, I estimate the number of defenseless people slaughtered at three quarters of a million."

—Hermann Neubacher, special envoy of the German foreign office for the Southeast[2]

"Killing all the Serbs in as little time as possible. That is our agenda."
—Franciscan Father Šimić (p. 204)

THE PAPACY AND THE BALKANS UP TO THE FIRST WORLD WAR

"Sono tutti quanti barbari." ("*They are all so many barbarians.*")
—Pope Pius X, 1913[3]

The dividing line between Catholic and Orthodox Christianity goes right through the Balkans. They both built up their bastions against each other here; the papacy availed itself of the Austro-Hungarian monarchy and the fanatically Catholic Croats. The curia expected the conquering and Catholicization of the Balkans from Austria, as it would later the conquering of Russia from Hitler's Germany.

After the Russo-Turkish War, the Turkish areas of Bosnia and Herzegovina had been handed to the Habsburgs for administration in 1878. And in his document "The Papacy and Civilization among the South Slavs" in 1880, the Roman prelate Pressuti propagated the division of Turkey in order to strengthen the Roman Catholic influence in the Balkans—actually with Austria's help. This remarkable agenda received the "praise and warm recognition" of the pope and was handed on by the Austro-Hungarian envoy at the Vatican, Paar, to his foreign minister Baron Haymerle, immediately after its appearance. Haymerle had already suggested in a speech on January 7, 1880, "that the Austrian government had made an agreement with the Holy See for the purpose of regulating Church affairs in Bosnia and Herzegovina."[4]

In 1881 the Austrian emperor installed the Archdiocese of Sarajevo and the Dioceses of Banjaluka and Mostar, and in October 1908 the provinces were annexed. "I felt predestined," the monarch declared in a manifesto, "to extend the rights of my crown to Bosnia and Herzegovina."[5]

In 1912, Bishop Sereggi of Skutari also demanded the armed intervention of Austria in Albania at the Eucharist Congress in Vienna. The Catholics' language in general became clearer and clearer. The then mass-produced, leading Austrian church newspaper, *Österreichs katholisches Sonntagsblatt*, wrote in October 1912: "The stone that has plunged into the European pond of peace in the Balkans will gradually produce ever increasing circles until *the long-awaited European war* blazes, for all the joy the great powers have in making declarations. All the misery! The killing! The economic ruin! But will this not be necessary sooner or later? Even modern liberalism will collapse under the emotional values of a war like this. *It would do no harm for Europe to have its circumstances thoroughly shaken up for once.*" It continues: "And Europe's Catholic Emperor? If Austria is forced to unfurl its flags, then it should and will also take up its sword, as Habsburg and its people's traditions demand. And when, in the whirlwind of collapsing and fermenting relations, the Pope and the interests of the Church require a powerful arm and a weighty word, then the Catholic Emperor of Europe will certainly also show himself to be a *son of the Church* and like every layman, every Catholic sovereign of a Catholic State will place his influence at the disposal of the Holy Father as a son would his father and not as a *Crown's Commander in Chief would the Church.*"[6]

In the same year, the Viennese cardinal Nagel stated in the same paper: "This is not about the Balkan States but about the first opportunity to get a foothold on a broad basis with Slavdom, a race that is undoubtedly rising. We are missing *a Catholic Slavic Empire* for the future of Slavdom. . . . *The Church must not miss the moment,* miss what may be the crucial hour of Slavdom.[7]

Well, they did not miss it. They promoted Austrian interests in the Balkans, especially in Albania, Bulgaria, and Romania, to such an extent that a veritable shower of medals rained down on the curia at the beginning of 1914 as thanks. Twenty-eight Vatican prelates were decorated by Vienna at that time.[8] And in the middle of July, the German ambassador in Vienna, Prince Stolberg, reported to Berlin that the Austrian foreign minister Graf Berchtold, who was, incidentally, a pious Catholic, answered the question of what would happen if Serbia accepted all the Austrian demands thus: he thought it out of the question that even a government like Serbia's would swallow such demands. But if they should, there would be no choice other than to provoke Serbia even after they had accepted all the demands until Austria had the opportunity to invade.[9]

This is exactly what the Vatican wanted. Pope Pius X, who ruled from 1903 to August 20, 1914, said repeatedly: "The world war is coming. 1914 will not end before it breaks out."[10] And this pope informed the Austrian prince Schönburg, who had several audiences at the Vatican in the autumn of 1913: "Austria-Hungary would have been better off punishing the Serbs for all their misdeeds."[11]

And that famous telegram that the Bavarian embassy counselor at the Holy See, von Ritter, sent to Munich on July 26, 1914—a text of which there are admittedly so many different versions that even Baron von Ritter himself wanted to correct it—was in agreement with this. This telegram, which became well known in the Munich Fechenbach trial, stated (according to the document "The Fechenbach Verdict," written by Supreme Court Counselor Freymuth on the basis of the files): "Baron Ritter to Bavarian government. Pope approves Austria's clampdown on Serbia. The Cardinal Secretary of State hopes Austria will stand firm this time. He asks how it could wage war if it could not even have the determination to repel by force of arms a foreign movement that brought about the murder of the Archduke and endangers Austria's continued existence in view of its current situation. The fear of the Roman Curia of Panslavism is revealed in its declarations. —signed *Ritter*."

And indeed, Pope Pius X did not stand up for peace on the eve of the war, but regretted, as we now know from a completely incontrovertible document, that Austria-Hungary had not undertaken similarly determined steps before. The pope's thoughts were reflected in a report from the then Austro-Hungarian envoy, Graf Pálffy, to his foreign minister about a talk with Cardinal Secretary of State Mery del Val on July 27, 1914: "In the course of recent years, His Holiness expressed his regret on several occasions that Austria-Hungary has neglected to punish its dangerous Danube neighbor. . . . The Pope and the Curia see in Serbia a gnawing disease that is slowly destroying the marrow of the monarchy and will gradually cause its dissolution in time. The destruction of this bastion would, for the Church, mean the loss of the firmest base of support in its fight against Orthodoxy and the loss of its strongest pioneer." For his part, Cardinal Secretary of State Mery del Val expressed his hope that the monarchy would "go to extremes."[12] Now, this makes the enthusiasm of the German Jesuits at the outbreak of the war understandable.[13]

And of course, the Austrian Catholic press were in a rush of lust for conquest. They were demanding war even before the Serbian response to the Austrian ultimatum was received. In the Catholic weekly journal *Großösterreich,* which was close to Franz Ferdinand, the later vice mayor of Vienna, E. K. Winter, wrote: "We have been waiting since six years for the final release of all the onerous tensions that we have been so tortuously experiencing in our entire politics. Because we know that only after a war can the new and great Austria, the happy Greater Austria that can satisfy its people, can be born, *and this is why we want the war.* We want the war because it is our most passionate conviction that our ideal can only be achieved radically and suddenly by war: a powerful *Greater Austria* in which the idea of the Austrian State, the Austrian *missionary thoughts of bringing freedom and culture to the peoples of the Balkans*, will bloom in the sunshine of a great, happy future. Fate has already clenched our fists around the sword twice, and twice we put it back in its sheath. *Redemption is beckoning to us* at this third and final time. We have once more the opportunity to recall our historic task, *of being the supreme power in the Balkans*, once again, the *finger of God is showing us the way* we must go if the torrent of coming events is not to wash us away from the stage of life as if Austria had never existed.

It is about to be or not to be! If we want to live on as a great, culture-bringing, powerful state and do justice to the future *of our historic calling in the Balkans and Western Russia in the name of Catholicism* and European culture, then we *must* reach for the sword. . . . But we pray to God that they (i.e., the conciliatory, war-shy circles) do not succeed this time (in prevailing), and *God, whose instrument on Earth we are*, will hear us."[14]

PACELLI'S THREAT

After the collapse of the Danube monarchy, the curia took up what was, in view of the threatened Catholic "bastion" in the Balkans, a distinctly hostile position to the new South Slav state, the "Kingdom of the Serbs, Croats and Slovenes" (after 1929, the "Kingdom of Yugoslavia"). It was not until a year later, on November 6, 1919, that the pope recognized it, and not until the summer of 1920 that his nuncio, Monsignor Cherubini, appeared in Belgrade.[15]

The Vatican now unleashed intensive activity in Yugoslavia, above all via *Katholische Aktion.* Its intentions here speak for themselves. In August 1936 the one leading Prague Catholic paper, *Deutsche Presse*, said: "Croatian Catholicism can be described as the actual bridgehead from which the abyss that separates two worldviews could, *at a suitable point in time*, be overcome." The Roman Church, it continued, was in a "continuous offensive against Orthodox Christianity" here, and it was, in their consensus, Croatia's religious function "to form a strategic bridgehead that would pave the way for a link between Rome and the Orthodox Church *as long as the latter was willing*, but not to make way for an unclear and dangerous 'fraternization' at the expense of the Catholic Church."[16]

Before the Second World War, the Catholic Church enjoyed complete freedom and equality in Yugoslavia, as countless witnesses would concur. Catholics also ensure that Catholic daily, weekly, and monthly newspapers flourished there, Catholic schools and colleges were active, Catholic hospitals were built, and Catholic organizations spread.[17] Even Dr. Anton Korosec, the Slovenian Catholic leader, admitted: "Even without the concordat the Catholic Church enjoyed complete freedom of activity."[18]

Because the curia suffered a defeat in 1937 with the rejection of the Vatican-Yugoslavian concordat at the hands of the Yugoslavian people. All the religious groups were against the concordat, including most Croatian Catholics.[19] But the nineteen Catholic bishops of Yugoslavia declared in October 1937: "The Catholic episcopate will definitely know how to protect the rights of the Catholic Church and the six million Catholics in this state and has undertaken the required measures to put right all injustices."[20]

Pius XI and his secretary of state Pacelli, who was involved in drafting the concordat, felt particularly piqued. Pacelli threatened bluntly in a speech to the consistory in December 1937: "The day will come [he didn't want to say it, but he was sure of his position] when the number of those who really regret having rejected a noble and magnanimous good work that Christ's representative offered their country will increase dramatically."[21]

On April 6, 1941, this threat by Eugenio Pacelli would start to fulfill itself in a way that exceeded the worst massacres of the Christian Middle Ages and yet is still totally unknown in Germany, or even in the greater part of Europe, to this day. The work, originally written in French by the author Edmond Paris and precisely documented and providing shocking picture material, *Genocide in Satellite Croatia, 1941–1945. A Record of Racial and Religious Persecutions and Massacres*, was published by only one American publisher, which faced bankruptcy after the book was published.[22]

A PAPAL BLESSING FOR CRIMINALS

After the German troops had invaded Yugoslavia on April 6, 1941, and occupied this country too, they cooperated with Croatia's Fascist-Catholic movement, the Ustaša Party ("Ustaša" = "rebel"). Their intellectual progenitor Ante Starčević was of the view that there should not be any Serbs at all, that everything called "Serbian" must disappear, which was why, as Starčević wrote, "the Serbs [are] work for the slaughterhouse."

The Ustaša now proceeded against the Serbs according to this principle, led by Dr. Ante Pavelić, a former lawyer from Agram. Pavelić certainly viewed himself as a scholar of Starčević, who was glorified in the so-called Independent State of Croatia as "the greatest Croatian political ideologue," as "the creator of the ideological basis," and as an "example for Ustaša fighters."[23]

Since 1929 the Italian government had allocated a house in Bologna for Pavelić and his family that served as the Ustaša headquarters for years.[24] With the help of the Fascist chief of the secret police, Conti, and the minister of police, Bocchini, Pavelić had young Croatians living abroad and Ustaša supporters who had fled trained in Italy; and in a "statute," he set out the liberation of Croatia from the "foreign yoke" as the main task of the "armed resistance." Each Ustaša member had to bind himself by an oath "to Almighty God" to obey the statutes.[25]

They already had no hesitation in resorting to acts of violence. One of the first spectacular attacks was the murder of the chief editor of the Zagreb newspaper *Novosti*, Anton Šlegel, on March 22, 1929. His closest colleague, Gustav Perčec, was shot by Pavelić himself in an Italian prison after being tortured by his people.[26] He also organized the assassination of King Alexander of Yugoslavia, who had landed in Marseilles on October 9, 1934, to visit the allied French. But along, with French foreign minister Barthou, was murdered by Pavelić's minions already in the harbor area.[27] In October 1936, Pavelić released a memorandum "on the Croatian Question" that later reached the foreign office. In this document, the head of the Ustaša hoped for "understanding for his heroic struggle . . . from the new Germany"; he called Hitler Germany's "greatest and best son" and saw in "Hitler's Germany . . . the most powerful fighter for living law, true culture and higher civilization."[28]

As early as April 6, 1941, when Belgrade started to burn under the constant German air raids, Pavelić ordered the Croatian soldiers via a secret transmitter to take up arms against the Serbian troops. "From now on we will fight side by side with our new allies, the Germans and Italians."[29] At the same time, Hitler, in an "Appeal to the German People," cursed the "clique of Serb criminals" who had "already brought the world into nameless misfortune with the assassination of Sarajevo in 1914" and stressed that the German people need not "fight against Croats and Slovenes."[30]

On April 10, 1941, when Pavelić was still absent, an "Independent State of Croatia" was proclaimed, which also included Bosnia, Herzegovina, part of Dalmatia, and some purely Serbian borderlands. Of the roughly six million inhabitants of this state, only about three million were Catholic Croatians, two million were Orthodox (Serbs or Bosnians), and more than half a million were Bosnian Muslims. The rest were ethnic Germans, Magyars, Jews, Slovenians, Czechs, and others.[31]

The proclamation begins and ends with the name of God: "God's providence, the will of our great ally, the centuries-old struggle of the Croatian people and the great willingness to sacrifice for our leader Ante Pavelić and the Ustaša movement both at home and abroad have ordained that today, before the resurrection of the Son of God, our independent state of Croatia will be resurrected." And at the end of the proclamation, it says again: "God be with the Croats! Ready for the Fatherland!"[32] In the night of April 13, Pavelić crossed the Italian-Yugoslavian border; on April 17, he appointed his first cabinet. Then southern Serbia was given to the Bulgarians, a part of the northern province was occupied by the Hungarians, and in May, Pavelić traveled to Rome with his ministers and some clergy, including Archbishop Stepinac's vicar general, Bishop Salis-Sewis, and ceded more than half of Dalmatia to Italy, to which he also made further major concessions. The so-called crown of Zvonimir (the last independent Croatian king from the eleventh century) was offered to King and Emperor Victor Emanuel III for Duke Aimone of Spoleto, who had already appeared at the Vatican as the designated king of Croatia on May 17,[33] but who, for reasons of caution, never entered his kingdom.

The day after, Pavelić—sentenced to death in absentia because of the double murder of Marseilles twice, by France and Yugoslavia—in addition to his sizeable entourage (Pavelić, "surrounded by his bandits," as the Italian foreign minister Count Ciano had already written in his diary some weeks previously[34]) was also received and blessed in a particularly solemn private audience by Pius XII. Croatia's Catholic press were very moved by the attention and warmth of the pope,[35] who finally dismissed Pavelić and his retinue amicably with best wishes for their "further work."[36]

"FURTHER WORK"

> *". . . that the Croatian people must destroy all the foreign elements that have been weakening its power, these elements are the Serbs and the Jews."*
>
> —Foreign Minister Dr. Mladen Lorković[37]

> *"We will kill some of the Serbs, expel others and the rest, who must take on the Catholic religion, will be absorbed into the Croatian people."*
>
> —Minister of Education Dr. Mile Budak[38]

> *". . . but it is easy to recognize the hand of God in this work."*
>
> —Archbishop Stepinac[39]

This "further work," which Pavelić performed not least with the help of the Catholic clergy, looked like this: 299 Serbian Orthodox churches were plundered and destroyed in the "Independent State of Croatia"; 172 of these were in the provinces of Lika, Kordun, and Banija.[40] The churches of Jasenovac, Velika Kladuša, Surduk, Svinica, Suha Mlaka, Veljun, and Belegiš were converted into slaughterhouses; the churches of Hadžići, Plaški, Drvar, Travnik, Modrić, and Gomirje were turned into department stores; those at Vreoce, Drinjača, Mrkonjić Grad, Cvijanovićevo Brdo, and Jajce became public toilets; and the churches of Čitluce, Donji Vakuf, Stari Majdan, Sanski Most, and Mojkovac became stables. In areas where Orthodox Serbs formed the majority of the population, their churches were mostly completely obliterated; where they were in the minority, their churches were refitted for Catholic purposes. This all indicates that a well-planned policy was being pursued. Indeed, the conversion of Serbian Orthodox churches into Catholic ones took place on the orders of the ordinariates. On the orders of the Episcopal ordinariates of Djakovo (no. 2733/42, April, 1942), Serbian Orthodox churches were converted into Catholic ones in Bračevci, Majar, Dopšin, Tenje, Dalj, Markušica, Kapelna, Kućanci, Paučje, Budimci, Poganovci, Bijelo Brdo, Borovo Selo, Trpinja, Pačetin, Bršadin, Čepin, Martinci, Čačinski, Trnjani, Klokočevik, Topolje, and Brod na Savi.[41] The entire possessions of the Serbian Orthodox Church were transferred to the Catholic Church.[42]

Of course the "further work" did not stop at plundering, burning, and dispossessing: In April 1941, Serbs were forced to wear a blue armband with the letter *P* for *Pravoslav* ("Orthodox"); Jews, the Star of David. Jews and Orthodox were also banned from walking on the sidewalk. Signs were hung up in all offices, shops and restaurants, streetcars and omnibuses: "No entry for Serbs, Jews, Nomads or dogs!"[43]

And in the very first days of the occupation, the Serbian Orthodox patriarchs Dr. Gavrilo Dožić and Bishop Dr. Nikolaj Velimirović were picked up and taken off to Dachau, where they stayed until the end of the war. In November 1941 the Italians also arrested the Serbian Orthodox bishop of Dalmatia, Dr. Irinej Djordjević, who also disappeared in a concentration camp until 1945.[44]

But that was still not enough.

Countless Serbian clergy suffered horrific torture. In Zagreb, where Archbishop Stepinac and the Apostolic nuncio Marcone resided, the Orthodox metropolitan Dositej was beaten and tortured to such a bestial extent that it made him insane.[45]

Three princes of the Orthodox Church, Bishop Platon of Banja Luka, the metropolitan of Sarajevo, Peter Zimonjić, and the bishop of Sava as well as several hundred Orthodox clergy were murdered.[46] Bishop Platon and his companion, the priest Dušan Subotić, had their eyes gouged out while a fire burned on their chests, and their noses and ears were cut off before they were finally given the death blow.[47] The Catholic clergy demanded that the Orthodox convert everywhere. "When you have come over to the Catholic Church," Bishop Akšamović of Djakovo promised, for instance, "you will be left in peace in your homes."[48] Many became Catholic in this way but even more were massacred.

Just a few pieces of evidence.

One night at the end of April 1941, Ustaša surrounded the Serbian villages of Gudovec, Tuko, Brestovac, and Dolac in the district of Bjelovar. Then they had the Orthodox priest Božin, the teacher, Ivanković, and 250 peasants, men and women, dig a grave, tied their hands behind their backs, and buried them alive.[49]

In Otočac, 331 Serbs were liquidated and the Orthodox priest, Branko Dobrosavljević, was forced to pray in front of the tortured and dying while his little son lay literally cut into pieces before his eyes. Then the priest's hair and beard were torn off, his eyes were gouged out, and he was tortured until he died.[50]

The same crime happened in Svinjica, in the province of Banija.[51]

In Kosinj, where the Ustaša had gathered six hundred Serbs, a mother had to catch the blood of her four sons in a bowl.[52]

In Mliniŝte, in the district of Glamoč, a former member of parliament, Luka Avramović, and his son were crucified.[53]

When Pavelić held an audience with the Catholic episcopate on June 26, 1941, and Archbishop Stepinac said, "we attest our deference with all our heart and promise devoted and loyal cooperation for the brightest future of our fatherland,"[54] three Orthodox bishops, more than one hundred Orthodox priests and members of the Order, and 180,000 Serbs and Jews had been murdered in Catholic Croatia within six weeks.[55]

In the following month, July 1941, the Ustaša killed more than 100,000 Serbian women and children in just a few days in houses, schools, prisons, and Orthodox churches, on streets and in fields. The church at Glina, for example, was converted into a slaughterhouse according to a report from the Ustaša involved, Hilmia Berberović. "The bloodbath lasted from 10 in the evening until 4 in the morning and went on that way for eight days. The killers' uniforms had to be changed because they were drenched with blood. Later, impaled children with limbs still bent in pain were found."[56] Two thousand Serbian men, women, and children were killed in the butchery that had been ordered by the justice minister Dr. Mirko Puk, who came from Glina, and the prior of the Franciscan monasteries of Cuntic, Hermenegildo alias Častimir Hermann.[57]

The death lists are nearly endless. Every small subordinate commander went on a manhunt and quickly reported his successes to the authorities in order to be decorated by them. The Ustaša commandant of Vojnić called Zagreb, saying: "Hunt plentiful today. 500 in total."[58]

This included atrocities that nearly make the deeds committed by Hitler's concentration camp minions pale into insignificance. The Ustaša pushed red-hot nails under fingernails and rubbed salt into open wounds. They mutilated all possible body parts. One penchant was to cut their victims' noses and ears off and gouge their eyes out. The Italians photographed an Ustaša who wore two chains of human tongues and eyes around his neck.[59]

The Italian author Curzio Malaparte interviewed Pavelić in Zagreb.

"While he spoke," Malaparte wrote, "I looked at a wicker basket that was on his desk to the right of the Poglavnik. The basket was opened and a lot of sea creatures or something similar appeared.

'Oysters from Dalmatia?' I asked.

Ante Pavelić lifted the lid and showed me what looked like a mass of sticky, gelatinous oysters. He said with a tired, friendly smile: 'A gift from my loyal Ustaša. Forty pounds of human eyes!'"[60] This was the man Pius XII had blessed.

EVEN THE GERMANS PROTESTED

At the Führer's headquarters, the special envoy of the foreign office for the southeast of Europe, Hermann Neubacher—who was therefore Pavelić's "State Enemy no. 1"—repeatedly reported of "truly horrific events in my Croatian neighborhood," to which Hitler replied: "I have also told the Poglavnik that such a minority cannot simply be wiped out: it is too big!"[61] And on another occasion, Hitler said: "I will finish with this regime one day—but not now!"[62] "Now" he had a blatantly cynical "understanding" for the butchery and spoke out against "staying the hand of the Croatians' actions against the Serbs."[63]

And why not? Especially when even the pope kept silent!

But the German envoy in Zagreb interceded with both oral and written communications to the Ustaša government.[64] And the German general Glaise von Horstenau also told Pavelić of "his serious doubts about the Ustaša's excesses . . . and he substantiated his communications with numerous concrete examples from most recent times."[65]

On July 10, 1941, Ambassadorial Counselor Troll wrote to the foreign office saying that many acts of terror were "a cause of serious concern even to the more circumspect Croatian circles."[66] And just one day later, Troll was communicating further "shocking" reports that had reached the embassy from the army headquarters from the head of the security police task force and the SD security service in Zagreb and "from numerous private individuals." Troll finally sought out the Croatian foreign minister Lorković and handed him "all the material, which was proved in part by photos."[67] The SS security service later made a longer report on the Ustaša massacres.[68] And the chief of the security police and the SD stressed in a detailed communication to Himmler on February 17, 1942, "that ultimately the Catholic Church, with its conversion measures and enforcement, had forced these atrocities by the Ustaša by also using the Ustaša to carry out their conversion measures."[69]

The crimes committed by this movement even provoked clashes with German troops who had themselves committed some scandalous acts on many fronts[70] and executed hostages to an almost unprecedented degree, especially in Yugoslavia. After the envoy, Benzler had already reported from Belgrade on April 10, 1942: "German unit reports from the Drina that the killing of Serbs has started again on the west bank and can be observed clearly by the unit," the SD wrote in a telegram to the Reich Security Central Office two days later: "Since April 10, 1942, triggered by the senseless slaughter of the Serb population in Bosnia, there have been serious clashes and fights between German border security troops and Ustaša units at different points along the Serbian–Croatian border."[71] And the German commander of the 718th Infantry Division had an entire company of the Ustaša regiment led by Colonel Francetić disarmed and arrested because of renewed atrocities against the Serb population in June 1942.[72] It is of note here that the Ustaša that were often fatigued as a consequence of their atrocities over the years were repeatedly urged to take drastic measures, as in general the massacres were never initiated by the people in general but always by the Ustaša leaders, those in uniform and those in a priest's or monk's attire.[73]

The German intelligence service at the Zagreb Information Center stressed on August 7, 1941, that the regime was rejected by a "not inconsiderable part of the Croatian population" even "by Croatian Nationalists and former Ustaša supporters."[74]

CONCENTRATION CAMP AND CARITAS

Concentration camps sprouted everywhere in the Catholic "Independent State of Croatia": in Jasenovac, Jadovno, Pag, Ogulin, Jastrebarsko, Koprivnica, Krapje, Zenica, Stara Gradiška, Djakovo, Lobograd, Tenje, Sanica, and so on. Deportation to these camps was outside any jurisdiction. In a decree law dated November 26, 1941, there was an outright affirmation that this was a preventative measure against "undesirable persons" who *could* be dangerous to "public order and safety" and threaten "the achievements of the liberation struggle of the Croatian Ustaša movement."[75] "There is no right of appeal or objection against the decision of the Ustaša Police regarding consignment to forced detention."[76] The leader of all these camps, Vjekoslav Luburić, the right hand of Interior Secretary Artuković, the Croatian Himmler, lives in Franco's Catholic Spain today [that is, in 1965] under the name of Max Luburić. At the time, about 350,000 people died in the Croatian concentration camps.[77]

Thousands of children were also slaughtered there.[78] Indeed, there were even concentration camps set up especially for them in Lobor, Jablanac, Mlaka, Brocice, Ustici, Gradiška, Sisak, Jastrebarsko, and Gornja Rijeka. In 1942 there were about twenty-four thousand children in Jasenovac alone; half of them were murdered.[79]

But gradually it began to seem more useful to the state and church authorities to spare the children. Since the parents were mostly dead or imprisoned, the young were easy to convert to the church as the one and only true institution of salvation. The Catholic "Caritas," of which Archbishop Stepinac was president, now took care of the orphans and their reeducation was that much easier since many could no longer find any relatives at all. Some were also too young to know their origins, their village, or even their names when they ended up in the "care" of Caritas. So today, in 1965, there are countless young people who live as devout Catholics, even priests, without knowing what circumstances they have to thank for their Catholicism.

Yugoslavs are still looking for their parents or siblings under the motto of "searching for relatives." Pars pro toto just one such voice: "My whole family was sent to the camp at Stara Gradiška. We were separated from our parents and sent away. Before, a man had ordered me to bring my young sister, who was only three, to the office. Two nuns took her away and I never saw them again. If you can give me any information, please write to Vaso Radovanović, architect, Gaglin."[80] Many of these Serb children were registered in the theological faculties of Italy, Argentina, Australia, and the United States.[81]

THE DEEDS OF THE USTAŠA WERE DEEDS OF THE CHURCH

> *"The image of a Catholic state of God, in which the Ustaša appeared as an Order of Knighthood, was formed in the popular Catholic papers and sermons from the pulpit."*
>
> —Hory and Broszat[82]

> *"The image of the Virgin Mother of God has appeared as a sign in the heavens above our new, young and free Croatia. . . . The Croatia of God and Mary from ancient times has risen again."*
>
> —*Katolički Tjednik*, Sarajevo, May 11, 1941

> *"Christ and Ustaša, Christ and the Croatians, marching along through history together."*
>
> —*Nedelja*, Zagreb, June 6, 1941

Let us expressly stress that there were not only religious but, of course, also racial differences that played a big part in the slaughter of the Serbs by the Croats—although this hardly exonerates the Catholic Church, for it cooperated very closely with the Ustaša movement from the beginning to the end of this regime. There were bishops in the Ustaša parliament, priests working as police chiefs and officers in Pavelić's guard, Franciscans in charge of concentration camps, members of *Katholische Aktion* and organizations affiliated to it were also frequently Ustaša[83]; even nuns, their chests often plastered with Ustaša medals, greeted in the Fascist style and took part in the parades, marching directly behind the soldiers.[84]

The country's Catholic press affirmed their sympathy for the Ustaša party at every opportunity. In a plethora of articles, it welcomed "the new and free

Croatia as a Christian and Catholic state," declared their loyalty to the Godsent Pavelić, and celebrated Adolf Hitler as the "Crusader of God."[85]

The newspaper *Nedelja*, printed in Zagreb, wrote on April 27, 1941: "God, who controls the fates of nations and rules the hearts of kings, has given us Ante Pavelić and moved the leader of a nation that is friendly and allied to us, Adolf Hitler, to disperse our oppressors with his victorious troops and enable the founding of the Independent State of Croatia. Glory to God, our gratitude to Adolf Hitler and eternal loyalty to our Poglavnik, Ante Pavelić."[86]

The Croatian radio station in Zagreb reported on July 29: "There are no Serbs and there is no so-called Serbian Orthodox Church in Croatia. . . . There can be no Serbs and no Orthodoxy in Croatia; the Croats will make sure of this as soon as possible."[87]

In June 1941, the seriously incriminated Archbishop Ivan Šarić praised the revolutionary methods in the name of truth, justice, and honor in his weekly *Katolički Tjednik* and called it "stupid and unworthy of disciples of Christ to think that the fight against evil could be conducted with gloves on in a gentlemanly manner."[88]

Indeed, the newspaper of the Archdioceses of Sarajevo affirmed: "until now, God has spoken through the papal encyclicals. But people closed their ears. . . . Now God[!] has decided to use different methods. He wants to prepare missions. Europe missions. World missions. And they will not be supported by priests but by army commanders. These sermons will be heard with the help of cannons, machine guns, tanks, and bombers."[89]

This was not an unusual tone. It was the rule.

On July 7, 1941, Dr. Ivo Guberina, a priest and a leader of *Katholische Aktion* who was also a captain in Pavelić's guard, said: "Croatia should purge its system of all poison in any possible way, including with the sword."[90]

Another prominent priest, Dionis Jurićev, wrote that only Croats will still be able to live in this country. "It is no longer a sin to kill a seven-year-old child if it violates Ustaša legislation. Although I wear the garb of a priest I often have to resort to a machine gun."[91]

One clergyman from the town of Udbina preached: "Until now, my brothers, we have worked for our religion with cross and Brevier. Now the time has come for revolver and rifle."[92] He gave the go-ahead for the slaughters of Serbs in the district of Udbina with such speeches.

The Jesuit Dragutin Kamber, who celebrated Hitler's soldiers as fighters for "political and social justice" and builders of the "foundations of a happy world for future generations" in *Novi List* on August 16, 1941, was chief of police in Doboj (Bosnia) and solely responsible for the murder of hundreds of Orthodox Serbs. Like many other Ustaša, the Jesuit lives in the United States as Dr. Charles Kamber today (that is, in 1965).[93]

The clergyman Božidar Bralo, "a main accomplice of the murdering bishop Šarić of Sarajevo," only traveled through the country with his machine gun after being appointed prefect, constantly shouting: "Down with the Serbs!" He was involved in the butchery of 180 Serbs at Alipašin Most and did a dance of joy with the Ustaša around the slain.[94]

In Prebilovci and Surmanci, Herzegovina, where 559 Serbs, all old men, women, and children, were slaughtered; the two Catholic priests Ilija Tomaš and Marko Hovko were also among the murderers.[95]

Branimir Zupančić, a curate in Rogolje, massacred four hundred people.[96]

THE FRANCISCANS' LEADING ROLE

> *"I have discovered from a safe source that the Franciscans of Bosnia and Herzegovina have behaved regrettably."*
> —curia cardinal Tisserant (p. 211)

The sons of St. Francis of Assisi, whose monasteries had already served as arms depots for the Ustaša for a long time, distinguished themselves in particular in exterminating the Orthodox. This was no accident.

The following appeared in the Christmas edition of the *Independent Croatia* newspaper in 1941 under the title "The Role of the Clergy in the Independent Croatian State": "The universities of the Franciscans in Sinj, Široki Brijeg and Visoko, the seminaries in Makarska, Mostar and Split and the Theological Faculty of the University of Zagreb were the real centers of national conscious-ness, the breeding grounds from which not only groups of Levites and workers poured out into God's garden every year, but also national fighters who spread the convictions of the Ustaša."[97] And on July 4, 1941, the Ustaša newspaper

Hrvatski Narod praised the Franciscan Dr. Radoslav Glavaš as a great organizer of the Ustaša who had then put himself "at the front of the fighters."[98] The Franciscan Glavaš worked as an advisor around Pavelić and had, as a note from the German embassy in Zagreb states, "daily" access to him.[99]

And the role the Franciscan order played in the overthrow in Yugoslavia became immediately known abroad. For instance, an essay in the Slovakian Catholic newspaper *Gardist*, an organ of the Hlinka Guard, in August 1941, was called: "The Franciscans, the First Fighters for Independence."[100]

On May 21, 1941, the Franciscan father Šimić came to the commander of the "Sassari Division" in Knin with two escorts in order to assume civil administration in his area. The Franciscan answered the general's question about the guidelines of their policy: "To kill all the Serbs in as short a time as possible." The general could not believe his ears and asked him to repeat it. The father promptly did: "To kill all the Serbs in as short a time as possible. That is our agenda."[101]

The Franciscan Berto Dragićević from the monastery of Široki Brijeg was in command of the local Ustaša, supported by the Franciscans Ante Cvitković and Andrija Jeličić.[102]

The Franciscan father Augustino Cievola appeared on the streets with a revolver under his habit and called upon the people to murder the Orthodox.[103]

The Franciscan Tugomir Soldo organized the massacres of Čapljina.[104]

The Franciscan Silvije Franković was frequently in the company of the biggest throat cutters. When they asked him one day in Bugojno when they could confess, he said: "Much too soon for you. Come when you've killed them all." When the prefect of Bugojno wanted to confess to Franković because he had killed fourteen Serbs, the Franciscan said: "Confess when it's forty and I'll forgive you everything."[105]

Several monks assumed executioners' posts in a concentration camp. The Franciscan Zvonko Brekalo was an officer at the death camp of Jasenovac, notorious because of his mass beheadings. About 120,000 Serbs died there. In the fall of 1942, the Franciscan Miroslav Filipović-Majstorović, called "Brother Devil," actually ran this camp, supported by a series of clergy—Brkljanić, Matković, Matijević, Brekalo, Celina, Lipovac and others. Forty thousand people were liquidated in four months under the command of the Franciscan father.[106] The

Franciscan scholar Brzica alone beheaded 1,360 people with a special knife in one night, on August 29, 1942.[107]

Edmond Paris, who lists a "horrific litany" of Franciscan crimes, affirms that this list could be "extended infinitely."[108]

After the collapse of the Catholic regiment, it was, tellingly, foreign Franciscan monasteries that became refuges for the mass murderers, Klagenfurt in Austria, Modena in Italy, and also monasteries in France. "All these monasteries hid the escaped Ustaša. These criminals received Church help and support everywhere. This was only too understandable since the deeds of the Ustaša were deeds of the Church."[109]

Alois Mišić of Mostar was the only bishop in Croatia to condemn roundly the excesses in a pastoral letter on June 30, 1941. And the priest J. Lončar of Zagreb, who protested against the atrocities in a sermon on the commandment "Thou Shalt Not Kill" on August 23, 1941, was sentenced to death and then had his sentence commuted to hard labor for life. "Apart from these two spirited men, all the Catholic clergy in Croatia approved of or tolerated the butchery, some out of fanaticism, others out of fear, and the others subordinated themselves to Church discipline."[110]

Let us also mention en passant that the Ustaša movement, with the help of clerical circles, also murdered 80 percent of the Yugoslavian Jews.[111]

THE PRIMATE OF THE CROATIAN CATHOLICS, ARCHBISHOP Dr. STEPINAC, ALSO SUPPORTED THE MURDERERS

He collaborated with them from the first hour of the regime to the last. Pavelić arrived in Zagreb on April 13, 1941. On the very next day, the Archbishop conveyed congratulations from the church to the assassins of Alexander and Louis Barthou and held a banquet on the evening at which "Blackshirts and clerical robes mingled like brothers."[112]

On Easter 1941, Stepinac announced, from the pulpit of the Cathedral in Zagreb, the foundation of the "Independent Croatian State" and also immediately pushed for its diplomatic recognition by the pope.[113]

In *Nedelja*, Stepinac told of his first talks with the Poglavnik, who, on this occasion, confided to him his intention to eradicate the Old Catholics and the Orthodox. After this communication, Stepinac affirmed: "The Archbishop [i.e., he himself] had the impression throughout our conversation that Pavelić was a devoted Catholic and the Church would have full freedom to act."[114] In a pastoral letter dated April 28, 1941, the Croatian primate wrote: "Who could reproach us for also supporting, as spiritual shepherds, the joy and enthusiasm of the people when we *turn to the Divine Majesty in deep gratitude*? Although current events, which are so important, are very complicated, although the factors that influence their course are very different, it is still easy *to recognize the hand of God in this work. Ab domino factum est istud et est mirabile in oculis nostris* ["This is the Lord's doing: and it is wonderful in our eyes," Psalm 117:23]. Which is why you will follow our appeal and thereby support the preservation and development of the independent state of Croatia. *We know the people* who hold the fate of the Croatian people in their hands and we are firmly convinced that the Church will be able to proclaim the infallible principles of truth and eternal justice in the restored Croatian State in complete freedom."[115]

Stepinac expressly demanded cooperation with the Ustaša from the episcopate.[116] He instructed the clergy to celebrate the anniversary of the proclamation of "Independent Croatia" and the birthday of its leader, Pavelić, with particular solemnity.[117]

In January 1942, Archbishop Stepinac was even appointed military vicar of the Ustaša by the Vatican, upon which nearly 150 priests joined the Ustaša army as field chaplains.[118]

On February 23, 1942, Stepinac, surrounded by church dignitaries, received Pavelić, the man blessed by the pope and sentenced to death twice, at the portal of St. Mark's Church in Zagreb and celebrated the foundation of the Croatian parliament with resounding phrases.[119] Only three weeks earlier, the London weekly *New Review* had written of Pavelić: "He is unanimously viewed as the greatest criminal of the year 1941."[120]

Archbishop Stepinac had also spoken when the Ustaša Parliament, to which he and ten of his clergy belonged, was actually opened. When, at a meeting on February 25, Justice Minister Mirko Puk declared in the name of the state that the Old Catholics and the Serbian Orthodox Church would no longer be recognized, the eleven official representatives of the Roman Catholic Church supported it unanimously.[121]

On Pavelić's saint's day (June 13, 1942) Stepinac ordered the Te Deum to be sung in all churches the following Sunday.[122]

On May 18, 1943, the archbishop sent a memorandum to Pius XII asking for support for Pavelić's regime. Stepinac stressed the Ustaša services in converting the Orthodox. And he was already expressing great fears. "The victory of the pan-Serbian idea," he wrote, "would mean the destruction of Catholicism in the north-west of the Balkans, that is, in Croatia. There is not the slightest doubt about that." Furthermore, he prophesied, the waves of the Orthodox offensive would also wash over the Italian coast. Stepinac then thanked the Croatian clergy for their services, "especially the Franciscans," and implored the Holy Father to turn to the Croatian people. "The new Croatian state, born under more difficult and terrible circumstances than any state in recent centuries, is now desperately fighting for its own survival. At every opportunity, it has proven its will to remain loyal to its Catholic traditions and secure a brighter and better future for the Catholic Church in this part of the world." Stepinac also wrote to the pope that not only could 240,000 converts be lost, "but the entire Catholic population of this area with all the churches and monasteries."[123]

In 1944 the Croatian War Ministry edited the soldiers' prayer book *The Croatian State* full of ardent prayers for the criminal regime—with permission to print from the archbishop.[124] Even as late as March 24, 1945, Stepinac, awarded the "Great Cross with the Star" by Pavelić a year before, published a manifesto in favor of the Ustaša state and offered his palace as a refuge to numerous political murderers who were being hunted by the police.[125]

Only once in all these years did Archbishop Stepinac mention the tragedy of the Serbs and Jews in a speech in "Independent Croatia." "There are people," he said on October 31, 1943, "who accuse us of not having been outraged in time or not having taken appropriate measures against the crimes committed in the various parts of our country. Our answer is: we are not anyone's political tool and we do not want to be. . . . We have always publicly stressed the principles of eternal and divine law. . . . We cannot be deemed responsible for some of these reckless fanatics in the ranks of the Church."[126]

Edmond Paris fittingly comments on this: "What cynicism from a prince of the church! Whose 'political' tool would he have been if he had raised his voice against the butchery of the innocent?"[127] [Stepinac was beatified in 1998 by Pope John Paul II, PG]

THE MOST BLOODTHIRSTY CRIMINAL OF ALL SATELLITE COUNTRIES WAS PROTECTED AND BLESSED BY THE CATHOLIC CHURCH RIGHT TO THE END

Pavelić's rule already began to falter seriously when Italy surrendered.[128] Some of his accomplices therefore sought to save themselves. The national defense minister, Vokić, and Foreign Minister Lorković organized a palace revolt but were shot after the attempt failed. Pavelić then tried to save himself in November with an act of treachery. He offered the chief of the Allied High Command in the Mediterranean the Ustaša army to fight against the Germans, but in vain.

On March 24, 1945, the Catholic bishops of Croatia published a pastoral letter aimed less at their diocesans than the Allies. They emphasized the letter Pavelić sent to the British and Americans and his fight against communism and volunteered to support the democratic powers (whom they had so far been fighting against) with all their might, which the Allies, however, also ignored. Finally, Pavelić tried in vain for several more days to make Archbishop Stepinac his successor. Then he took his leave at a secret meeting at the Episcopal palace on May 4, 1945, and left Stepinac a pile of documents and whole chests full of gold, jewels, and watches behind that were stored in Stepinac's palace and various churches. On the next day, Pavelić fled with his family and a few thousand gangsters, including about five hundred Catholic priests, including in turn the archbishop of Sarajevo, Ivan Šarić, who died in Madrid in 1960, and the bishop of Banja Luka, Jozo Gavić.

Pavelić and Artuković found sanctuary in the monastery of St. Gilgen near Salzburg, "laden with stolen gold." They were then arrested by British troops but soon released again as a consequence of a "mysterious intervention."[129] Artuković went to Switzerland in November 1946, then later to Ireland, and finally to the United States, where he now lives in Los Angeles [he was finally extradited to Yugoslavia and sentenced to death but died in 1988 of ill health after winning a stay of execution on these grounds].

Pavelić, who did not feel safe in Austria because of the Yugoslavian government's efforts to extradite him, went to Rome disguised as a priest where he lived in a monastery as Father Gomez and Father Benarez. At the end of 1948 he went to Buenos Aires as Pablo Aranyoz, still in possession of 250 kg of gold and 1,100 carats of precious stones[130]—and he was accompanied by the former liaison between Archbishop Stepinac and the Vatican, the priest Krunoslav Draganović, with whom he had been provided by the *Commissione d'assistanza* pontifica.[131]

Pavelić had to go underground after the overthrow of Peron in 1955. On April 10, 1957, he escaped an assassination attempt with a revolver and later the Argentinian police as well. He somehow managed to reach Franco's Spain and, undisturbed by judiciary, found refuge in a Franciscan monastery in Madrid. The criminal died in the German hospital in the Spanish capital on December 26, 1959, and, on his death bed, received yet another blessing from the Holy Father.[132] (There is still [in 1965], incidentally, a strict Ustaša organization in Spain, led first by Archbishop Šarić and now by Vjekoslav Luburić, the former commandant of all Croatian concentration camps.[133]) Hitler's photographer, writes Edmond Paris at the end of his documentation, was sentenced to ten years merely for committing the crime of photographing the Führer. By contrast, thousands of serious Ustaša criminals went unpunished, despite countless protests and memoranda, just because they were under the protection of the Catholic Church.

DID THE POPE KNOW NOTHING?

> *"What is happening in Croatia and alarming the whole world?"*
> —undersecretary of state Montini

> *"Indeed, it is horrific."*
> —curia Cardinal Tisserant

Even Italian newspapers reported openly on the massacres at the time. For example, the following could be seen in a Bologna newspaper on September

18, 1941: "The First Brother of Assisi spoke with the birds and fishes and called them brothers and sisters, but his disciples and spiritual heirs, full of hate, are massacring people in the Independent State of Croatia who are their own brothers before God the Father, brothers of the same blood, the same language and the same Mother Earth that has fed them from her tender breast. They are massacring, killing and burying people alive, throwing their victims into rivers, the sea and ravines. There are hordes of these murderers and they are in a state of insane agitation, led by the priests and Catholic officials."[134]

Former Yugoslav minister Većeslav Vilder said on the radio in London on February 16, 1942: "And now the most horrific crimes are happening in Stepinac's surroundings. There are rivers of brothers' blood flowing. Orthodox are being forced to go over to the Catholic faith and the voice of Archbishop Stepinac is not being raised to preach resistance. But we read that he is taking part in these parades of Fascists and Nazis. And what is even worse, the Bishop of Zagreb, Salis-Sewis, roundly praised Pavelić in his New Year's address and Archbishop Šarić of Sarajevo composed a long ode to Pavelić on December 24, 1941."[135]

The Roman Catholic Croat and former Yugoslav minister Dr. Prvislav Grisogono, who now [in 1965] lives in England, asked the archbishop of Belgrade, Dr. Ujčić, to ask the pope to intercede in order to stop the butchery. The archbishop's response: "Thank you for your letter. We have already received information on the massacres from the most varied of sources. I have passed everything on to the Vatican and believe everything possible will be done."[136] But nothing was done.

And this, despite the fact that protest letters arrived at the Vatican from all over the world, including all the Allied governments. But Pius XII remained silent—just as he did about Auschwitz and other matters.

But Croatia, the Croatia of mass murders and torture, was a predominantly (if not purely) Catholic problem. The pope's voice held the greatest weight there. "All our actions," said the minister of education and later Croatian envoy in Berlin, Mile Budak, "are based on loyalty to religion and the Catholic Church."[137] And Archbishop Stepinac himself wrote to the pope about this Croatian state: "It has, at every opportunity, proved its will to remain loyal to its Catholic traditions and guarantee a brighter and better future for the Catholic

Church in this part of the world."[138] But Undersecretary of State Montini, later Paul VI, asked "right at the beginning of the discussion" with Nikola Rušinović, one of the two unofficial representatives of Pavelić at the Vatican: "What is happening in Croatia and alarming the whole world? Is it true that crimes have been committed and deportees are being treated so terribly?"[139]

And curia cardinal Tisserant admitted to Pavelić's Croatian confidant: "If you only knew how the Italian officers stationed on the Adriatic coast are talking about you! Indeed, it is horrific. It is hardly possible to imagine that such atrocities are being committed. I have discovered from a safe source that the Franciscans of Bosnia and Herzegovina have behaved regrettably. Such deeds should not be committed by civilized and educated people, and most certainly not by priests."[140]

But the pope remained silent.

A few days after Tisserant's statement Pius XII replied graciously to a communication from the Ustaša chief.[141]

On February 6, 1942, Pius XII received 206 Croatian youths in Ustaša uniforms in a private audience held in "one of the holiest halls of the Vatican," according to the paper *Katolički Tjednik*. "The most moving moment was when the young Ustaša asked the Pope to bless their Poglavnik, the Independent State of Croatia and the Croatian people. Every member received a medal as a souvenir."[142]

But Pavelić's attaché in Rome, Nikola Rušinović, reported on May 9, 1942: "We have many enemies. Even so-called friends attack us everywhere with intrigues, especially in the Vatican. They refer to gangsters and gangsterism in Croatia. They are saying 8,000 photographs had been collected as evidence for Ustaša crimes against the Serb population."[143]

And indeed, the Vatican state secretariat did have photograph albums of the massacres and mass conversions in its possession.[144] There was also a liaison between the archbishop of Zagreb and the Vatican, Krunoslav Draganović, a member of the conversion committee and chaplain at the Jasenovac concentration camp,[145] who later accompanied Pavelić on his escape to South America.

There was also the Benedictine Giuseppe Ramiro Marcone, whom Pius XII had already appointed as representative of the curia in Zagreb on June 13, 1941, Pavelić's saint's day, giving him the title of "Papal Visitor." The delegate, who was de facto acting as a nuncio, took part in public events, sat in the diplomats' box in the Ustaša parliament, appeared among high-ranking officers of Hitler's, Mussolini's, and Pavelić's, inspected the Ustaša Youth side by side with the latter[146] and made a wish for him on his saint's day on June 13, 1942, "that Croatia may overcome all its difficulties and begin to blossom under the leadership of Ante Pavelić."[147]

And Archbishop Stepinac was himself in Rome twice during the terror regime and was received by the pope.

But the pope remained silent.

In a report to the foreign ministry in Zagreb on February 8, 1942, Nikola Rušinović mentioned a visit to Monsignor Pietro Sigismondi, the head of the Croatian Department in the Vatican: "During our discussion we talked about the conversions in Croatia. He said the Holy See was glad about them but the American and British press were condemning us because the conversions were taking place under great pressure from the authorities, which the Holy See did not believe, of course. It would appear advisable to proceed somewhat more slowly to save the Holy See reproaches, accusations and dilemmas. He mentioned that even the Italian press was publishing articles about the mass conversions of Orthodox to Catholicism from time to time."[148] But the *Osservatore Romano* guaranteed that the conversion of the Serbs was happening "without the slightest pressure from civil or religious authorities."[149]

Compare this claim from the papal journal with the memorandum the leaders of the *Catholic* Slovenes sent to the Catholic bishop Ujčić of Belgrade on March 1, 1942, via whom it was to be passed on to the Vatican: "In the Independent State of Croatia all Orthodox bishops and priests have been either killed, imprisoned or sent to concentration camps; their churches and monasteries have been destroyed or confiscated. It is the avowed main goal of the politicians in Zagreb to eradicate the Serb population in Croatia. The conversions to Catholicism there have nothing to do with religious conviction and are humiliating processes for the Catholic Church, whose standing and dignity they compromise extremely. Any impartial observer must admit that the conversions of Serbian Orthodox to Catholicism have taken place under terrible political pressure. For there is no doubt that the Orthodox of Croatia who have converted out of inner conviction can be counted on one hand." The Slovenian

Catholics conclude: "We are convinced that the Vatican will, on learning of this report, protest against the tragic fate awaiting the Serbs and save the standing of Yugoslavian Catholicism. Familiar with the situation in our fatherland, we consider it necessary that:

1. the Holy See publicly condemns the bloody persecution of the Serbs and their Church;
2. the Holy See bans all conversions to Catholicism under the existing reign of terror;
3. persons wanting to convert to Catholicism despite the general ban require a special permit from the Holy See, which will check each case individually;
4. the Holy See orders the Croatian bishops to protect the Serbian Orthodox Christians and their priests."[150]

So this is what the Holy See should have done according to the conviction of *Catholics*.

And what did it do?

It appointed the primate of the Croatian Church military vicar of the Ustaša. It expressed its "gratification" at the approach of the Croatian bishops on March 27, 1942, and conveyed its apostolic blessing in recognition of its great service.[151] It also blessed the greatest gangster of all the satellite states at the beginning of his bloody career, during it, and on his deathbed. And it appointed this man's closest ally, Archbishop Stepinac, who was still expecting the West to "use its atomic power" after the war "to bring Western civilization to Moscow and Belgrade before it is too late,"[152] cardinal. And Stepinac had already long been sentenced to sixteen years of forced labor by the Supreme People's Court in Zagreb. But even now Pius XII still supported him before the whole world. And rightly so! Because the bishop, whom the pope was now praising as "an example of apostolic zeal and Christian strength of mind,"[153] had only tolerated what the pope had also tolerated. And so the latter wrote on January 12, 1953: "Although he is absent, We embrace him with fatherly love—and We wish passionately for everyone to know that Our decision to decorate him with the honor of the Roman Purple is for no other reason than to repay him for his great achievements in an appropriate manner."[154]

Archbishop Stepinac performed his "great achievements" as the primate of a state in which, of two million Orthodox Serbs, 240,000 were forcibly converted to Catholicism and 750,000[155] murdered, often after the cruelest of torture.

Stepinac, who had neither killed anyone nor burned down a single church himself, benevolently kept this quiet for four years.

As did the pope.

And is Stepinac not guiltier than that Ustaša who wore two chains of human tongues and eyes around his neck?

If one considers the attitude of Eugenio Pacelli to the politics of Mussolini, Franco, Hitler, and Pavelić, it hardly seems an exaggeration to say: Pius XII is probably more incriminated than any other pope has been for centuries. He is so obviously involved in the most hideous atrocities of the Fascist era, and therefore of history itself, both directly and indirectly, that it would not be surprising, given the tactics of the Roman Church, if he were to be canonized.

APPENDIX

DISCUSSION ABOUT KARLHEINZ DESCHNER'S CRITICAL CHURCH HISTORY, *ABERMALS KRÄHTE DER HAHN* (*AND AGAIN THE COCK CREW*) IN *DIE TAT*, ZURICH

Few critical works have been vilified so maliciously as Karlheinz Deschner's church history *Abermals krähte der Hahn*. Yet no Catholic journal provided an anti-critique or even a correction, not even when, as in the *Kölnische Rundschau* paper, the book was slandered in several major articles and the editor repeatedly refused a right of reply. It is not possible to print even a small part of those offensively untrue reviews together with some (prudently suppressed) replies from the author here. Let us view just one case as an example of what remains of all the denigrations, distortions, and lies that are being spread about Deschner's work on church history when he is permitted an answer and then, beyond this, a theologian, striving for objectivity, makes a quasi-arbitrary judgment as the editors of the Zurich newspaper *Die Tat* fairly did.

The Protestant priest Wolfgang Hammer wrote the following in this newspaper on May 4, 1963, under the title "A Hit below the Belt at Christianity":

"A critical Church history from its beginnings through to Pius XII," the title page promises—truly a praiseworthy, weighty undertaking! Because the Church histories of recent decades overflow with moral simple-mindedness and harmlessness insofar as they flourished beyond school editions and monographs at all! So our interest is awakened. We know that there were a number of dark points: witch mania, persecution of the Jews, burning of heretics....

215

How important such a presentation would be if it were truly "critical"! But Deschner's book is only dressed as a Church history. In truth it is, unfortunately, just a pamphlet. "What has Christ taught the world? Shoot each other dead, protect the moneybags of the rich! Suppress the poor, take their lives in my name!" is the quotation from an unknown Mr. Belzner on the first page. Aha, the reader notices, this is supposed to be irony—and starts reading.

It would be pointless to prove individually even Deschner's main omissions, errors and retouching. But lest he (and his friends, who in our allegedly so pious times only quietly, their teeth grinding, utter Voltaire's "Écrasez l'infame!") think we have nothing to give by way of reply, let us casually take a few details:

Napoleon and the young Goethe assuming that Jesus had never lived are quoted as serious judgments. On the other hand, our author (in the conclusion) accuses all Catholic theologians of bias and mockingly contrasts their results to "critical" or "free" theology, whose supporters can admittedly only be quoted until about 1925 because even this direction has long ceased championing the kind of exaggerated theses that suit Deschner.

An example of artistic distortion can be found on page 30: "The most significant men have hardened the Christian truth with lies. Even Paul must be suspected of this. For he writes: 'For if the truth of God has more abounded through my lie unto his glory; why yet am I also judged as a sinner?'" (Romans 3:7). If you look there you will find that Paul talks of people who argue in this way and whose "condemnation is deserved" (Romans 3:8). The result: Deschner unscrupulously takes a sentence out of context and suggests the Apostle is bragging about of lying for the honor of God!

The young critic expends infinite energy on releasing the "laymen" from their theological ignorance in which they are imprisoned by sinister clerics! Deschner spent five years on his work in order to elucidate for the laymen the results of historical criticism of the Bible that has been available to everyone for 200 years and as his *dernier cri* reveals that academics can in no way prove in all cases which words Jesus himself actually said, how they were recorded or that five of the books of Moses were not written by Moses at all! And the four Gospels were not written *by* their authors! If he had cared to open a Greek New Testament he would have noticed that it already says on the first page: "The Gospel *according to* Matthew!"

The fact that our angry young author is not embarrassed to quote obscure books in his extensive appendix that claim Jesus has never lived only reveals his true intention: pamphlets are listed there such as that by the Dutch late Hegelian *Bolland*: "De groote vraag voor de Christenheid onzer dagen" ["The Great Question for Modern Christianity"] (1911), or the "work" by the Polish author *Niemojewski*: "Astral Secrets of Ancient Christianity" (1913). The "famous Danish literary historian" Georg *Brandes* contributed: "The Jesus Saga" (1925). All that is missing is Mathilde Ludendorff!

Why am I going into the details of such references? Because it gives away Deschner's method: he writes for the theological layman. But how is a layman supposed to differentiate between the fantasies of Mr. Niemojewski and the results of Karl Barth, Rudolf Bultmann, Emil Brunner, Paul Tillich or Karl Rahner? He must now say that there are still many authors who have been printed and who are highly esteemed in other fields who have disputed the existence of Jesus with good reasons! So may the "Savior" have never really lived after all . . . ?

Once Deschner's method has been seen through, his results become self-explanatory: Jesus's prophecies are errors, he borrowed his thoughts partly from the Jews, partly from Gnostic Greeks, there were many miracle workers, even more wandering prophets and most of all people who were crucified! There were hordes of resurrected reported from India and Jesus's ethics were cobbled together from rudiments of other religions! Deschner busily rolls out the long passé trick of "comparative" religious studies, which proceeds as follows: "Hamburg is a city. Leningrad is also a city. So why talk about their individual features?"

One could ignore this spirited concoction if there were not sufficient people who will now hurl themselves at it in order to welcome this collection of old hat from the historical-critical period of Protestant theology with the same rapturous applause and wheezing pathos of a sensation-hunting contemporary criticism as *Spiegel* [left-wing German weekly magazine]—faithful students cheer Yevtushenko today and Presley tomorrow. By doing this they feed the early liberal, anti-Catholic complex that Deschner puts on with bravura and perfection.

Puts on? Yes! One can tell this by his only borrowing weapons from the armory of the liberal muzzle-loaders and grapeshot but not their colorful flags from the patriotic Jesus, the idealist Jesus or the moral force of Christianity. For the sake of brevity he simply omits the positive things the liberal theologians and philosophers thought about Jesus. He only takes the negative—and that made me wonder.

There are three arguments, I find, that one must not use against him because he is just waiting for them so that he really feels vindicated due to misunderstanding on the part of his "uncritical" and limited readers:

1. Deschner's attack is "grist to the mill of the communists"! Of course it is that *too*. Our author does not expend a syllable on communist persecutions of Christians; but neither does he share the official communist godless propaganda. He wields a finer blade and assumes the pose of "objectivity" (something that is anathema to communists).
2. Deschner would be outraged if he were to be called an enemy of religion. He takes care not to attack the person of Jesus, to whom he, like many enemies of the Church, dedicates a few clauses: Jesus was a poor devil whose work only stood out from other top religious men in its intensity and radical nature.
3. It would only serve Deschner's purpose if he were to be misrepresented as being an uncompromising youth, hypercritical but definitely right in places, or words to that effect! He would reject such false benevolence proudly and—rightly—feel misunderstood. Because he is not only, in places, definitely not right, but thanks to his distortions of the truth definitely wrong both in places and as a whole.

But what does he really want? Nothing disguised, no pseudo-communist propaganda, no enterprising contemporary criticism à la Kuby or *Spiegel*!

Deschner is nothing less than—*a prophet of the truth himself*! He runs amok with his subjective truthfulness; he is a secularist Kierkegaard. The big lie (of Christianity) must be exposed! For Deschner is a *poet*, and an excellent one at that! That must be taken into consideration. His books *Die Nacht steht um mein Haus* [Darkness at My Door] and *Florenz ohne Sonne* [Florence without Sun] show an eye-catching talent for the indirect, the lovable, the distantly tender from a farsightedness that is in no way grim, but esthetically pensive.

Now he is daring to go among the prophets with his "critical Church history." He manages to produce 700 pages without leaving the slightest trace of goodness on two thousand years of Christianity. Instead, he tears away its hypocritical mask, as he hopes: finally, finally the prophet has arisen who will show the most powerful taboo of our times its limits: *the* (in particular Roman Catholic) *Church*. He reveals that the—precisely registered—dead of Hiroshima are nothing more than victims of Christian morality (p. 597 in *Abermals krähte der Hahn*).

Is my judgment malicious? Absolutely not! Anyone is free to convince themselves by reading it. On the contrary, my judgment stems from the same kind of seriousness that Deschner offers. The roots of his drive may be explained by a psychologist! Deschner, in his footnote-heavy appendix, refers to the fact that he was raised a Catholic—presumably something went wrong there. He portrays himself as liberal, but he is pathologically one-sided to the point of injustice. He pretends to be "critical" but avails himself of the dustiest shelf-warmers of the discipline from 60 years ago!

Therefore I have to confess: the Jesuit *Alighiero Tondi*, who went over to the communists eleven years ago and whom Deschner so often presented as a star witness, is not one iota more likeable or credible for me because he preaches red propaganda at the University of East Berlin today instead of Vatican propaganda at the Roman Pontifical Gregorian University!

So a word on the final chapters, where the Prophet of the Free Spirit elucidates on the ruinous effect of the Church on politics of the recent past, is appropriate! One thing he must definitely be credited for is that he is the first to detail the material on the slaughter of Serbs in Dr. Ante *Pavelić's* fascist "Kingdom of Croatia" (1941–44). Another point to his credit is that he quotes from documents—that are well worth keeping—of martial enthusiasm from high German and Italian clergy. But these achievements become immediately wrong, in fact, they become a fault, when Deschner, for example, quotes two stray propaganda sentences from today's regional bishop D. *Lilje*, but does not mention that the same man was in prison after July 20th and that apart from him there was a whole series of much weightier and serious admonishers, witnesses and even martyrs of the Protestant Church in Germany such as Karl Barth, Niemöller, Gross, Niesel, Steinbauer and hundreds of unknown clergy and laymen. They all sacrificed their freedom, and frequently their lives, for Christ, including the *Scholls*, the twentieth anniversary of whose death was on February 22 [1963]. They died for Christ and *for freedom at the same time*, because they saw both in a positive, inseparable context on the basis of their faith.

And did the Catholic Church only have bishops like Bornewasser or Faulhaber? Does Deschner not know the martyr priest Dr. *Metzger*, who was executed in Regensburg? Never heard of him? No? Why does he not mention him?

Deschner distinguishes himself from any genuine liberal on account of his lack of fairness. There will be voices that accuse him not only of disseminating propaganda for the East unconsciously, but also consciously. But his pathos lies elsewhere. He draws an adventurous line from Jesus via Paul, the Church Fathers (liars, Emperors' bootlickers and criminals, the whole lot of them!) to Augustine, touches (without even showing the slightest understanding for the Reformation—Deschner's Catholic upbringing!) on Martin Luther, reports briefly and simply on John Calvin's burning of witches, and goes on nimble of pace to Pius XII, Mussolini, Hitler, Pavelić and the Slovakian Nazi puppet Dr. Tiso, who in turn were considerable Catholic-Christian role models for Adenauer and the West German State!

No one has ever recognized this direct line from Calvary to Hiroshima before, not even the boldest enemies of Christianity such as Nietzsche or (according to Deschner) Goethe, except Karlheinz Deschner! He, finally, exposes all the meanness, all the infamy, all the mania, all the hypocrisy and imperiousness, all the tyranny that has ever been carried out in the name of Jesus! And how!

It is a shame about Deschner's plentiful material. Because of course there are certain relations between Mussolini and the papal social doctrine of 1931, of course there was a Catholic movement that wanted to re-Catholicize Europe with Hitler's weapons, of course it is a bitter affair when a Lutheran clergyman blesses the first atomic bombs, of course the tragedy of a nationally oriented German people's churchdom is reflected in people like Lilje or Bornewasser, and of course "Christian" politicians make mistakes today that are definitely tantamount to a betrayal of the Gospels.

But on account of his blindness, Deschner renders himself incapable of any *genuine* criticism by whispering to us that *only* these negative aspects are the true and real foundations of the Church. Everything else is propaganda, lies and hypocrisy.

And what about the phenomenal achievements of the papal relief organization? The care of the nuns and deaconesses in hospitals and children's homes? The martyrdoms of the missionaries, the prayers of the faithful, the sacrifices of the upstanding? Is this nothing but self-deceit, skillful exploitation by predators dressed in black or purple at the Vatican or elsewhere?

This is where criticism becomes nonsense. "So in everything, do to others what you would have them do to you," is Jesus's golden rule (Matthew 7:12). Who knows—Will Deschner now inform us of whether Jesus even said this himself in this way? With which he claims to have shown once more that the whole of Christianity is a swindle . . .

The author responded to this on June 1, 1963, under the title "A Hit below the Belt at Karlheinz Deschner" [the following remarks have been only slightly adapted in terms of style, and printing errors have been corrected]:

During the five years I spent writing my Church history *Abermals krähte der Hahn* [*And Again the Cock Crew*] I was certain that it would either be silenced or be comprehensively slandered. It was slandered on May 4 in the Zurich newspaper *Die Tat* by Wolfgang Hammer, and with such completeness that I asked the editors for a right to reply. I would like to thank them for their fairness.

Mr. Hammer, although you left nothing out in slandering my work virtually in its entirety, you were not able to prove one single untruth in a volume of 700 pages, apart from the "example of artistic distortion" that you wrongly tried to accuse me of. Because with the best will in the world I cannot help but recognize in Romans 3:7 a word of Paul, apart from the fact that you are not able to contradict the other quotations I provided that attest the same as Romans 3:7. You, on the other hand, have crammed your four-column article with untruths.

1. You claim that I was only able to "quote" the representatives of critical theology "only until about 1925" because even this discipline has not championed any such exaggerated theories "that suit Deschner" for a long time.

The truth is that I refer to dozens of critical theologians whose papers were published long after 1925: these include F. Buri with three publications, the most recent of which appeared in 1946; C. Schneider with three publications, the most recent of which appeared in 1956; J. Groß with three publications, the most recent of which appeared in 1961; K. Aland with two publications, the more recent of which appeared in 1957; H. Braun with two publications, the more recent of which appeared in 1957; H. Conzelmann with three publications, the most recent of which appeared in 1959; E. Hirsch with five publications, the most recent of which appeared in 1941; K. Heussi with seven publications, the most recent of which appeared in 1955; M. Werner with seven publications, the most recent of which appeared in 1959; G. Bornkamm with four publications, the most recent of which appeared in 1959; M. Dibelius with eight publications, the most recent of which appeared in 1953; R. Bultmann with nine publications, the most recent of which appeared in 1958; J. Leipoldt with eighteen publications, the most recent of which appeared in 1958. The vast majority of these academics still write today. But I have also referred to the works of numerous other critical theologians who published long after 1925. Nonetheless, you state that the representatives of free or critical theology could only "be quoted until about 1925." The truth, Mr. Hammer, is not your domain.

2. "He pretends to be 'critical,'" you write, "but avails himself of the dustiest shelf-warmers of the discipline from 60 years ago!"

This is an accusation that is already rebuffed by the works referred to above. But I want to be more precise. Of the roughly 1,000 documents I used, only about 20 were from last [the nineteenth] century. Furthermore, I only mention nearly all of them peripherally. They hardly play any part. But most of my secondary literature stems neither from 60 years ago, nor 50, nor even 40. Here, as evidence pars pro toto, are the years in which all the publications that appear under the letter *A* in my bibliography were published: 1928, 2. A. 1925, 1952, 1961, 5. A. 1928, 1960, 1955, 1957, 1952, 1938, 1956, 1958, 1937, 1959, 1950, 1951, 1955, 6. A. 1956, 1932, 1959, 1955, 1937, 1939, 1926. It is similar with the publishing years of all the books I used—"the dustiest shelf-warmers of the discipline from 60 years ago!" The truth, Mr. Hammer, is not your domain.

And incidentally, of course, the latest academic theses most certainly do not have to be the right ones. And on the subject of dusty shelf-warmers, what about Church theology, which adheres to the same tenets as in ancient times?

3. "Our author does not expend a syllable on communist persecutions of Christians." It is true that I almost exclusively write about persecution by the Christian churches. Because firstly, Christianity, not communism, is the subject of my book. Secondly, the Church systematically persecuted all those of different faiths from the fourth century until well into modern times, torturing and killing millions of innocent people as it did so. Thirdly, the crimes of communists against Christians are piffling in comparison—not to mention that it is not the *Communist Manifesto* that binds one to love one's enemy, but the Bible. And independently of all that, it says in my Church history, which allegedly contains "not a single syllable" about communist persecution of Christians: "And indeed, the Soviets did not leave out any rigorous measures. Church schools, theological seminars, and monasteries were closed, chapels were confiscated, churches were heavily taxed, clergy members were exiled, and Christian teachers were replaced by communists at public schools." The truth, Mr. Hammer, is not your domain.

4. You claim, after—almost incredibly—admitting to some achievements of mine, that "these achievements become immediately wrong, in fact, they become a fault, when Deschner, for example, quotes two stray propaganda sentences from today's regional bishop D. *Lilje*, but does not mention that the same man was in prison after July 20th and that apart from him there was a whole series of much weightier and serious admonishers, witnesses and even martyrs of the Protestant Church in Germany."

As regards the men of "July 20th," I only respect those who had been opponents of Hitler since the beginning of the war at the latest. But if they had supported him before, while he was wallowing in the blood of victory and reducing half of Europe to ashes, and only turned against him when his defeat was imminent, then I despise them doubly, and that also applies to Bishop Lilje.

Mr. Lilje quite expressly stated support for the declaration from the representative of the German Protestant Church Committee from April 25, 1933, "We say a thankful Yes to this turning point in history. God has sent it to us" and the appeal of the Protestant military district priest Ludwig Müller the day after, "I go to work with the trust of God and in awareness of my responsibility toward God. The aim is the fulfillment of German Protestant longing that has existed since the Reformation." So he had sympathized with Hitler at least since 1933. And as late as the third year of the war, Hanns Lilje published his own document with the telling title "Der Krieg als geistige Leistung" ["War as an Intellectual Performance"].

But you further claim that I have remained silent about a series of weightier and more serious admonishers, witnesses, even martyrs. But I actually write, and just a few lines after mentioning Lilje's (Nazi-inspired)—"Krieg als geistige Leistung," which means that you should not have missed it: "But of course there were Protestants who were not only immune to the National Socialist ideology but also testified in public to this stance. Remember the Confessing Church, men such as Karl Immer, Paul Schneider, Regional Bishop Wurm, and Martin Niemöller, whose letters to Hitler's ministers must be read so that their intrepidness can be honored." And in my detailed examination of clerical anti-Semitism—several regional Protestant churches had even excommunicated baptized Jews under Hitler, something that had not even happened in the darkest Middle Ages—I also stress the courageous behavior of individual Protestant theologians and church leaders. The truth, Mr. Hammer, is not your domain.

5. You also claim that I only gave Jesus "a few clauses," which you then follow up with a colon as if this quotation were from me: "Jesus was a poor devil whose work only stood out from other top religious men in its intensity and radical nature." The expressions "top men" and "poor devil" are from you. I do not speak about Jesus in this way, and I describe his preaching as follows at one point: "Jesus, through the consistency and uncompromising attitude [of his preaching] that are taken to the limit, by their exclusion of the unnecessary and limitation to the essential, goes beyond much of what preceded him. He was able to shock and attract, *and he still can today*." Even the Catholic Bernard von Brentano recognized in a defense of my book: "My deep admiration of Jesus the

person has not been reduced; on the contrary, it has become greater, deeper, clearer while reading this passionate pamphlet."

Jesus's not being quite a singular phenomenon is taught by a long series of the most outstanding Protestant exegetes of the New Testament and comparative religious studies, the latter of which, however, proceeds thus according to you: "Hamburg is a city. And Leningrad is also a city. So why talk about their individual features?" A judgment that says nothing about comparative religious studies but everything about you.

Furthermore, a large part of my book is dedicated directly or indirectly to the preaching of Jesus, because it is, as is my fundamental issue, confronted with what has become of it. For this reason I talk of Jesus on hundreds of pages, a whole chapter was dedicated to him, there are exclusively and always positive references to the man to whom, according to you, I only give "a few clauses," on pages 170–171, 258–259, 292–294, 410–412, 493–500, among others. The truth, Mr. Hammer, is not your domain.

6. Then you continue to fib that in my work, the Church Fathers are "liars, bootlickers to the Emperors and even criminals, the whole lot of them!" All these types of people are most certainly to be found among the fathers and saints of the Catholic Church, as no serious historian could deny. But my describing the "whole lot of" the Church Fathers as such is pure invention on your part.

The editor of the Hamburg journal *Lynx*, which is excellent but unfortunately only appears in hectographed form, Dr. Wolfgang Beutin, writes: "He [Deschner] always tries to do justice to the men of the Church. He differentiates. If you were to drop the name of John XXIII into the debate, Deschner would probably be the last to deny the achievements of this Pope of peace and the first to emphasize the qualities of the person of Roncalli. But does respect for the figure of John XXIII also mean forgetting the history of the Christian churches, in particular the Catholic one?" I can only agree. And wherever it seemed justified to me I have acknowledged or praised the achievements of the Church Fathers, especially those of the Church teachers Basil, John Chrysostom and others on social matters, of Tertullian, Cyprian and others in questions of war, military service and the death penalty; in the matter of Jews I referred to the benevolent intentions of Saint Gregory the Great, just to name a few cases that you ignore completely. Because the truth, Mr. Hammer, is not your domain.

7. It is so little your domain that you insinuate: "He manages to produce 700 pages without leaving the slightest trace of goodness on two thousand years of Christianity. He believes"—this in your closing remark—"that the whole of Christianity is a swindle . . ." I just ask myself why it is, then, that Christian theologians can acknowledge my book and recommend it? Why could there even be a positive review in the *Hamburger Sonntagsblatt* [a Sunday newspaper]? And why did an important pastor, whose opinions I admittedly do not necessarily subscribe to, write in the *Bremer Nachrichten*: "Deschner is a radical pacifist in the sense of original Christianity, he intends a fundamental restoration of original Christianity as a religion of absolute love without any secular considerations, church or the outside political world"?

Mr. Hammer, have you actually read my book, which you spend four columns slandering, at all? Even flicking through it must have drawn your attention to the fact that I have spent entire chapters defending Christian men or movements! A chapter on the greatest Christian of the second century, for instance, Marcion, whom, according to a well-known Protestant theologian, I even praised too greatly! I dedicate another positive chapter to montanism. The chapter "The Social Direction of Christianity" praises the stance of Catholic Church leaders. I honor Origen, the most important theologian of the major churches of the first three centuries, in a series of sections, just to name these examples. But according to you, I do not leave "the slightest trace of goodness on two thousand years of Christianity on 700 pages" and believe "that the whole of Christianity is a swindle . . ." The truth, Mr. Hammer, is not your domain.

"And did the Catholic Church only have bishops like Bornewasser or Faulhaber?" Oh, no! At last I can agree with you. It also had Archbishop Gröber von Freiburg, Regional Bishop Burger, Cardinal Bertram of Breslau, Cardinal Schulte of Cologne, Bishop Wilhelm Berning of Osnabrück, Cardinal

Innitzer of Vienna, Prince-Archbishop Weitz of Salzburg, the Augsburg bishop
Kumpfmüller, the celebrated Catholic resistance fighter, the "Lion of Münster,"
Bishop von Galen, who guaranteed under Hitler that "the Christians will do
their duty," the German soldiers "want to fight and die for Germany" and so
on. The Church also had Prince-Bishop Ferdinand of Seckau and the Bamberg
Archbishop Kolb, who still supported Hitler in the fifth and sixth years of the
war. And not least it had the Catholic Wehrmacht field bishop, Franz Justus
Rarkowski, who veritably gushed with Nazi-friendly slogans. He was not an outsider. "The entire German-Austrian episcopate behaved as he did." This is what it
says, correctly, in my Church history, in which you should not have missed this
sentence, especially since it is emphasized as a title and then proved in detail:
"The German (and, after 1938, also the Austrian) Catholic bishops supported
one of the greatest criminals in world history with increasing intensity until the
final years of the Second World War." No, the Catholic Church, as you quite
rightly say, did not only have bishops like Bornewasser and Faulhaber. *All* the
German bishops professed their support for National Socialism in a mutual pastoral letter in 1933. And all, did you hear, all the German and Austrian Catholic
bishops still followed the Second World War "with gratification" in 1941—
and hardly in contradiction to Pius XII!—in a mutual pastoral letter: fifty-five
million dead!

Incidentally: to my knowledge no one, not even a Catholic critic, has so far
defended the (in Germany) much-celebrated Cardinal Faulhaber; my material
on him is too damning.

And I do not want to miss out on a reference to the truly tragicomic continuation of your so victorious sentence "And did the Catholic Church only have
bishops like Bornewasser or Faulhaber?" Now everyone expects the names of
other princes of the Church. But what do you write? "Does Deschner not know
the martyr priest Dr. Metzger, who was executed in Regensburg?" Of course not.
You can only name one priest? No cardinals? No bishops or regional bishops?
Not even one of the lower prelates, perhaps? "Never heard of him?" you ask. "No?
Why does he not mention him?" Why not? I will tell you. Because I, not being
as petty as you, trust the Catholic clergy to have more than just one decent and
courageous man. This is why it says in my Church history, which you should
perhaps try reading: "Not one German bishop, incidentally, ever became a martyr

at the time or even sat in a concentration camp. Lower clergy were good enough for those purposes." Or: "But in fact, the episcopate and the Curia were both on the side of the Axis powers, while a considerable number[!] of members of the lower clergy in all the occupied countries were actively taking part in resistance against the German occupants and often[!] paying with their lives for doing so." You see, I do not, like you, credit the Catholic Church with just one hero among its clergy. Anyone who reads my book carefully will also recognize that I differentiate between the low and high clergy in matters that are not exactly peripheral, which is why, however, I in no way assume the absolute worst in everyone and even less the absolute best. I have Catholics to thank for the most beautiful memories of my life, including a Catholic clergyman, and there is definitely not, as you tactfully assume, anything that "went wrong" in my upbringing.

But I am happy that you at least do not defend Pius XII as well. For this I would like to bow to you, who are presumably a pastor or at least a Protestant of the Karl Barthsch school, in reverence. Because the incriminations Hochhuth makes in his play *Der Stellvertreter* [*The Deputy*] are virtually chicken feed compared to my material. Near the end of your lousy article, which is in need of considerable correction, you write "No one has ever recognized this direct line from Calgary to Hiroshima before, not even the boldest enemies of Christianity such as Nietzsche or (according to Deschner) Goethe, except Karlheinz Deschner!"

Dear Mr. Hammer, it is not enough that I have proved your incessant untruth—now you are also making yourself ridiculous. And how! Think about it: the Hiroshima crime. Nietzsche. Goethe. Understood? And you also made a grammatical error—indeed, I do not envy you for your German in general.

In view of all your qualifications: if *Tat* has another important review for someone to write—anyone who is seriously interested in my Church history should heed Lichtenberg's words: "If you have two pairs of trousers, sell one and buy this book"—then I would offer to write instead of you, who are exactly what you accuse me of being: "wrong both in places and as a whole."

⋘⋙

Now the editors of *Tat*, "in view of the severity of the dispute and the important subject being disputed," asked the Zurich church historian

Prof. Fritz Blanke to take a stand. So the theologian made the following judgment under the title of "Kirchengeschichte ohne Mythus" ["Church History without Myth"] on August 18, 1963, as follows:

I.

I would like to start with a quotation from which the content and stance of Deschner's "Critical Church History" (as the subtitle says) follow well. It says on page 241/42: "How strange Jesus and his message seem in the presence of these (Roman Catholic) hierarchs and their claim to be the vicars of Christ. How strange the appearance of their splendid residence and their almost Oriental courts in view of Jesus's words: 'Foxes have burrows and the birds of the heavens have nests; but the Son of Man has nowhere to rest his head.' How strange is their centuries-long greed for ever greater riches in view of Jesus's instruction: 'Go, sell what you have and give it to the poor.' How strange their fixed prices for each episcopal nomination, each honor, dispensation and decision they convey in light of Jesus's command to his disciples: 'As you have received it for nothing, so you shall give it for nothing.' How strange their habit of having themselves called Holy and Holiest Father next to Jesus's exhortation: 'And call no man your father on earth, for you have one Father, who is in heaven.' How strange the constant emphasis of their priority over all other bishops, and even over all the rulers of the world in comparison to Jesus's proclamation: 'If anyone wants to be first, he must be the very last, and the servant of all.' How strange their excommunications that rush through the millennia that even the purest Christians have pronounced next to Jesus's command: 'Judge not lest ye be judged.' How strange their executions of heretics, burning of witches, pogroms against Jews and religious wars in the light of Jesus's teaching: 'Love your enemies, do good to those who hate you, bless those who curse you and pray for those who vilify you.'"

For Deschner, the history of Christianity is a story of the betrayal of the Gospel by the Church. This is already implied in the title *And Again the Cock Crew*. In Matthew 26:72–74 Peter denies "again" and then a third time and "immediately"—not "again"—"the cock crew." So Deschner aims to allude to Peter's denial with this (slightly unfortunate) title and clearly means: as Peter denied the Lord, so has the Christian Church also done the same. Deschner's sights are set above all (but not exclusively) on the Catholic Church.

So the main thesis of the book is that the development of the Church has led away from Jesus. This is shown by the origin of the Christian cult, which Jesus did not know, the veneration of the saints, which developed with inspiration from ancient hero worship, the infiltration of Christian teaching with Greek philosophy, the transformation of the Church from a free community of love into a hierarchical, political entity of power. But these adaptations, rigidities and atrophy were not all. There were, in the Christian Church, clear and glaring contraventions of the message of Christ: by the maintaining of slavery, the condemnation of women, Church anti-Semitism (from the Church Fathers through to Luther) and the bloody persecution of witches and heretics. One major cause of this entire degeneration was (according to Deschner) Emperor Constantine, who gave Christianity the state's blessing in the fourth century, after which the actual perversion and depletion of Christian teaching began.

Deschner primarily takes his examples, in accordance with his topic, from early Christian history (1st–6th centuries), but he also includes the Middle Ages, the Reformation and the modern era. His most recent example is the unworthy submissiveness of leading German churchmen of both confessions to National Socialism (in which, among others, the names of the now highly regarded theology professors Joseph Lortz, Michael Schmaus and Ethelbert Stauffer appear) and the horrific persecution of the Serbs in the fascist Kingdom of Croatia (1941–5), approved by the Roman Curia.

II.

Deschner stresses that his book has been written "by a layman for laymen." This is the expression of a modesty that honors the author. In reality, it is not only theological laymen but also theologians themselves who will benefit from this work. Furthermore: the author is in no way a mere layman; he studied at a Catholic university of philosophy and theology for a while (p. 128 in *Abermals krähte der Hahn*) and later obtained a PhD. So theological questions and academic methods are familiar to him. This can be seen in every aspect of the work. Deschner has really worked through the books he refers to—there are nearly a thousand of them!—and is familiar with the latest discussions on the matter. He has read many other sources in addition to the literature. All such information is documented by footnotes. Deschner has not conducted any new research of his own—that was also not his intention—but he has summarized today's knowledge and understanding of church history so extensively that even a church history specialist must be grateful to him for his information, which frequently illuminates the little known. Deschner, who prefers to stay close to the works of the Bultmann school, is also very well informed about the New Testament and its current interpretation. I did not find any printing errors in this 703-page volume.

So that is the formal information on this Church history. As far as its contents are concerned, it is difficult to prove any false claims on the part of Deschner. As a Protestant theologian, I consider his portrayal of the genesis of the papacy and Roman Catholicism (essentially) objective. The "cultification" of Christianity and its Hellenization are also correctly portrayed, as are the misogyny and anti-Semitism of the Church Fathers (with all their devastating consequences). The same applies, in my opinion, to the interpretation of the cult of the saints and the documents about the suppression of witches and heretics. What Deschner writes about the significance of Constantine for the Christian Church corresponds to the facts. It was not possible for me to check Deschner's statements regarding support for the far-right Croatian Ustaša by Pope Pius XII. Deschner refers to Serbian confidential sources and an essay from Professor Viktor Novak (Belgrade, 1954) on the relationship between the Vatican and the South Slavs, which unfortunately I have no access to. A reasoned opinion to this delicate matter from the Catholic side would be most desirable. On page 433, Deschner presents precise information in table form regarding the financial interrelations of the Vatican, with reference to a book by Professor Heinz Mohrmann, lecturer in economics at the Humboldt University in Berlin. Is Mohrmann's information correct? It would be crucial to obtain authentic information about these conditions from Catholic experts themselves. How long will the Vatican leave it to its opponents to inform us about its finances?

What must be agreed with is the standard Deschner sets for the course of Christian history. He measures Christianity by its origins, by Jesus of Nazareth. He confronts the proclamations of this Jesus with what has become of it. What was the "preaching of Jesus"? Its focal points were (p. 135 in *Abermals krähte der Hahn*) the proclamation of the coming Kingdom of God, love of God, one's neighbor and one's enemies, the fight against cult and any open display of piety, against the self-righteous and those who judge, against the oppression of the weak, the exploitation of the poor, violence, retaliation and murder. Deschner stands before the figure of Christ with deep admiration. He says of him (his own emphasis on the last four words): "He was able to shock and attract, and *he still can today.*"

III.

As implied above, the Christian Church has failed (according to Deschner) in two respects. Firstly, it has weakened the preaching of Jesus and adapted it increasingly to support mass requirements. It must be noted that this process was, to a certain extent, unavoidable. Every high, world-changing message has had to pay for its historic victory with a certain dilution of its substance. Secondly, the Church has not only played down Jesus's teachings but also inverted them. As soon as Christianity had power in its hands, it turned the love of one's enemies into hate. It persecuted the Jews in an unprecedented manner. The witch trials, to which millions of people fell victim, only came about in the Christian era and did not peak in the Middle Ages, but in the post-Reformation, Protestant era. Deschner restricts himself to the Middle Ages with the persecution of heretics. He could have added the Reformation century, in which about 5,000 Anabaptists lost their lives in both Catholic and Protestant countries. Deschner's "scandal chronicles" are in general incomplete. He says nothing of indigenous Americans being wiped out by Catholic Spaniards and Protestant Puritans. And the Orthodox Church in Russia, which allowed itself to be misused for centuries as an instrument of power by the state, remains undiscussed. But the facts reported by Deschner are certainly sufficient to confirm the words of the English historian William E. H. Lecky: "It is no exaggeration to say that the Christian Church has caused more undeserved suffering to people than any other religion."

It is to the credit of the work *Abermals krähte der Hahn* that it presents us with these findings. It does not help to cover this up or silence it. We have to take up a position on it and explain the nightmarish events that the rage of persecution and cruelty in Christian peoples has spread. One answer to this question is provided by Friedrich Wilhelm Foerster, who writes in *Erlebte Weltgeschichte* [*Experienced World History*] (1953, p. 341): "Christianity has increased the strength of emotionality in human life to an extraordinary degree. But if the highest good at which this emotional life was directed is lost, then its dynamic comes to serve elemental passions and we are then faced with intellectual and emotional barbarians that are much more dangerous than those who once stood at the gates of Rome under Alarich."

In my opinion, Foerster has seen the crucial thing: the extremes of the human soul have been intensified under the influence of Christianity. Toward evil, but also, we must add (certainly in agreement with F. W. Foerster): toward good as well! It is precisely the brutality used by Christian nations and churches toward people who were different that led to individual Christians, spurred by their consciences, took up the fight against the inhumanities. The Catholic bishop Las Cases protected the Indians from the whites' rapacity. The Catholic Friedrich von Spee stood up against the witch trials. The English Protestant William Wilberforce pushed through the liberation of slaves. They and many others—let me just mention Francis of Assisi, Vincent de Paul, Johann Friedrich Oberlin, Johann Hinrich Wiehern, William Booth, Friedrich von Bodelschwingh, Albert Schweitzer—have, working against the evils of their times with the heroic power of love, turned curses to blessings and shown that the proclamation of Jesus repeatedly shows through in Christianity.

IV.

The weakness in Deschner's Church history is that he does not emphasize the positive achievements of the spirit of Christ. But there have been enough others before him who have done this (not infrequently in a purely glorifying way), and it was not Deschner's task. I would especially recommend his book, aimed at laymen, to those theologians who are professionally occupied with church history. We must ask ourselves if we should not "rewrite" our current version. Not in the style of Deschner, whose total blackening is one-sided. But in such a way that we make the low points more clearly visible as well as the high ones, the bright sides as well as the blemishes. What we need is not a (as Huizinga puts it) "perfumed history," but definitely one without myth and incense. Only observation of the history of the Church, in which the sharp winds of truth blow, has a right and a mandate, that is, the mandate to enthuse the reader for real Christianity and guiding him toward self-examination.

<hr>

ABERMALS KRÄHTE DER HAHN AS REVIEWED BY THEOLOGIANS

> *"This clearly and very interestingly written book, at the basis of which there is immense literary knowledge, provides, on 600 pages of text, an overview of the results of modern Bible criticism and the history of dogma, and then the acts of violence committed by the Church throughout world history up to the pitiful dealings with the seductive anti-Christian forces of the twentieth century. It anticipates Hochhuth's theme in 1962 [a year before Hochhuth's play was published] but contains material for hundreds of 'The Deputy'-style tragedies. Deschner has uncovered the weaknesses and crimes of leading Christians so mercilessly that one can understand that they take a dim view of it. Anyone who does not notice the beam in their own eye will, with Deschner, have to deal with the splinters. . . . The specialists may have familiarized themselves with all the facts of Deschner's Church history one hundred times over but they have drawn no practical reformatory consequences from their great post-Reformation knowledge and understanding. Most of this has remained unknown to laymen to this day. They have not had it explained to them from the pulpits or in Bible lessons in the Protestant churches either. . . . I hope this book— the performance of a non-theologian—is widely read amongst lay people because only when they become mature will the theologians— perhaps—revise their position."*
>
> —the priest Dr. Carl Anders Skriver, *Der Vegetarier* [*The Vegetarian*], Hanover, December 1964

<hr>

"I would especially recommend his book, aimed at laymen, to those theologians who are professionally occupied with church history."
—Prof. Dr. Fritz Blanke, *Die Tat,* Zurich, August 18, 1963

"The book is so interesting as a phenomenon that it is worth going into. Although the author is not a theologian, but an author, so he has no special inherent educational background for the task he tackles, he has expended an extraordinary amount of effort on this book. . . . The whole of modern theology is on the march here."
—Prof. Dr. Kurt Aland, *Sonntagsblatt,* Hamburg, April 21, 1963

"The sections that penetrate the recent past in particular are extremely topical: papal policy in the Third Reich and during the war, the bishops' joy in collaboration and—especially impressively—the struggle of annihilation against the Orthodox Church in Yugoslavia with the assistance of Catholic forces is particularly stimulating reading."
—Prof. Dr. Karl Kupisch, *Evangelische Theologie,*
Munich, April 1963

"Deschner is well informed. He will rely on nothing but—information."
—Prof. Dr. H. Conzelmann, *Evangelische Theologie,*
Munich, June 1964

"All in all, a bleak overall picture is painted of the Church and its long historical development. But historically it is true and basically nothing more than an illustrating commentary on the fitting, sober statement by the well-known opinionated theologian from Tübingen, Adolf Schlatter, according to which 'doubt about the Church can become bitter scorn in view of the enormous amount of folly and evil we call the history of Christianity.'"
—Prof. Dr. Martin Werner, *Schweizerische Theologische Umschau,*
June 1963

———

"Deschner . . . is well orientated. Let us say in advance that it is the most exhilarating—and annoying—presentation of Church history, which persistently unilaterally withholds all the positive achievements of Christianity and only shows the abysses and blemishes in its history. Perhaps this was due as a healing correction of a church historical work that elegantly slides from one church historical pinnacle of achievement to the next and forgets the other things that have happened in terms of betrayal of the Gospel by the Church. . . . But the decisive facts from his 'scandal chronicles' remain watertight."

—Prof. Dr. Erich Beyreuther, *Pastoral-Blätter*, Stuttgart,

January 1965

———

"Deschner . . . is mercilessly honest. . . . His presentation makes demands on critical readers but above all those who always get agitated by the discrepancy between the words and deeds of Jesus on the one hand and the words and deeds of his disciples and church on the other. Deschner deserves thanks for holding up this mirror in front of the Christians. We would not recommend putting it to one side. Looking into it would be more honest."

—student priest Martin Stöhr, *Weg und Wahrheit* [*Path and Truth*],

Evangelisches Kirchenblatt für Hessen, Frankfurt, July 21, 1963

———

"Deschner comes from the Catholic Church and accordingly had a much further and more difficult way to the Gospel than a Protestant would have, especially one who has been familiar with academic Bible and dogma criticism since his youth. This was all alien to Deschner, which is why he had to fight for it—also internally—which was good for his book because it was not satisfied with great lines like ours but had to explain everything thoroughly right down to the last details. I am therefore left with no choice but to refer my readers to it at the end of my book."

—The priest Dr. Adolph Seeger, author of *Staatsgott oder Gottesstaat? Eine religionssoziologische Untersuchung*, 1965

*"The author, undoubtedly a good stylist, aims to write in a way under-
standable to everyone and requires nothing but interest and love of
historical truth. And indeed, the book is very readable and remains
lucid, not least because of its frequently individual and also ironic
subheadings, despite its length. But above all the author proves what
he says by means of* immense utilization of sources and literature.
*Although it was impossible to check the vast amount of evidence piece
by piece individually, samples did prove the reliability of the information. The form of quotation is also . . . correct. Furthermore, the
author also had his work checked by several theologians before it was
published. So I must urgently warn anyone who considers viewing the
book as an academically 'cheap' publication."*
   —Prof. Dr. Richard Völkl, Caritas, Freiburg, December 1963

*"He [Deschner] has drawn a picture of the thoughts, words and deeds
of Christianity composed of an immense amount of information,
secured this picture with careful literary references and finally aimed
the entire behemoth of his work like a monstrous cannon on the present-
day Catholic Church, to the extent that this church will require an
army of specialists to defend its entire two-thousand-year history."*
   —Father Max Schoch, *Neue Zürcher Zeitung*, August 8, 1963

*"This book is the fulfillment of a necessity, a turn to the truth and libera-
tion from the old and fateful error that burdens the whole of Occidental
[Western] humanity, so that we can finally move freely again and ask the
question of what good is and what values we should be aiming to have. . . .
In this light, Deschner forces modern Christianity to undertake a reformation and a new Qumran 'without temples' and a cult of pure spirit. In this
way, Deschner's book is an entirely unprecedented kind of Church history;
a testament of immense erudition and years of devoted hard work . . .
a passionate confirmation of the statement of the Danish Reformer Sören
Kierkegaard: the Christianity of the New Testament is not here at all!"*
   —Pastor Hermann Raschke, *Die Pforte*, 1963

ABERMALS KRÄHTE DER HAHN AS REVIEWED BY RATIONALISTS AND FREE RELIGIOUS

"The book proves clearly and immaculately that the freedom, humanity and human dignity, peace and safety of the individual and community alike have only been obtained by the opponents of Christianity and the Church against the Church and the clerical states. Everyone should own a copy of what is the most important new publication of the 20th century!"

—*Mitteilungsblatt der Freireligiösen Landesgemeinde Bayern*, March 1963

———

"It is to his particular credit that Deschner thoroughly illuminates the role of the Church in the political problems of our century. . . . An indispensable book for every rationalist."

—Dr. Dr. Josef Rattner, *Freidenker*, Zürich, June 1963

———

"Deschner has given us a handbook of the historical and ethical criticism of Christianity that is unrivaled in the 20th century."

—Dr. Friedrich Pzillas, *Die Freigeistige Aktion*, Hanover, February 1963

———

"A fundamental book that gives a unique and comprehensive criticism of the Church!"

—*Freies Denken*, Dortmund, February 1963

———

"Only a man of outstanding learning could have written this book. . . . It is undoubtedly to the credit of the author that he has written a church history with admirable application that takes up its task from this otherwise unusual viewpoint. Since he clearly presents all lines of development—dogmatic, cultic, organizational, ecclesio-political and social—and writes excitingly and comprehensibly to all,

everyone who is interested in the question of how the Church came
about, has the opportunity to obtain an objective picture."

—*Der Freireligiöse*, Ludwigshafen, April 1963

<hr>

"If the reader wishes to form a sound judgment about this multifaceted
subject, he should read Deschner's book and I guarantee he will learn a
great deal from it."

—*Europäische Freimaurerzeitung*, Strasbourg, January 1964

OTHER REVIEWS

"If a book has . . . a subject that is so central in cultural terms, a presenta-
tion that is so temptingly clear and exciting, such a fascinating style with
a calm, modest, elegant prose that is never man-of-letters intellectual,
combined with splendidly passionate objective intolerance and complete
honesty, then one can only say that this book is absolutely essential for
any spiritual person. That is meant very seriously, very literally. This is
the first *great* current criticism *of* truly *valid and* real *Christianity."*

—Dr. Kurt Port, *Die Pforte*, 1963

<hr>

"Deschner's achievement is above all the writing of a critique of the
Churches, primarily the Roman Church, from a moral and political
viewpoint, that is unprecedented in its openness, implacability, aca-
demic thoroughness and width. . . . A shining theoretical performance
and, what is more, a social and political act."

—*Blätter für deutsche und internationale Politik*,
Cologne, April 1964

<hr>

"Comprehensive source and literature studies, couple with the will
for honesty and clarity, made this outstanding work possible. . . . The
German public, indeed, the world public, will not be able to ignore this
'J'accuse.'"

—*Forschungsfragen unserer Zeit*, March–April 1963

"A compendium of the sins and depravities of the ancient and medieval Church which is unique in its detail. The author has spent five years of admirable assiduity coming to grips with the sources and presentations of history."

—*Der Bund*, Bern, May 31, 1963

"Undoubtedly a symptomatic event for the era of the second Enlightenment, on whose threshold we stand according to Ernesto Grassi."

—*Nachrichten der Evangelisch-Lutherischen Kirche in Bayern*, first issue, July 1963

"This is the most important book by a young author who is definitely on the side of Ormuzd that has been brought to light in Germany since 1945. . . . A book in the spirit of Reuchlin and Voltaire, Nietzsche and Freud."

—Wolfgang Beutin, *Lynx*, Hamburg, May 1963

"Why is nobody sounding the alarm? Because this is theology that has, out of academic consequence, more consistently and advanced than even David Friedrich Strauß, changed into anti-theology. . . . The challenge is immense when one picks up this compendium, that much should be clear in advance."

—*Zeit geschehen*, July 1963

"A phenomenon of our time of the first order . . . it is tremendous and outrageous material that Deschner disseminates here. . . . The sharpness of the diction, the hardness of the judgment and the condemnation of historical Christianity in Deschner's Church history are centered here: Karlheinz Deschner is convinced that leading Christians, laymen, theologians and men of the Church, desire and are consciously active in preparing the Third World War just as much as they did the First and Second World Wars. The evidence he provides

*for the Christian, spiritual and political preparation for nuclear war
cannot simply be pushed aside by turning the page."*
—Prof. Dr. Friedrich Heer, *Süddeutscher Rundfunk*,
August 11, 1963

---

*"The accusations made against Pope Pius XII by the author Hochhuth
are almost petty compared with those leveled by Dr. Deschner at the
head of the Catholic Church for the period of the Second World War."*
—*Braunschweiger Presse*, February 27, 1964

---

*"In former times Deschner would have been burned at the stake for
this book."*
—Gerhard Zwerenz, *Twen*, Munich, April 1963

---

*"It is an overwhelming book, a constant waterfall of documents,
quotations and facts . . . , a work of great topicality and far-reaching
significance."*
—Radio Hilversum, June 5, 1963

---

*"No diatribes, no unfounded suspicions and no empty collection of
words, as one would usually, sadly, expect from products with similar
themes all too often. Deschner has retraced the path of Christianity
from Nazareth to modern times critically but dispassionately. . . .
Broad circles in Germany will not like what Deschner says. His concerns will be rejected as unfounded and he will be presented as a quib-
bler or troublemaker. They will mainly be angry with him because he
addresses the layman. A well-known Church historian put it like this:
'If the book were only for bishops, priests or theologians, then I would
say: excellent!' But as it is, Deschner lets the simple believer know
what has been known to the clergy for a long time, and they will really
hold that against him."*
—*Der Mittag*, Düsseldorf, March 16, 1963

———

"His method is compiled academically, unrhetorical, aimed at the plethora of facts and written with a view to unchallengeable foundation by sources and evidence. Everything that can be objected to about the Church and its manifestation has been compiled and designed in a clear form."

—*Österreichischer Rundfunk*, March 18, 1963

———

"As a whole, Deschner's presentation remains watertight. . . . This work will meet with a lot of resistance but will be able to assert itself thanks to its internal truthfulness."

—*Neues Winterthurer Tagblatt*, March 2, 1963

———

"The first thing anyone will want to do after reading this book is to thank Karlheinz Deschner for the courage he has written it with and for the seemingly infinite work that has been put into it. . . . It is quite amazing how a Catholic 'layman' has also worked through the whole mass of Protestant church and dogma history research without getting buried in it. It is precisely the distance of the 'layman' that sharpens the view of the fall from the spiritual basis upon which the Church and Christianity arose. Deschner's book is a 'critical' Church history that has a radical quality that has not been seen since the days of Gottfried Arnold."

—*Freies Christentum*, Frankfurt, September 1964

———

"Demonstrations against a book like Deschner's work signify nothing at all. . . . Deschner is a pupil of Friedrich Nietzsche, the greatest German thinker of the nineteenth century, let us not forget that, and anyone who attempts to reject books like Deschner's to any degree is the one who causes damage and never a book like this Church history."

—Bernard von Brentano, *Rhein-Neckar- Zeitung*,
Heidelberg, April 2, 1963

NOTES

Authors of whom only one work has been used are mentioned only by name in the following. The titles of their respective works are listed in the bibliography.

CHAPTER 1: THE VATICAN AND ITALIAN FASCISM

1. Manhattan, German edition, 111.

2. Tondi, Die Jesuiten [The Jesuits], 73 ff.

3. Quotation in Gontard, 253.

4. Mark 6:8 f.

5. Matt. 10:10; Luke 9:3, 10:4.

6. Luke 12:33, 14:33; also cf. Luke 16:9, 16, 11, 6:24 ff., 16:19 ff., 1:52 f.; Mark 10:25. For the position of Jesus: Deschner, 410 ff.

7. Troeltsch, 49.

8. Acts 4:32–35, also cf. 2:42 ff. For the tendency to idealize the apostles' story: Heussi, Der Ursprung des Mönchtums [The Origins of Monasticism], 19 f.; Pöhlmann II, 483; Haenchen, Die Apostelgeschichte [The History of the Apostles], 191 ff. But Lohmeyer writes in Galiläa und Jerusalem [Galilee and Jerusalem], 65 f.: "The sacrifice of all possessions is the absolute duty of original Christian faith." Also cf. Gottesknecht and Davidson, 138. And also in this respect Troeltsch, 50, and cf. Kautsky, Der Ursprung des Christentums [The Origins of Christianity], 347 ff.

9. Cyprian op. et al. 25. St. Basil, see in particular his sermon given at the time of a famine and drought, c. 8.

10. Joh. Chrys. hom. in ep. 1 ad Ti. 12, 3 f. For the communist preaching of the Early Fathers, cf. Deschner, 414 ff.

11. Kautsky, Geschichte des Sozialismus I [The History of Socialism I], 34.

12. For details, see Deschner, 493 ff., especially 506 ff. Ude is important.

13. cf. "The Destruction of Paganism" and "The Fight against the 'Heretics'" in Deschner, 465 ff. and 471 ff.

14. The church may have kept slaves for the longest. cf. in particular Troeltsch, 355 ff.

15. Heussi, Kompendium [Compendium], 110.

16. Theiner, I., 146 f.

17. C. Schneider, II., 269, with reference to Euseb. h. e. 10, 6 f.; Joh. Chrysost. in Act. hom. 18, 4; also cf. Tondi, Die Jesuiten [The Jesuits], 50 f.

18. cf. in particular "Why Jesus Cannot Have Founded a Church" and "The Beginnings of the Papacy," in Deschner, 213 ff. and 243 ff.

19. cf. esp. Haller, Das Papsttum [The Papacy], 388 ff. Heiler, Altkirchliche Autonomie [Old Church Autonomy], 235ff., 276.

20. Heiler, Altkirchliche Autonomie [Old Church Autonomy], 239.

21. Heiler, Der Katholizimus [Catholicism], 297; also cf. Altkirchliche Autonomie [Old Church Autonomy], 236.

22. Neues Münchener Tagblatt, February 15, 1929.

23. cf. p. 188 ff. I write in more detail on this in the anthology Das Jahrhundert der Barbarei [The Century of Barbarism], published by Desch in Munich in 1966. Winter, II, 425 ff. is important.

24. Münchener Telegramm-Zeitung, February 8/9, 1929. Deutsches Volksblatt, February 27, 1929. For the justification of the mistrust cf. Winter, II., 582.

25. Münchener Telegramm-Zeitung, February 8/9, 1929.

26. cf. Winter, II., 608 f.

27. Hamburger Fremdenblatt, February 12, 1929, Deutsches Volksblatt, February 13, 1929.

28. Kurella, 252.

29. Allgemeine Rundschau, Munich, February 23, 1929.

30. Paris, The Vatican, 69.

31. Neisser Zeitung, March 12, 1929.

32. Borgese, 175.

33. Kurella, 252.

34. Borgese, 287.

35. Allgemeine Rundschau, Munich, February 23, 1929.

36. Neisser Zeitung, March 12, 1929.

37. Ibid.

38. cf. Benito Mussolini, VII., 30 ff.

39. Ibid., 33 and 107; also cf. 96 and others.

40. Sieben, 394.

41. Borgese, 175.

42. Rumpelstilzchen, 13.

43. Paris, The Vatican, 69.

44. Neues Münchener Tagblatt, February 16, 1929.

45. Mussolini, 123.

46. cf. Borgese, 293.

47. Germania, February 12, 1929; also cf. Mussolini, VII., 76.

48. Nitti, 10.

49. Ibid., 31.

50. Paris, The Vatican, 97.

51. Ibid.

52. Ibid.

53. cf. Borgese, 227 f. It is a pleasure to read this book, which is steeped in wonderful mockery.

54. Manhattan, German edition, 104.

55. Ibid.

56. January 13, 1928.

57. February 13, 1929.

58. Manhattan, 112 ff.

59. cf. table in Deschner, 432 ff. For more information, see Mohrmann, 52 f.

60. Ibid. See also Breza, 544 ff.

61. Manhattan, 112 ff.

62. Ibid.

63. Ibid.

64. Ibid.

65. If any village voted socialist, armed Fascists would surround it very quickly, round up the men of voting age, bind their trousers together at the bottom, drip castor oil into them, and have them walk around in double time for an hour and a half. Castor oil flowed so plentifully at that time that the shortage hiked up its cost in Italy, which supplied the whole world with it. But afterward, the revolution took a victorious path in hundreds of villages. "Every resistance was broken with castor oil." Rumpelstilzchen, 38 f.

66. Borgese, 248.

67. Nitti, 38 f.

68. cf. e.g., Allgemeine Rundschau, February 23, 1929, 130.

69. According to Nitti, 38.

70. Manhattan, 115.

71. Augsburger Postzeitung, September 1929.

72. Article 20.

73. Claar, 64.

74. Augsburger Postzeitung, September 20, 1929.

75. Ibid.

76. Bayerischer Kurier, February 20, 1929.

77. Mussolini, VII., 78.

78. Ibid., 87. According to the Bayerischer Kurier of February 20, 1929, "one hundred and nineteen times"; according to others, two hundred times.

79. Mussolini, 87.

80. Dresdner Anzeiger, March 14, 1929; also cf. Kurella, 250 ff.

81. Dresdner Anzeiger, March 14, 1929.

82. Ibid.

83. Tondi, Die geheime Macht [The Secret Power], 34, and Die Jesuiten [The Jesuits], 73; Manhattan, 118.

84. Augsburger Postzeitung, February 20, 1929, and February 22, 1929.

85. Deutsches Volksblatt, March 11, 1929.

86. Manhattan, 118.

87. cf. note 26.

88. Bayerischer Kurier, February 19, 1929.

89. Altkatholisches Volksblatt, March 29, 1929.

90. Münchner Zeitung, February 13, 1929.

91. Bayerischer Kurier, February 16, 1929.

92. Ibid.

93. Allgemeine Rundschau, Munich, February 23, 1929.

94. Ibid.

95. Germania, Berlin, February 12, 1929.

96. Ibid., February 19, 1929.

97. Völkischer Beobachter, February 22, 1929.

98. Ibid., February 21, 1929; February 27, 1929; and others.

99. Quotation in ibid., February 21, 1929.

100. Ibid.

101. Ibid., also cf. February 27, 1929.

102. Ibid.

103. Ibid., February 22, 1929.

104. Ibid.

105. I demonstrate to what incredible grotesqueness this leads in my Church history, 265 ff.

106. Manhattan, German edition, 111.

107. Schwäbischer Merkur, April 24, 1932; also cf. Borgese, 295.

108. Ibid. Officially, however, the reasons given for Pacelli's award were "apolitical."

109. Manhattan, 120. With reference to New York Times, January 20, 1938, and T. L. Gardini.

110. Quotations in Der romfreie Katholik [The Rome-Free Catholic], February 2, 1936.

111. Friedländer, 17.

112. On this cf. Stimmen der Zeit, vol. 67, no. 132, 107 f.

113. Ibid.

114. Deutsche Freiheit, 1936, vol. 5, no. 12.

115. Schönere Zukunft, June 7, 1936, 943.

116. Germania, April 5, 1936.

117. Schönere Zukunft, June 7, 1936, 943.

118. According to Stimmen der Zeit, vol. 67, no. 132, 107.

119. Klein, 53.

120. Siebert, 32.

121. Manhattan, 121 ff. The speech is printed in Reichspost, Vienna, August 30, 1935.

122. Reichspost, Vienna, August 30, 1935.

123. Salzburger Chronik, September 6, 1935.

124. Manhattan, 121 f.

125. Ibid.

126. June 7, 1936.

127. December 8, 1935.

128. Reichspost, Vienna, June 30, 1935. Schönere Zukunft, March 15, 1936, and many others.

129. Buchheit, 395 f.

130. Linzer Volksblatt, December 3, 1935.

131. cf. Germania, December 1, 1935; also Frankfurter Volksblatt, November 30, 1935.

132. Germania, December 3, 1935.

133. Ibid.

134. Salzburger Chronik, December 20, 1935.

135. cf. Germania, December 1, 1935.

136. Borgese, 400. And they indemnified themselves later in Abyssinia and stole and plundered what was most worth stealing and plundering: imperial thrones, imperial crowns, imperial coaches, imperial sabers, imperial cutlery, including many heavy gold pieces and others that were bejeweled. And thirty years later, in early 1965, they were even prepared to give some of it back. cf. Frankfurter Allgemeine, April 17, 1965.

137. Germania, December 9, 1935.

138. Linzer Volksblatt, October 17, 1935.

139. Kirchenzeitung, Salzburg, October 24, 1935.

140. Manhattan, 121 ff.

141. Tondi, Die geheime Macht [The Secret Power], 36.

142. Werner, 205.

143. Manhattan, 123.

144. For the heathen origin of the Blessed Mother, the history of the Marian cult and the origins of the dogmas of her virginity, immaculate conception, and bodily ascension, cf. Deschner, 360 ff.

145. Goethe, diary, October 8, 1786.

146. Höcht, 85 f.

147. Miller, Informationsdienst zur Zeitgeschichte [Information Service on Contemporary History], Leonberg-Stuttgart, 9, 1962.

148. Höcht, 23 f. and 61.

149. Deschner, 367.

150. Höcht, 25.

151. Ibid., 29.

152. Ibid., 30 ff.

153. Ibid., 33 f.

154. Ibid., 38 f.

155. Which was, however, called such only by Pius V's successor, Pope Gregory XIII, ibid., 42.

156. Ibid., 48 ff.

157. Ibid.

158. Ibid., 57, 61 f.

159. cf. esp. 12 f. and 114, and others.

160. Ibid., 114 f.

161. Ibid.

162. Ibid.

163. Ibid.

164. Ibid., 85 f.

165. Illustration in Becker, 103.

166. Manhattan, 121 ff.

167. Basler Nachrichten, vol. 92, no. 10. There, on the front page, is the picture of the prelate, the Madonna, and the Fascists.

168. Germania, April 5, 1936; also cf. Deutsche Freiheit, 1936, vol. 5, no. 12.

169. Borgese, 400.

170. Germania and Schwäbischer Merkur, Stuttgart, March 1, 1936. Afterward, telegrams of homage were sent to the king, Mussolini, and the pope, tellingly in Pacelli's presence.

171. According to Borgese, 398.

172. Quotation in ibid., 296.

173. Manhattan, German edition, 116.

CHAPTER 2: THE VATICAN AND THE SPANISH CIVIL WAR

1. Manhattan, German edition, 89 ff.

2. Duff, 74.

3. Quotation in Deutsche Freiheit, vol. 6, no. 10.

4. cf. Deschner, 453 f.

5. Troeltsch, 350, note 160.

6. Dahms, 302, note 7.

7. Ibid.

8. Ibid., 302 f., notes 8 and 9.

9. Thomas, 45.

10. Manhattan, 88. For the massive land possessions, the share ownership, and the capital of the Catholic Church in general, cf. Deschner, 429 ff. Materialreich Mohrmann.

11. Duff, 109.

12. Ibid.

13. Deutsche Freiheit, vol. 5, no. 29.

14. Thomas, 55.

15. Ibid.

16. Ibid.

17. Neue Zürcher Zeitung, no. 1413, 1936.

18. Blätter aus Spanien [Letters from Spain], June 1936.

19. Der Bund, Bern, September 12, 1936.

20. Germania, August 27, 1936.

21. Ibid., September 15, 1936.

22. Timmermanns, 22.

23. Die Welt, October 18, 1956.

24. Manhattan, 87.

25. Ibid.

26. Thomas, 45.

27. Quotation in Manhattan, German edition, 84.

28. Ibid., 81.

29. Trend, J. B., 61.

30. Schweizerische Republikanische Blätter, July 10, 1937.

31. Quotation in Deutsche Freiheit, vol. 5, no. 32, 1936.

32. Ibid., vol. 6, no. 10.

33. Ecclesia militans, Rome, Vienna, Lucerne, August 1936.

34. Katholisches Kirchenblatt, Berlin, June 14, 1936. But it tellingly seeks to exonerate those who bore primary guilt: the bishops.

35. Entscheidung, Luzern, October 15, 1936. Honest.

36. Linzer Volksblatt, August 22, 1936. Otherwise hypocritical and mendacious.

37. Quotation in Katholisches Kirchenblatt, Berlin, June 14, 1936.

38. Reichspost, Vienna, September 15, 1936.

39. Manhattan, 88.

40. Brenan, 53.

41. Thomas, 51.

42. Ibid., 65.

43. Ibid.

44. Ibid., 66.

45. cf. Keller, 135 f.

46. Völkischer Beobachter, May 9, 1935.

47. Schweizerische Rundschau, no. 8, 1939, 559.

48. Thomas, 42.

49. Detwiler, 2.

50. Fernsworth, 131.

51. Detwiler, 3.

52. Manhattan, 91.

53. Ibid.

54. Ibid.

[55. Thomas, 66f.]

56. Longo, 12 f.

57. Quotation in Reichspost, Vienna, December 21, 1936.

58. cf. the letters printed in the Grazer Volksblatt of December 6, 1936.

59. Völkischer Beobachter, May 9, 1935.

60. Ibid.

61. Thomas, 81.

62. Völkischer Beobachter, May 9, 1935.

63. Thomas, 150 f.

64. Scheinmann, 274, with reference to Current History, June 1942.

65. cf. the foreword by the Duchess of Atholl in A. Koestler, 8.

66. Deutsche Freiheit, vol. 5, no. 28, 1936.

67. Thomas, 79 f.

68. Ibid.

69. Longo, 14.

70. Thomas, 73.

71. Ibid.

72. The [London] Times, February 17, 1936.

73. Manhattan, German edition, 88; and National-Zeitung, Basel, September 28, 1937.

74. Blätter aus Spanien [Letters from Spain], June 1936, quoted in Deutsche Freiheit, vol. 5, no. 28.; cf. also the statement made by the republican Spanish minister of justice in the National-Zeitung, Basel, September 28, 1937.

75. Manhattan, German edition, 88.

76. Thomas, 72.

77. Blätter aus Spanien [Letters from Spain], June 1936. Quotation in Deutsche Freiheit, vol. 5, no. 28.

78. Thomas, 89.

79. National-Zeitung, Basel, September 28, 1937; also cf. Timmermanns 12.

80. Quotation in Detwiler, 12.

81. Duff, 24.

82. Bob Edwards, MP, in Konkret, October 1, 1960.

83. Quotation in Dahms, 249.

84. Detwiler, 6 f.

85. cf. ibid., 8; also M. Merkes, 170.

86. Siebert, 52.

87. Longo.

88. Thomas, 183 f.

89. Ibid.

90. Ibid., 216.

91. Ibid., 135.

92. Ibid., 194.

93. Beumelburg, 22 ff., 36. Dahms, 101.

94. Thomas, 185.

95. According to Dahms, 145.

96. Thomas, 186.

97. Ibid.

98. Duff, 23.

99. Stuttgarter Zeitung, February 28, 1963.

100. For further information, see Beumelburg, 56 ff.

101. Thomas, 263.

102. Ibid., 196.

103. Longo, 28.

104. Thomas, 202.

105. Longo, 28.

106. Dahms, 154.

107. Duff, 23.

108. Thomas, 259 f.

109. Ibid., 259.

110. Ibid., 423.

111. Detwiler, F.

112. Thomas, 227.

113. Dahms, 193.

114. Thomas, 229.

115. Siebert, 52.

116. Thomas, 259.

117. Dahms, 136 f.

118. Detwiler, 148.

119. Ibid., 131 ff.

120. Thomas, 472.

121. Manhattan, German edition, 98.

122. Dahms, 285.

123. Detwiler, 144.

124. Manhattan, German edition, 98.

125. Quotation in Thomas, 230 f.

126. Bley, 36.

127. Ibid., 38. The style of books of this nature is emetic; also cf. Deutsche kämpfen in Spanien [Germans Fighting in Spain], published by Legion Condor, 461.–485. T., 1940.

128. Thomas, 238.

129. Ibid., 242.

130. Longo, 26.

131. Duff, 147.

132. Manhattan, 92.

133. Germania, February 25, 1937.

134. Ibid., January 30, 1937.

135. Ibid., August 27, 1936.

136. cf. and others, ibid. April 19, 1937, and August 5, 1937.

137. Bates, 24.

138. Duff, 147.

139. Thomas, 89.

140. Duff, 147.

141. National-Zeitung, Basel, September 28, 1937.

142. Ibid.

143. Quotation in Deutsche Freiheit, vol. 6, no. 10.

144. Ibid., 9, 1937.

145. National-Zeitung, Basel, March 31, 1937.

146. Ibid.

147. Ibid.

148. Ibid., September 23, 1937.

149. Ibid., January 16, 1939.

150. Thomas, 268.

151. Duff, 72.

152. Germania, April 19, 1937.

153. Dahms, 313.

154. National-Zeitung, Basel, July 2, 1938.

155. The bishop of the northern Spanish diocese of Pamplona; cf. Salzburger Chronik, September 22, 1936.

156. The bishop of Gerona, Cartana Ingles; cf. Die Ostschweiz, January 10, 1939.

157. Grazer Volksblatt, January 30, 1937.

158. J. Overmanns, Zwei Kriege im heutigen Spanien [Two Wars in Today's Spain], Stimmen der Zeit, vol. 68, no. 134.

159. Salzburger Chronik, November 16, 1936.

160. A. R. Villaplana, Questo è Franco, 1945, 139 ff. Quotation according to Tondi, Die Jesuiten [The Jesuits], 76 f.

161. National-Zeitung, Basel, September 28, 1937.

162. Reichspost, Vienna, August 28, 1936.

163. Ibid., September 3, 1936.

164. Ibid.

165. Kirchliches Amtsblatt für die Diözese Münster [Official Church Gazette of the Diocese of Münster], no. 21.

166. Ibid., no. 34. Emphasis by the author.

167. cf. Deschner, 434 f.

168. Ibid.

169. Linzer Volksblatt, July 30, 1937.

170. Ibid. Emphasis by the author.

171. For details, see Deschner, 334 ff.

172. cf. Germania, February 3, 1937.

173. Neue Basler Zeitung, March 1, 1937.

174. Thomas, 144.

175. Deschner, 489.

176. Thomas, 145.

177. Dahms, 122.

178. Thomas, 131.

179. cf. Stimmen der Zeit, vol. 68, no. 134, 407 f.

180. Madariaga, 377.

181. According to Thomas, 144.

182. National-Zeitung, Basel, September 28, 1937.

183. Grazer Volksblatt, August 15, 1937.

184. For the lack of love of truth of his successor, Pacelli, too, cf. Deschner, 429 ff.

185. Germania, August 5, 1937.

186. Deutsche Freiheit, vol. 6, no. 10.

187. National-Zeitung, Basel, February 4, 1938.

188. Emphasis by the author.

189. cf. Deschner, 515 ff.

190. Germania, January 30, 1937.

191. Deschner, 518.

192. Entscheidung [Decision], October 15, 1936.

193. A. Koestler, 13.

194. Grazer Volksblatt, January 30, 1932. Nero did not persecute the Christians as such at all. This was only an arson trial; "Christianity," as the theologian Carl Schneider says in his outstanding Spiritual History of Ancient Christianity, "played no part in the discussion at all." cf. Deschner, 336 f. For the Diocletian persecution, see Deschner, 339 ff.

195. Duff, 22.

196. Thomas, 278.

197. Dahms, 157. Thomas, 139.

198. Dahms, 157.

199. Ibid., 119 f.

200. Ibid.

201. Thomas, 197.

202. Quotation in Deutsche Freiheit, vol. 5, no. 32, 1936.

203. Das große Kirchenblatt, Vienna, December 13, 1936.

204. Thomas, 150.

205. Deutsche Freiheit, vol. 5, no. 34, 1936.

206. Ibid., vol. 5, no. 29. Shortly afterward, it was hit by a bomb.

207. Keding, 27.

208. Deutsche Freiheit, vol. 5, no. 34, 1936.

209. Ibid.

210. Ibid.

211. Ibid.

212. Dahms, 419 f., Echo der Zeit [Echo of the Times], May 18, 1958.

213. Duff, 73.

214. Ibid.

215. Ibid., 112.

216. Germania, August 5, 1937.

217. Thomas, 141.

218. Ibid.

219. Stuttgarter Zeitung, February 28, 1963.

220. An oral communication from Edmond Paris to me.

221. Coles, 92.

222. Schweizerische Republikanische Blätter, October 31, 1936.

223. Quotation in Grazer Mittag, February 17, 1937.

224. Linzer Volksblatt, September 28, 1936.

225. Manhattan, 95 ff.

226. Germania, August 5, 1937.

227. Manhattan, German edition, 92, and Neue Zürcher Zeitung, September 15, 1936.

228. cf. Germania, August 5, 1937.

229. Corsten, 162.

230. Thomas, 216.

231. Duff, 26.

232. Ibid., 24.

233. With close reference to Duff, 19 ff.

234. Ibid.

235. Thomas, 218.

236. Coles, 92.

237. Manhattan, German edition, 96.

238. For more detail, see Duff, 75 ff.

239. Thomas, 130.

240. Neue Basler Zeitung, January 4, 1937.

241. Detwiler, 13 f.

242. Ibid., 14.

243. Thomas, 216.

244. Ibid., 374.

245. Manhattan, 99.

246. Ibid.

247. Quotation in Tondi, Die Jesuiten [The Jesuits], 80 f.

248. Ibid.

249. National-Zeitung, Basel, July 2, 1938.

250. Neue Züricher Zeitung, April 30, 1938.

251. Basler Nachrichten, April 3, 1939.

252. Neue Zürcher Zeitung, April 30, 1938.

253. Basler Nachrichten, June 12, 1939.

254. Ibid.

255. Bates, 29.

256. National-Zeitung, Basel, April 17, 1939.

257. Dahms, 276.

258. National-Zeitung, Basel, April 17, 1939.

259. Ciano's diplomatic papers, 1948, 293f.

260. Duff, 27.

261. Konkret, October 1, 1960.

262. Manhattan, 100. Duff, 34 ff.

263. Duff, 27 and 37.

264. Ibid.

265. Ibid., 28.

266. Ibid., 18.

267. Feis, 269.

268. Detwiler, 10.

269. cf. J. Overmans, SJ, in Stimmen der Zeit, vol. 67, no. 131, 108.

270. Katholisches Kirchenblatt, June 24, 1938.

271. Thomas, 139.

272. Duff, 17.

273. Ibid., 14.

274. Ibid., 13.

275. Ibid., 16.

276. Konkret, October 1, 1960, 7.

277. Duff, 68.

CHAPTER 3: THE VATICAN AND HITLER'S GERMANY

1. Von Papen, Der 12. November 1933 [November 12, 1933], 5.

2. For details, see Manhattan, 138 ff., which I am following here.

3. Fest, 220. On the following, apart from Fest, see 209 ff. Gisevius, 144 ff. Glum, 180 ff.

4. Glum, 180, with reference to von Rimelen, The Dark Invader.

5. Picker, 396.

6. A. François-Poncet, Souvenirs d'une ambassade à Berlin [Memories from a Berlin Embassy], 1946, 42 f. I quote here from Glum, 180 f.

7. Das Urteil von Nürnberg [The Nuremberg Verdict], 26.

8. Der Neue Herder [The New Herder], 1949.

9. Fest, 215.

10. Goebbels, 152.

11. Glum, 199 f. Von Papen disputed Schröder's version in Nuremberg.

12. Goebbels, 42 f.

13. Hallgarten, 110 and footnote 92.

14. Ibid.; also Glum, 198.

15. Glum, 207.

16. Das Urteil von Nürnberg 1946 [The Nuremberg Verdict of 1946], dtv. Documents vol. 8, 1961, 275.

17. Von Papen, 7 f. Emphasis by the author.

18. cf. S. Einstein, Herrn von Papens Pension [Mr. von Papen's Pension], Die Andere Zeitung, Hamburg, April 19, 1962.

19. Ibid.

20. Das Urteil von Nürnberg [The Nuremberg Verdict], 275 f.

21. Ibid., 244.

22. S. Einstein, Herrn von Papens Pension [Mr. von Papen's Pension], Die Andere Zeitung, April 19, 1962.

23. Ibid.

24. cf. the explanation in Das Urteil von Nürnberg [The Nuremberg Verdict], 274 ff.

25. Von Papen, Der Wahrheit eine Gasse [A Path for the Truth], 302.

26. Gisevius, 191.

27. Miller, I. D., 3/1963, 10.

28. Gisevius, 189.

29. Theodor Heuss, Die Zitate [The Quotations], p. 25, 3 f., 5, 18, 121, 123, 119, 130, 14, 109, 22, 4, 6, 124, 27.

30. Bundestag protocol dated June 11, 1949. Quotation in Miller, I. D., 12/1962, 1.

31. Kölnische Volkszeitung, October 19, 1917, quotation according to Miller, I. D., August 1964, 3. Emphasis by the author.

32. Kölnische Volkszeitung, October 19, 1917.

33. Quotation in A. Miller, I. D., August 1964, 3f.

34. Ibid., 1, 1962, 7 f.

35. First quotation from a telephone conversation between Kaas from the Vatican on July 2 or 3 with Centre leader J. Joos in Matthias/Morsey, 398. For the second quotation, see Manhattan, 175.

36. Matthias/Morsey, 370.

37. Lewy, 75.

38. Quotation in Spiegel, November 18, 1964, 117.

39. Quotation in Manhattan, 175.

40. Shuster, 188.

41. Gisevius, 190.

42. Stimmen der Zeit, 1960, 426.

43. Report from the Bavarian envoy at the Holy See, cf. Lewy, 70.

44. Von Papen, Der Wahrheit eine Gasse [A Path for the Truth], 314.

45. Matthias/Morsey, 379.

46. Fleischer, Das Schanddokument des Konkordats von 1933 [Fleischer, The 1933 Concordat: A Scandalous Document], Das Andere Deutschland [The Other Germany], September 18, 1959.

47. Görlitz, Hitler, 88 f.

48. Glum, 209.

49. Ibid., 210.

50. cf. Anger, 17, 24. Görlitz, Hitler, 91. Glum, 212.

51. Glum, 216.

52. Glum, 210. Görlitz, Hitler, 93.

53. Anger, 55.

54. Görlitz, Hitler, 94. Glum, 230. For details see Ball-Kaduri.

55. Fleischer, Das Schanddokument des Konkordats von 1933 [Fleischer, The 1933 Concordat: A Scandalous Document].

56. Görlitz, Hitler, 97.

57. Fleischer, Das Schanddokument des Konkordats von 1933 [Fleischer, The 1933 Concordat: A Scandalous Document].

58. Spiegel, November 18, 1964.

59. Binder, 234.

60. For details see Deschner, 442–464.

61. Quotation in Fleischer, Das Schanddokument des Konkordats von 1933 [Fleischer, The 1933 Concordat: A Scandalous Document].

62. Hitler, 379, 631.

63. Picker, 289.

64. Völkischer Beobachter, July 24, 1933. Emphasis by the author.

65. Binder, 244 f.

66. Ibid.

67. Quotation in Fleischer, Das Schanddokument des Konkordats von 1933 [Fleischer, The 1933 Concordat: A Scandalous Document].

68. Amtsblatt für die Erzdiözese München und Freising [Official Gazette of the Archdiocese of Munich and Freising], 1936, no. 6, Supplement II. Emphasis by the author.

69. Ibid. Emphasis by the author.

70. Neuhäusler, II., 26.

71. Lewy 30 f., 70.

72. Fleischer, Das Schanddokument des Konkordats von 1933 [Fleischer, The 1933 Concordat: A Scandalous Document].

73. Deschner, 587.

74. cf. e.g., Schmaus, 7; Bates, 39.

75. Wucher, A., Der politische Katholizismus 1933 vor Hitlers Karren gespannt [Political Catholicism in 1933 Exploited by Hitler], Süddeutsche Zeitung, August 1961. On this, cf. R. Leiber, SJ, Reichskonkordat und Ende der Zentrumspartei [The Reich Concordat and the End of the Centre Party], Stimmen der Zeit, 1960/61, 217.

76. Dirks, 242.

77. Allgemeine Rundschau, April 19, 1933, no. 16, 243.

78. Lewy, 47.

79. Dirks, 246.

80. Amtsblatt für die Erzdiözese Bamberg [Official Gazette of the Archdiocese of Bamberg], vol. 56, 1933, March 28, 1933, no. 11, 83.

81. Heldt, 168 f.

82. Ibid.

83. Emphasis mostly by the author.

84. cf. H. Müller, Zur Behandlung des Kirchenkampfes in der Nachkriegsliteratur [On the Treatment of the Church Struggle in Postwar Literature], in Politische Studien [Political Studies], July 1961, 478 ff.

85. cf. Ibid., 477.

86. Ibid., 481.

87. Amtsblatt für die Erzdiözese Bamberg [Official Gazette of the Archdiocese of Bamberg], vol. 56, 1933, no. 13, May 5, 1933, p. 99 ff. Emphasis by the author.

88. Quotation in Fleischer, Der Mythos vom heiligen Widerstandskämpfer, Die "Generallinie" des Kardinals von Galen [The Myth of the Holy Resistance Fighter. The "General Line" of Cardinal von Galen], Die Andere Zeitung, December 13, 1956.

89. Lewy, 100.

90. Heldt, 169.

91. Ibid.

92. Ecclesiastica, vol. 13, 475.

93. Quotation in Schmaus, 7.

94. Ibid., 43 f.

95. Picker, 395 f.

96. Lewy, 103.

97. E. F. J. Müller, 76 f.

98. Ibid., 72 f.

99. Ibid., 78.

100. Unser Wille zur Tat [Our Will for Action], Zeit und Volk I., 181.

101. Augsburger Postzeitung, October 5, 1935.

102. Miller, I. D., 11/1962, 2, with reference to Wächter der Kirche [Guardians of the Church], with Church approval to print from the Episcopal Ordinariate, Munich, 1934.

103. Ibid.

104. H. Müller, 170 f.

105. Ibid.

106. Quotation in J. Fleischer, Noch einmal in den Abgrund [Into the Abyss Once Again], Das Andere Deutschland [The Other Germany], 16/56.

107. Lewy, 102.

108. Quotation in Miller, I. D., 8, 1964, 5.

109. Der Spiegel, March 7, 1962, 54.

110. Schmaus, 12 f., 21.

111. Ibid., 23, 31, 44.

112. Lortz, 5 f.

113. Ibid., 6, 15.

114. Ibid., 4, 9, 15, 26.

115. Ibid., 9 f.

116. Ibid., 5.

117. Frankfurter Allgemeine, July 29, 1964.

118. Pieper, 3.

119. Deutsches Volksblatt, January 23, 1934. Emphasis by the author.

120. Quotation in A. Miller, I. D., 3/1963, 6.

121. Germania, no. 306, November 6, 1933.

122. Ibid., no. 248.

123. Lewy, 46 f.

124. Quotation in H. Müller, 192.

125. F. Arnold, V/5.

126. Amery, 28.

127. Ibid., 31.

128. Ibid., 20 ff.

129. Ibid., 32.

130. Ibid., 31 f.

131. cf. note 75.

132. Lewy, 75.

133. cf. ibid., 181 and 217.

134. Stern, 41, October 11, 1964, 181.

135. Neuhäusler II., 44.

136. On Pzillas's differentiations, see 92 ff. I would expressly recommend this imaginative, accurate, and cynical brochure. It can be obtained from the editor, Dr. Friedrich Pzillas, Bad Godesberg, Kronprinzenstrasse 41. On Pzillas himself, see Deschner, 129.

137. Manhattan, 187.

138. Quotation in Binder, 424 ff.

139. Altmeyer, 144.

140. Documents in Manhattan, 182 ff.

141. Quotation in J. Fleischer, Der Christ als perfekter Staatsroboter [The Christian as the Perfect State Robot], Gesamtdeutsche Rundschau, May 27, 1955.

142. J. Fleischer, Katholischer Wehrbeitrag. Gestern und Heute [Catholic Contribution to Defense. Then and Now], 8 f.

143. cf. Deschner, 506 ff. For details on the real and alleged persecutions of Christians and the (relatively) extremely low number of Christian martyrs: Deschner, 334–352.

144. Begegnung, Monatsschrift deutscher Katholiken [Encounter, the German Catholics' Monthly Journal], Berlin, 6, 1964, 18 ff.; also cf. Miller, I. D., 6/1963, 1 f.

145. Amelunxen, 130.

146. Quotation according to Fleischer, Adolf Hitler, Sein Krieg und die Bischöfe. Wo bleibt

das Schuldbekenntnis der Katholischen Kirche? [Adolf Hitler, His War and the Bishops. Where Is the Catholic Church's Admission of Guilt?], Die Andere Zeitung, October 8, 1964.

147. Here I am following the two articles by Fleischer in a compact manner. Schuldbekenntnis der versäumten Pflichten [Acknowledgement of Guilt of Neglected Duties], and Sprache der Tatsachen [The Language of Facts], Tagesspiegel, Berlin, January 12, 1947, and February 16, 1947.

148. Ibid.

149. Ibid.

150. Ibid.

151. Lewy, 234.

152. Kreutzberg, 86.

153. Der Spiegel, November 18, 1964, 123.

154. Picker, 293, note 1.

155. Miller, I. D., 6/1964, 12.

156. Supplement to the Amtsblatt für die Diözese Münster [Official Gazette of the Diocese of Münster], October 1935, 1.

157. Amtsblatt für die Diözese Münster [Official Gazette of the Diocese of Münster], March 12, 1936, 44.

158. P. Smith, The Bishop of Münster and the Nazis, London, 1943, 7 ff. Catholic publication. Quoted according to Scheinmann, 393.

159. Quotation in Fleischer, Der Mythos vom heiligen Widerstandskämpfer [The Myth of the Holy Resistance Fighter], Die Andere Zeitung, December 13, 1956.

160. Ibid.

161. cf. on this: Deschner, 497 f. For Jesus' position on war and the stance of the pre-Constantine church, see Deschner, 493–510.

162. Kirchenblatt, March 9, 1941. Quotation in Fleischer, Der Mythos vom heiligen Widerstandskämpfer [The Myth of the Holy Resistance Fighter].

163. Lewy, 311.

164. Quotation in Herman, 74.

165. Breza, 319.

166. A copy of the letter "An die Ritenkongregation des Heiligen Stuhls [To the Congregation of Rites of the Holy See], Città del Vaticano," dated October 16, 1959, which the author allowed me to view.

167. H. Mueller, Zur Behandlung des Kirchenkampfes [On the Treatment of the Church Struggle], 474. Spaced out by the author. However, I also notice a contradiction between the claim of a "long time" and its following limitation to the first year.

168. Miller, I. D., no. 9, 1961, 10.

169. Faulhaber, Die Sittenlehre der Katholischen Kirche [The Ethics of the Catholic Church], 114.

170. Berning, 122 f.

171. Ibid., 129.

172. Scheinmann, 184, with reference to F. Thyssen, I paid Hitler, New York, 1941, 214.

173. Süddeutsche Zeitung, January 30, 1964.

174. Gröber, 17 f.

175. For details, see Deschner, 9 ff. Regarding the position of pre-Constantine Christianity to the state, see Deschner, 499 ff.

176. Gröber, 21 f.

177. Ibid., 27.

178. Ibid., 51.

179. To see the frenetic support for the war on the part of Catholic and Protestant theologians on both sides, cf. the numerous documents in Deschner 514–522.

180. Quotation in Fleischer, Der absolute Pazifismus—ein verpflichtendes Gebot der katholischen Kirche [Absolute Pacifism—a Binding Commandment of the Catholic Church], 18.

181. Ibid.

182. Gröber, 120.

183. Quotation according to Fleischer, Adolf Hitler, Sein Krieg und die Bischöfe. Wo bleibt das Schuldbekenntnis der Katholischen Kirche? [Adolf Hitler, His War and the Bishops. Where Is the Catholic Church's Admission of Guilt?].

184. Ibid.

185. cf. Miller, I. D., 6/1963, 3.

186. Lewy, 165.

187. According to Mueller, H., Zur Behandlung des Kirchenkampfes [On the Treatment of the Church Struggle], 476.

188. Corsten, 118.

189. Lewy, 202.

190. Ibid., 310.

191. Supplement to the Amtsblatt der Erzdiözese München und Freising [Official Gazette of the Archdiocese of Munich and Freising], June 12, 1936, 7.

192. Lewy, 208.

193. Quotation according to Fleischer in Katholischer Wehrbeitrag [Catholic Contribution to Defense], 10 f.; cf. also Fleischer, Adolf Hitler, Sein Krieg und die Bischöfe [Adolf Hitler, His War and the Bishops]. Spaced out by Fleischer and the author.

194. cf. the extracts to all these points in Fleischer, Katholischer Wehrbeitrag. Gestern und heute [Catholic Contribution to Defense, Then and Now], 3 ff.

195. Quotation in Fleischer [The Myth of the Holy Resistance Fighter], D. A. Z., December 13, 1956.

196. Ordinance dated May 29, 1933, in the Reichsgesetzblatt [Reich Law Gazette]. On this, see Binder, 265.

197. Text of the agreement in Binder, 267.

198. Manhattan, 250; also cf. Scheinmann, 45.

199. Picker, 438.

200. Gisevius, 414.

201. Wiener Neueste Nachrichten, March 28, 1938, vol. 14, no. 5501.

202. Ibid.

203. Ernst, 111.

204. Scheinmann, 48.

205. Lewy, 212.

206. Ibid., 218.

207. Amtsblatt für die Erzdiözese Bamberg [Official Gazette of the Archdiocese of Bamberg], no. 10, vol. 62, April 5, 1939.

208. Lewy, 221.

209. Ibid.

210. Ibid.

211. Quotation in Miller, I. D., 11/1962, 3.

212. Quotation in Fleischer, Gewalttat unter kirchlichem Segen [An Act of Violence with the Church's Blessing], Freisoziale Presse, July 25, 1964.

213. Quotation in Fleischer, Adolf Hitler, Sein Krieg und die Bischöfe [Adolf Hitler, His War and the Bishops].

214. Fleischer, Katholischer Wehrbeitrag [Catholic Contribution to Defense], 5ff.

215. Quotation in Fleischer, Das wahre Gesicht der Militärseelsorger [The True Face of the Military Chaplains], Das Andere Deutschland [The Other Germany], March 10, 1956.

216. cf. Kirchliches Amtsblatt für die Diözese Münster [Official Church Gazette of the Diocese of Münster], vol. 73, no. 25.

217. Katholisches Kirchenblatt für das Bistum Berlin [Catholic Church Gazette of the Episcopate of Berlin], February 27, 1938, 10.

218. Quotation in Fleischer, Adolf Hitler, Sein Krieg und die Bischöfe [Adolf Hitler, His War and the Bishops].

219. Gemeinsames Wort der Deutschen Bischöfe [A Collective Message from the German Bishops], Martinusblatt, September 17, 1939.

220. cf. note 205.

221. Amtsblatt für die Erzdiözese Freiburg [Official Gazette of the Archdiocese of Freiburg], September 5, 1939.

222. Amtsblatt für die Erzdiözese Rottenburg [Official Gazette of the Archdiocese of Rottenburg], September 8, 1939, 223.

223. Amtsblatt für die Erzdiözese Eichstätt [Official Gazette of the Archdiocese of Eichstätt], September 21, 1939.

224. cf. Lewy, 227 f.

225. Manhattan, 196.

226. Quotation in the Münchner Katholische Kirchenzeitung, January 7, 1940.

227. Ibid., February 25, 1940, 45.

228. Quotation in Fleischer, Adolf Hitler, Sein Krieg und die Bischöfe [Adolf Hitler, His War and the Bishops.].

229. Quotation in Gesamtdeutsche Rundschau, March 14, 1958, 3.

230. Lewy, 256.

231. Ibid., 228.

232. Amtsblatt für die Diözese Osnabrück [Official Gazette of the Diocese of Osnabrück], November 13, 1940.

233. Amtsblatt für die Erzdiözese Freiburg [Official Gazette of the Archdiocese of Freiburg], February 12, 1941.

234. Lewy, 230.

235. cf. Werkhefte, Zeitschrift für Probleme der Gesellschaft und des Katholizismus [Workbooks, Journal for Problems of Society and Catholicism], vol. 15, July 1961, 217.

236. Quotation in Gesamtdeutsche Rundschau, March 14, 1958, 3. Emphasis by the author.

237. cf. the documents in Lewy, 231.

238. Amtsblatt für die Erzdiözese Bamberg [Official Gazette of the Archdiocese of Bamberg], no. 4, vol. 64, February 24, 1941, 21ff. Emphasis by the author.

239. Quotation in Miller, I. D., 11/1962, 3.

240. Quotation in Gesamtdeutsche Rundschau, March 14, 1958, 3. Spaced out by the author.

241. cf. e.g., the documents in Manhattan, 207; Scheinmann, 392; Lewy, 231, 256.

242. Fastenhirtenschreiben über die Vorsehung Gottes und den Ernst der Zeit [Lent pastoral letter on the Providence of God and the seriousness of the times], 1944, 1.

243. Amtsblatt für die Erzdiözese Bamberg [Official Gazette of the Archdiocese of Bamberg], no. 1, January 31, 1944, 5, and ibid. no. 29, September 22, 1944, 200 f.

244. Amtsblatt für die Erzdiözese Paderborn [Official Gazette of the Archdiocese of Paderborn], February 11, 1942, 17. On this, see Lewy, 231.

245. Amtsblatt für die Erzdiözese Paderborn [Official Gazette of the Archdiocese of Paderborn], January 16, 1945.

246. Deschner, 591.

247. Quotation in Fleischer, Das wahre Gesicht der Militärseelsorger, Zur Berufung von Kardinal Wendel als Militärbischof [The True Face of the Military Chaplains. On the Appointment of Cardinal Wendel as a Military Bishop], Das Andere Deutschland 5/56, March 10, 1956.

248. Ibid.

249. Neuhäusler, II., 149.

250. Foreword on March 21, 1946, to Neuhäusler, 4.

251. Gisevius, 69.

252. Faulhaber, M., Die Sittenlehre der Katholischen Kirche [The Ethics of the Catholic Church], 114.

253. cf. Amtsblatt für die Erzdiözese München und Freising [Official Gazette of the Archdiocese of Munich and Freising], vol. 1936, no. 8, 70.

254. Manhattan, 219.

255. Ibid., 221.

256. Amtsblatt für die Erzdiözese Bamberg [Official Gazette of the Archdiocese of Bamberg], no. 5, vol. 68, July 4, 1945, 31.

257. Quotation in J. Fleischer, Die Fronten sind klar [The Fronts Are Clear], Das Andere Deutschland [The Other Germany], 1/1957.

258. Begegnung [Encounter], Berlin, 8/1964, 11.

259. J. Fleischer, Der absolute Pazifismus [Absolute Pacifism].

260. Michael Faulhaber, 25 Bischofsjahre [25 Years as a Bishop].

261. Neuhäusler, II., 118 f.

262. Amtsblatt für die Erzdiözese München und Freising [Official Gazette of the Archdiocese of Munich and Freising], 1941, no. 13, 162.

263. Manhattan, 221.

264. Neuhäusler, II., 100.

265. Faulhaber, Judentum, Christentum, Germanentum [Jewry, Christianity, Germanism], 19 and 10 f.

266. cf. the supplement to no. 20 of the Amtsblatt für die Erzdiözese München und Freising [Official Gazette of the Archdiocese of Munich and Freising], November 15, 1934.

267. Ibid.

268. Ibid.

269. Ibid.

270. Amtsblatt für die Erzdiözese München und Freising [Official Gazette of the Archdiocese of Munich and Freising], vol. 1936, no. 6, Supplement II.

271. Supplement to the Amtsblatt für die Erzdiözese München und Freising [Official Gazette of the Archdiocese of Munich and Freising], November 15, 1934.

272. Amery, 47. f., and the illustrated magazine Stern, no. 41, October 11, 1964, 182.

273. Quotation in Fleischer, Noch einmal in den Abgrund? Wenn Bischöfe unbesehen die Regierungspolitik bejahen [Into the Abyss Once Again? When Bishops Unthinkingly Approve Government Policy], Das Andere Deutschland [The Other Germany], 16/1956.

274. Pastoral letter, August 1, 1945. Quotation in Fleischer, Katholischer Wehrbeitrag [Catholic Contribution to Defense], 11.

275. Quotation in Fleischer, Adolf Hitler, Sein Krieg und die Bischöfe. Wo bleibt das Schuldbekenntnis der Katholischen Kirche? [Adolf Hitler, His War and the Bishops. Where Is the Catholic Church's Admission of Guilt?], Die Andere Zeitung, October 8, 1964.

276. Ibid.

277. Neuhäusler, II., 405 f.

278. Ibid.

279. Quotation in Fleischer, Die Freiheit, die sie meinen. Ein Jesuitenpater brandmarkt den kirchlichen Faschismus [Their Idea of Freedom. A Jesuit Father Brands Church Fascism], Die Andere Zeitung, May 17, 1956.

280. Detailed documentation in Deschner, 514 ff.

281. Klerusblatt [Clergy Gazette], February 19, 1941.

282. Katholisches Kirchenblatt für das nördliche Münsterland [Catholic Church Gazette for the Northern Münster Region], March 9, 1941.

283. Katholische Kirchenzeitung für die Erzdiözese Köln [Catholic Church Newspaper for the Archdiocese of Cologne], April 20, 1941.

284. Zahn, G. C., Die Deutsche Katholische Presse und Hitlers Kriege [The German Catholic Press and Hitler's Wars], in: Werkhefte [Workbooks], vol. 15, 1961, 205 ff.

285. Ibid., 209.

286. Kupisch, 38.

287. Quotation in W. Niemöller, 70.

288. Ibid., 71 f.

289. Ibid., 79.

290. Ibid., 80.

291. Kupisch, 258 ff.; Doerne, Jacobi, Künneth, Karl Ritter, Stählin, Riethmüller, G. Schulz, Schreiner, Heim, Gornandt, Wendland, Dannenbaum, and Anna Paulsen also signed.

292. W. Niemöller, 87.

293. Stauffer, 14 f.; 54 and various other places.

294. Niemöller, 170. Emphasis by the author.

295. Ibid., 197. Emphasis by the author.

296. Ibid., 198.

297. Ibid., 391 f.

298. Ibid.

299. Ibid.

300. Ibid., 393.

301. Ibid., 367 f.

302. H. Bunke, Kirchlicher Revanchismus in Reinkultur [Unadulterated Church Revanchism], Die Andere Zeitung, June 25, 1964.

303. Lilje, 13 f.

304. Der Spiegel, September 13, 1961, 56 f.

305. Asmussen, 86 ff.

306. Ibid.

307. Ibid., 28. However, there are also examples of opposite behavior there.

308. Quotation in W. Niemöller, 48.

CHAPTER 4: THE VATICAN AND THE SECOND WORLD WAR

1. On April 15, 1948, in a speech in Ortona. Quotation in Manhattan, 14.

2. Fleischer, Das Andere Deutschland [The Other Germany], 11/1956.

3. The well-informed Breza also has something interesting to say about this, 548 ff.

4. Ibid.

5. Newsweek, March 2, 1964; Spiegel, November 18, 1964, 110 and 107.

6. Deutsche Tagespost, March 17, 1964.

7. Frankfurter Allgemeine, March 27, 1963.

8. Quotation in Fleischer, Katholischer Wehrbeitrag [Catholic Contribution to Defense], 9.

9. Binder, 300.

10. Friedländer, 24.

11. Scheinmann, 65, with reference to The New International Year Book, 1939, New York, 1940, 681.

12. Friedländer, 20.

13. Giovannetti, 36 f.

14. Friedländer, 22.

15. Ibid., 23.

16. Ibid.

17. Neue Zürcher Zeitung, June 2, 1939.

18. Friedländer, 25. Emphasis by the author.

19. Ibid., 19.

20. Ibid., 19 f.

21. Giovannetti, 35.

22. Quotation in Giovannetti, 85, who adds: "This is how Himmler tried to make Ciano believe." But also Friedländer writes on p. 24: "Attacks on the Pope and the Vatican actually disappeared from the columns of German newspapers very quickly."

23. Quotation in Neutralität, Kritische Schweizer Zeitschrift für Politik und Kultur, 1964/65, no. 6/7, p. 19.

24. Lehman, 28.

25. The Trial of the Three Slovakian Bishops Jan Vojtassák, Dr. Th. Michal Buzalka, Pavol Gojdic, Prague, 1951, 15.

26. Quotation in Paris, The Vatican against Europe, 159.

27. Generalfeldmarschall Keitel [General Field Marshal Keitel], ed. Görlitz, 204.

28. Lehman, 28; also cf. W. Hagen, 170ff., esp. 186 f.

29. Manhattan, 267.

30. The Trial of the Three Slovakian Bishops, 50 f.

31. Ibid., 30 ff.

32. Two Years of German Oppression in Czechoslovakia, London, 1941, 134. f. According to Scheinmann, 251.

33. Manhattan, 267.

34. The Trial of the Three Slovakian Bishops, 15.

35. Quotation in Tondi, Die Jesuiten [The Jesuits], 363 f.

36. Scheinmann, 339.

37. Malvezzi-Pirelli, 264 f.

38. Picker, 396.

39. Breza, 189 f.

40. The pastoral letter is reproduced in its entirety in Begegnung, Monatsschrift deutscher Katholiken [Encounter, the Monthly Journal of German Catholics], Berlin, 9/1964, p. 11.

41. Ibid., 12.

42. Ibid.

43. Ibid.

44. Ibid.

45. Friedländer, 30 ff.

46. Ibid., 32.

47. Ibid., 33, for further documentation of similar efforts on the part of the pope.

48. Quotation in Manhattan, 277.

49. Binder, 307.

50. Scheinmann, 90, note 1.

51. Manhattan, 192 ff.

52. Ibid.

53. Ordinance Journal of the Catholic Wehrmacht Chief of Chaplains, 1939, 5.

54. Manhattan, 192 ff.

55. Friedländer, 36.

56. Giovannetti, 146 f.

57. Ibid., 145 f.

58. Bates, 11 f.

59. E. Revyuk, Atrocities in the Ukraine, 1931; according to Manhattan, 274; also cf. Roos, 138 f.

60. Giovannetti, 58.

61. Ibid.

62. Ibid.

63. Ibid., 15.

64. Ibid., 28.

65. Ibid., 168.

66. Ibid., 169.

67. Ibid., 157.

68. cf. the Catholic Deutsches Volksblatt, September 15, 1960.

69. Ziegler, 109 ff.

70. Lewy, 251.

71. Quotation in Giovannetti, 160.

72. Ibid.

73. Scheinmann, 127, with reference to R. Garaudy, l'église, le communisme et les chrétiens, Paris, 1949, 159, and La Pensée, Paris, 1949, no. 27.

74. Friedländer, 40. Emphasis by the author.

75. Quotation in Posser, 54.

76. Quotation in Giovannetti, 294.

77. Scheinmann, 161, with reference to C. Cianfarra, The Vatican and the War in Europe, New York, 1944, 238.

78. Scheinmann, ibid., with reference to the New York Times, July 2, 1940.

79. Manhattan, 199.

80. Giovannetti, 260.

81. Ibid.

82. Ibid., 263.

83. Friedländer, 47 f.

84. Giovannetti, 209.

85. Friedländer, 47.

86. Ibid., 48.

87. Ibid.

88. Ibid.

89. Ibid.

90. Miller, I. D., 4,/1962, 5.

91. Manhattan, 201.

92. Ibid., 289.

93. For details, see Paris, The Vatican against Europe, 127 ff.

94. Giovannetti, 211.

95. Ibid., 218.

96. Manhattan, 318 f.

97. Quotation ibid., 319.

98. Scheinmann, 180.

99. Ibid., 178, 222.

100. Friedländer, 49 f.

101. Basler Nachrichten, October 5, 1940.

102. Manhattan, 202 f.

103. Ibid., also cf. Scheinmann, 185.

104. Friedländer, 54 f.

105. Ibid.

106. Ibid., 56 f.

107. Quotation in Gesamtdeutsche Rundschau, March 14, 1958. Emphasis by the author.

108. Quotation in Manhattan, 207.

109. Good, concise information, which cannot, of course, replace Winter's weighty and superb work and is not intended to, is provided by Diether Posser in the paperback published by Stimme, Frankfurt, Answers 5. Deutsch-sowjetische Beziehungen, 1917–1941 [German-Soviet Relations, 1917–1941], 1963.

110. Posser, 57.

111. Paris, The Vatican against Europe, 139.

112. Scheinmann, with reference to Manhattan, Latin America and the Vatican, London, 1946, 27.

113. Scheinmann, 221 f.

114. Friedländer, 62.

115. Ibid.

116. This is what the German representative Menshausen writes to Weizsäcker on September 12, 1941. See Friedländer, 66.

117. Ibid., 63.

118. Gundlach, Die Lehre Pius' XII. zum Atomkrieg [The Teachings of Pius XII on Nuclear War], Stimmen der Zeit, April 1959, 14.

119. Friedländer, 65.

120. Lewy, 250.

121. Poliakov and Wulf, 33.

122. Sources documented in Scheinmann, 256.

123. Hagen, 453 f.

124. For more details on this, see The Trial of the Three Slovakian Bishops, 105 ff.

125. Miller, I. D., 4/1962, 5 f.

126. Ibid.

127. cf. ibid., 8/1962 and 6/1961.

128. Ibid., 8/1962.

129. Die Welt, November 20, 1964.

130. Miller, 1. D., 4/1962, 5 f.

131. Ibid.

132. cf. p. 157. See also J. Fleischer in: Freisoziale Presse, May 24, 1963, 5.

133. Friedländer, 66 f.

134. Ibid.

135. New York Herald Tribune, June 9, 1944.

136. cf. sep. Manhattan, 208 ff.; Scheinmann, 281 ff.

137. Friedländer, 132.

138. Ibid., 131.

139. Ibid., 134.

140. Ibid., 137 f.

141. Ibid., 135.

142. Ibid., 149.

143. H. D. Meyer, 30 f.

144. cf. p. 89; also Miller, I. D., 3/1963; 11/1962 and 11/1957.

145. Ambassador Dodd's Diary, 1941, 74; also cf. 62.

146. Manhattan, 212 f.

147. Spiegel, November 18, 1964, 124.

148. Manhattan, 341 ff.

149. Scheinmann, 344; also cf. The Trial of the Three Slovakian Bishops, 19.

150. Friedländer, 133.

151. Scheinmann, 420.

152. Quotation in Manhattan, 324.

153. Jacques Isorni, Souffrance et mort du Maréchal [The Suffering and Death of the Marshal], 1951, 227 f. I have Georg Schmitz, Uerikon am Zürichsee, to thank for directing me to this book.

154. The Bulletin of International News, September 2, 1944, no. 18. According to Scheinmann, 407.

155. Scheinmann, 250.

156. Konkret, June 20, 1961, 8.

157. For details, see Deschner, 442 ff.

158. Schoenberner, 108.

159. Deutsche Hochschullehrerzeitung, Tübingen, 1962, vol. 11, no. 3, 31.

CHAPTER 5: THE VATICAN AND THE CROATIAN ATROCITIES

1. Paris, Genocide, 189.

2. Neubacher, 31.

3. V. Novak, Die Beziehungen zwischen dem Vatikan und den Südslawen [Relations between the Vatican and the South Slavs], in Internationale Politik, Belgrade, July 16, 1954.

4. Quotation in Miller, I. D., 7/1964.

5. Ibid.

6. Ibid.

7. Ibid.

8. Winter, II., 559.

9. Miller, I. D., 7/1964.

10. Paris, The Vatican, 41 ff. esp. 46.

11. Ibid., 45 f.

12. V. Novak, Die Beziehungen [Relations], in Internationale Politik, Belgrade, July 16, 1954.

13. Documentation in plenty in Deschner, 517 ff.

14. Quotation in Miller, I. D., 7, 1964.

15. V. Novak, Die Beziehungen [Relations], Internationale Politik, Belgrade, July 16, 1954.

16. Grazer Volksblatt, September 6, 1936.

17. cf. Paris, Genocide, 13.

18. Ibid., with reference to Hrvatska Zora, Munich, September 1, 1954.

19. For details, see Paris, ibid., 30 ff.

20. Reichspost, Wien, October 30, 1937.

21. V. Novak, Die Beziehungen [Relations], in Internationale Politik, Belgrade, July 16, 1954.

22. Communicated orally to me by Edmond Paris.

23. Hory and Broszat, 15 f., with reference to the official brochure "The Ustaša Movement," Zagreb, 1943, 11 f.

24. Ibid., 21.

25. Ibid., 19 f.

26. Milićević, 50.

27. cf. e.g., Binder, 264 f. For details, see V. Milićević, 52 ff.

28. Hory and Broszat, 28 f.

29. Paris, Genocide, 47.

30. Völkischer Beobachter, April 7, 1941.

31. cf. G. Wolfrum, Die Völker und Nationalitäten [Peoples and Nationalities], tables 4 and 5 in the Eastern European Handbook, vol. "Yugoslavia," 1954.

32. Hory and Broszat, 53.

33. V. Novak, Die Beziehungen [Relations], in Internationale Politik, Belgrade, July 16, 1954.

34. Entry dated April 24, 1941. Quoted according to Hory and Broszat, 66.

35. Paris, Genocide, 75, with reference to Hvratski Narod and Katolički List.

36. V. Novak, Die Beziehungen [Relations], in Internationale Politik, Belgrade, July 16, 1954.

37. Miller A., Die "christlichen" Massaker in Kroatien 1941 bis 1945 [The "Christian" Massacres in Croatia 1941–1945], in: Die Freigeistige Aktion, Hannover, no. 11, November 1961.

38. Ibid.

39. Ibid.

40. Martyrdom of the Serbs, Chicago, 1943, 179; according to Scheinmann, 249. Miller, ibid.; also cf. Hagen, 238; 243 f.; 253 f.

41. Paris, Genocide, 213.

42. Ibid., 214.

43. Ibid., 62; also cf. Hory and Broszat, 96f.

44. Paris, Genocide, 49.

45. Ibid., 79.

46. Martyrdom of the Serbs, 179, according to Scheinmann, 149. Miller, A.; also cf. Hagen, 238; 243 f.; 253 f.

47. Paris, Genocide, 73.

48. Ibid., 96, with reference to J. Horvat and Z. Stambuk, Dokumenti o. protunarodmnom radu I zlocinima jednog dijela katolickog Klera (Documents concerning Antinational Activities and the Crimes of a Part of the Catholic Clergy), Zagreb, 1946, 55.

49. Paris, Genocide, 59.

50. Ibid.

51. Ibid.

52. Ibid., 60.

53. Ibid., 104.

54. Ibid., 88, with reference to Katolički List no. 26, 1941, and Hrvatski Narod, June 30, 1941.

55. Paris, Genocide, 88.

56. Miller, A., Die "christlichen" Massaker in Kroatien 1941 bis 1945 [The "Christian" Massacres in Croatia 1941–1945], in: Die Freigeistige Aktion, Hannover, no. 11, November 1961.

57. Paris, Genocide, 105.

58. Ibid., 107.

59. Ibid., 129. See also p. 189 for further atrocities.

60. Ibid., 130. Even if Malaparte may have made use of poetic license to a certain extent here, his sentences still precisely characterize the true nature of this man and his terror regime.

61. Neubacher, 32 and 156.

62. Ibid., 161.

63. Hory and Broszat, 138.

64. Ibid., 99.

65. Ibid., 99 f.

66. Ibid., 99.

67. Ibid., 100.

68. Ibid., 101 f.

69. Ibid., 119 ff.

70. cf. the compilations in Deschner, 562 ff.

71. Hory and Broszat, 126.

72. Ibid., 130 f.; also cf. Paris, Genocide, 102 f.

73. According to Paris, Genocide, 115.

74. Hory and Broszat, 85.

75. Ibid., 89.

76. Ibid.

77. Paris, Genocide, 189.

78. Ibid., 130 f.

79. Ibid., 133.

80. Ibid., 192. Further such texts there and on the following page.

81. Ibid., 193.

82. Hory and Broszat, 94.

83. Paris, Genocide, 65 and 97.

84. Ibid., 100; also cf. the corresponding illustrations in Paris's book.

85. Ibid., 64 ff.

86. Ibid., 51.

87. Ibid., with reference to Hrvatski Narod, July 30, 1941.

88. Ibid., 84, with reference to Katolički Tjednik, June 15, 1941.

89. Ibid., 51.

90. Ibid., 108, with reference to "Hvratska Smotra." 91. Ibid., 98.

92. Ibid., 110, with reference to Novi List, July 24, 1941.

93. Ibid., 99.

94. Miller, A., Die "christlichen" Massaker in Kroatien 1941 bis 1945 [The "Christian" Massacres in Croatia 1941–1945].

95. Paris, Genocide, 103.

96. Ibid., 111.

97. Ibid., 52.

98. Ibid., 54.

99. Hory and Broszat, 72.

100. Paris, Genocide, 113.

101. Ibid., 109.

102. Ibid., 113.

103. Miller, A., Die "christlichen" Massaker in Kroatien 1941 bis 1945 [The "Christian" Massacres in Croatia 1941–1945].

104. Paris, Genocide, 114.

105. Ibid., 110.

106. Ibid., 136 f.

107. Miller, A., Die "christlichen" Massaker in Kroatien 1941 bis 1945 [The "Christian" Massacres in Croatia 1941–1945].

108. Paris, Genocide, 114.

109. Miller, A., Die "christlichen" Massaker in Kroatien 1941 bis 1945 [The "Christian" Massacres in Croatia 1941–1945].

110. Paris, Genocide, 109 f.

111. Ibid., 79 f.

112. Ibid., 55.

113. Ibid., 55 ff.

114. Ibid., 67.

115. Miller, A., Die "christlichen" Massaker in Kroatien 1941 bis 1945 [The "Christian" Massacres in Croatia 1941–1945].

116. V. Novak, Prinzipium et Finis-Veritas, in: Review of International Affairs, vol. 2, no. 26, Belgrade, December 19, 1951.

117. Ibid.

118. Paris, Genocide, 165 f.

119. Ibid., 168.

120. New Review, February 1, 1942.

121. Paris, Genocide, 176.

122. Ibid., 179.

123. Novak, Magnum Crimen, 788 f.

124. Paris, Genocide, 208.

125. Ibid., 204.

126. Novak, Magnum Crimen, 128.

127. Paris, Genocide, 201.

128. The following closely follows Paris, Genocide, 208 ff.

129. Ibid., 259.

130. Miller, A., Die "christlichen" Massaker in Kroatien 1941 bis 1945 [The "Christian" Massacres in Croatia 1941–1945]. Also cf. Hagen, 261 f.

131. Paris, Genocide, 159.

132. Ibid., 218; also cf. 312.

133. For details of Ustaša propaganda after the war see, Paris, 259 ff.

134. Ibid., 219 f.

135. Miller, A., Die "christlichen" Massaker in Kroatien 1941 bis 1945 [The "Christian" Massacres in Croatia 1941–1945].

136. Paris, Genocide, 220.

137. V. Novak, Die Beziehungen [Relations], in Internationale Politik, Belgrade, July 16, 1954.

138. cf. p. 207, note 123.

139. Paris, Genocide, 220.

140. Ibid., 177.

141. Ibid.

142. Ibid., 167.

143. Ibid., 221.

144. Ibid., 220.

145. Ibid.

146. Ibid., 76 ff., cf. illustrations 251, 254, 314.

147. Ibid., 179.

148. Ibid., 142.

149. Ibid., 219.

150. Ibid., 163 ff.

151. Ibid., 146.

152. New Statesman and Nation, London, October 26, 1946.

153. New York Times, January 13, 1953.

154. Ibid.

155. Lowest estimate: 600,000; highest: approaching one million.

BIBLIOGRAPHY

Essays from newspapers and journals are named only in the notes.

Altmeyer, K. A. Katholische Presse unter NS-Diktatur [The Catholic Press under the Nazi Dictatorship]. 1962.

Amelunxen, R. Ehrenmänner und Hexenmeister [Honorable Men and Sorcerers]. 1960.

Amery, C. Die Kapitulation oder Deutscher Katholizismus heute [Capitulation or German Catholicism Today]. 1963.

Anger, W. Das Dritte Reich in Dokumenten [The Third Reich in Documents]. 1957.

Arnold, F. Anschläge, Deutsche Plakate als Dokumente der Zeit 1900–1960 [Attacks: German Posters as Documents of Their Times, 1900–1960]. 1963.

Asmussen, H. Zur jüngsten Kirchengeschichte, Anmerkungen und Folgerungen [Recent Church History: Notes and Conclusions]. 1961.

Ball-Kaduri, K. J. Das Leben der Juden in Deutschland 1933 [The Lives of the Jews in 1933 Germany]. 1963.

Bates, M. S. Glaubensfreiheit, Eine Untersuchung [An Examination of the Freedom of Religion]. 1947.

Becker, K. Sag nein zum Krieg [Say No to War]. 1962.

Berning, W. Glaube, Hoffnung und Liebe sind die Stützen des Staates. In: Hirtenbriefe der deutschen, österreichischen und deutsch-schweizerischen Bischöfe [Faith, Hope and Love Are the Pillars of the State. In: Pastoral Letters of the German, Austrian and Swiss German Bishops]. 1934.

Beumelburg, W. Kampf um Spanien. Die Geschichte der Legion Condor [The Fight for Spain. The History of the Legion Condor]. 1939.

Binder, G. Epoche der Entscheidungen. Eine Geschichte des 20. Jahrhunderts mit Dokumenten in Text und Bild [The Era of Decisions. A History of the 20th Century with Documents in Words and Pictures]. 1963.

Bley, W., ed. Das Buch der Spanienflieger. Die Feuertaufe der neuen deutschen Luftwaffe (82.–131. T) [The Book of the Spain Pilots. The Baptism of Fire for the New German Air Force]. 1939.

Borgese, F. A. Der Marsch des Faschismus [The March of Fascism]. 1938.

Brenan, G. The Spanish Labyrinth. 1943.

Breza, T. Das eherne Tor, Römische Aufzeichnungen [The Iron Gate. Roman Records]. 1962.

Broszat, Martin, and Ladislaus Hory. Der kroatische Ustascha-Staat [The Croatian Ustaša State]. 1st edition. 1964.

Buchheit, G. Mussolini und das neue Italien [Mussolini and the New Italy]. 3rd edition. 1941.

Claar, M. Deutschland von draußen gesehen: Rom [Germany as Viewed from Outside: Rome]. 1934.

Coles, S. F. A. Franco of Spain. 1955.

Corsten, W. Kölner Aktenstücke zur Lage der katholischen Kirche in Deutschland 1933–1945 [Cologne File Excerpts on the Position of the Catholic Church in Germany from 1933–1945]. 1949.

Dahms, H. G. Der Spanische Bürgerkrieg 1936–1939 [The Spanish Civil War 1936–1939]. 1962.

Deschner, K. *Abermals krähte der Hahn. Eine kritische Kirchengeschichte von den Anfängen bis zu Pius XII [And Again the Cock Crew. A Critical Church History from Its Origins to Pius XII]*. 2nd edition. 1964.

Detwiler, D. S. Hitler, Franco und Gibraltar. Die Frage des spanischen Eintritts in den 2. Weltkrieg [Hitler, Franco and Gibraltar. The Question of the Spanish Entry into World War II]. 1962.

Dirks, W. Das schmutzige Geschäft? Die Politik und die Verantwortung der Christen [Dirty Business? The Politics and Responsibility of the Christians]. 1964.

Duff, C. Spanien, Der Stein des Anstoßes [Spain, the Bone of Contention]. 1949.

Ernst, F. Die Deutschen und ihre jüngste Geschichte [The Germans and Their Most Recent History].

Faulhaber, M. Judentum, Christentum, Germanentum, Adventspredigten [Jewry, Christianity, Germanism. Advent Sermons]. 1933.

———. Die Sittenlehre der katholischen Kirche. In: Hirtenbriefe der deutschen, österreichischen und deutsch-schweizerischen Bischöfe [The Ethics of the Catholic Church. In: Pastoral Letters of the German, Austrian and Swiss German Bishops]. 1934.

———. 25 Bischofsjahre [25 Years as a Bishop]. 1936.

Feis, H. The Spanish Story. 1948.

Fernsworth, L. Spain's Struggle for Freedom. 1958.

Fest, J. C. Das Gesicht des Dritten Reiches, Profile einer totalitären Herrschaft [The Face of the Third Reich, Profiles of Totalitarian Rule]. 1963.

Fleischer, J. Der absolute Pazifismus—ein verpflichtendes Gebot der katholischen Kirche [Absolute Pacifism—a Binding Commandment of the Catholic Church]. 1962.

———. Katholischer Wehrbeitrag, Gestern und Heute [Catholic Contribution to Defense, Then and Now]. 1952.

Friedländer, S. Pius XII und das Dritte Reich. Eine Dokumentation [Pius XII and the Third Reich. Documentation]. 1965.

Gardini, T. L. Towards the New Italy.

Giovannetti, A. Der Vatikan und der Krieg [The Vatican and the War]. 1961.

Gisevius, H. B. Adolf Hitler, Versuch einer Deutung [Adolf Hitler: An Attempt at Interpretation]. 1963.

Glum, F. Der Nationalsozialismus. Werden und Vergehen [National Socialism. Genesis and Demise]. 1962.

Goebbels, J. Vom Kaiserhof zur Reichskanzlei. Eine historische Darstellung in Tagebuchblättern [From the Emperor's Court to the Reich Chancellory. A Historical Presentation in Diary Form]. 1937.

Gontard, F. Die Päpste, Regenten zwischen Himmel und Hölle [The Popes: Regents between Heaven and Hell]. 1959.

Görlitz, W. Adolf Hitler. 1960.

———, ed. Generalfeldmarschall Keitel, Verbrecher oder Offizier. Erinnerungen, Briefe, Dokumente des Chefs OKW [Field Marshal Keitel, Officer or Criminal. Memoirs, Letters and Documents of the Head of the OKW]. 1961.

Gröber, C. Kirche, Vaterland und Vaterlandsliebe, Zeitgemäße Erwägungen und Erwiderungen [Church, Fatherland and Love of the Fatherland. Contemporary Considerations and Responses]. 1935.

Haenchen, E. Die Apostelgeschichte [The History of the Apostles]. 10th edition. 1956.

Hagen, W. Die geheime Front [The Secret Front]. Year unknown.

Haller, J. Das Papsttum, Idee und Wirklichkeit [The Papacy, Idea and Reality]. 2nd edition. 1936.

Hallgarten, G. W. F. Hitler, Reichswehr und Industrie. Zur Geschichte der Jahre 1918–1933 [Hitler, Reichswehr and Industry. On the History of the Years 1918–1933]. 1962.

Heiler, F. Altkirchliche Autonomie und päpstlicher Zentralismus [Old Church Autonomy and Papal Centralism]. 1941.

———. Der Katholizismus. Seine Idee und seine Erscheinung [Catholicism. Its Idea and Its Appearance]. 1923.

Heldt, J. Gott in Deutschland. Eine Reportage über Glaube und Kirche [God in Germany. A Report on Faith and the Church]. 1963.

Herman, S. W. Die 7000 Zeugen, Kirche im Durchbruch [The 7,000 Witnesses. The Church Breakthrough]. 1952.

Heuss, T. Hitlers Weg. Eine historisch-politische Studie über den Nationalsozialismus [Hitler's Way. A Historical Political Study on National Socialism]. 4th edition. 1932.

Heussi. Kompendium der Kirchengeschichte [A Compendium of Church History]. 11th edition. 1957.

———. Der Ursprung des Mönchtums [The Origins of Monasticism]. 1936.

Hitler, A. Mein Kampf. 1933.

Höcht, J. M. Maria rettet das Abendland. Fatima und die "Siegerin in allen Schlachten Gottes" in der Entscheidung um Rußland [Mary Saves the Occident. Fatima and the "Victor in All God's Battles" in the Struggle for Russia]. 1953.

Kautsky, K. Geschichte des Sozialismus in Einzeldarstellungen I [The History of Socialism in Monographs I]. 1895.

————. Der Ursprung des Christentums. Eine historische Untersuchung [The Origins of Christianity. A Historical Examination]. 1910.

Keding, K. Feldgeistlicher bei Legion Condor, Spanisches Kriegstagebuch eines evangelischen Legionspfarrers [Field Clergyman with the Legion Condor. The Spanish War Diary of a Protestant Legion Priest]. 30.–35. T. Year unknown.

Keller, A. Church and State on the European Continent. 1936.

Klein, F. Warum Krieg um Abessinien? [Why the Abyssinian War?]. 1935.

Koestler, A. Ein Spanisches Testament [A Spanish Testament]. 1938.

Kreutzberg, H. Franz Reinisch. Ein Märtyrer unserer Zeit [Franz Reinisch. A Martyr of Our Times]. 1953.

Kupisdi, K. Quellen zur Geschichte des deutschen Protestantismus 1871–1945 [Sources of the History of German Protestantism, 1871–1945]. 1960.

Kurella, A. Mussolini ohne Maske [Mussolini Unmasked]. 1931.

Legion Condor, ed. Deutsche kämpfen in Spanien, 461.–485. T [Germans Fighting in Spain]. 1940.

Lehman, L. Vatican Policy in the Second World War. 1946.

Lewy, G. The Catholic Church and Nazi Germany. 1964.

Lohmeyer. Galiläa und Jerusalem [Galilee and Jerusalem]. 1936.

————. Gottesknecht und Davidsohn [God's Servant and the Son of David]. 1945.

Longo, L. Die Internationalen Brigaden in Spanien [The International Brigades in Spain]. 1958.

Lortz, J. Katholischer Zugang zum Nationalsozialismus [Catholic Access to National Socialism]. 2nd edition. 1934.

Madariaga, S. de. Spain. 2nd edition. 1942.

Maier, H. Soziologie der Päpste. Lehre und Wirkung der katholischen Sozialtheorie [The Sociology of the Popes. The Teachings and Effects of Catholic Social Theory]. 1965.

Malvezzi, P., and G. Pirelli. Letzte Briefe zum Tode Verurteilter aus dem europäischen Widerstand [Final Letters of European Resistance Fighters before Their Executions]. 1962.

Manhattan, A. The Vatican and World Politics. 1949. German version , Der Vatikan und das XX. Jahrhundert. 1958.

Matthias, E., and R. Morsey. Das Ende der Parteien 1933 [1933: The End of the Parties]. 1960.

Merkes, M. Die deutsche Politik gegenüber dem spanischen Bürgerkrieg [German Politics on the Spanish Civil War]. 1961.

Meyer, H. D. Amerika am Scheideweg [America at the Crossroads]. 1953.

Milićević, V. Der Königsmord von Marseille [The Regicide of Marseilles]. 1959.

Miller, A. Informationsdienst zur Zeitgeschichte [Contemporary History Information Service]. Archiv für Zeitgeschichte, Leonberg-Stuttgart.

Mohr, H. Das katholische Apostolat. Zur Strategie und Taktik des politischen Katholizismus [The Catholic Apostolate. On the Strategy and Tactics of Political Catholicism]. 1962.

Mohrmann, H. Über Finanzen und Kapital des hohen katholischen Klerus. In: Katholische

Soziallehre—klerikaler Volksbetrug [On the Finances and Capital of the high Catholic Clerics. In: Catholic Social Teachings—Clerical Betrayal of the People]. 1960.

Müller, E. F. J., ed. Der katholische Episkopat in der nationalen Revolution Deutschlands. Dokumente und Materialien [The Catholic Episcopate in the German National Revolution. Documents and Materials]. 1934.

Müller, H. Katholische Kirche und Nationalsozialismus. Dokumente 1930–1935 [The Catholic Church and National Socialism. Documents 1930–1935]. 1963.

Mussolini, B. Schriften und Reden 1929–1931 [Documents and Speeches 1929–1931]. Volume 7. 1934.

Neubacher, H. Sonder-Auftrag Südost 1940–1945, Bericht eines fliegenden Diplomaten [Special Mission: South East 1940–1945. The Report of a Flying Diplomat]. 2nd edition. 1957.

Neuhäusler, J. Kreuz und Hakenkreuz [The Cross and the Swastika]. 1946.

Niemöller, W. Die evangelische Kirche im Dritten Reich, Handbuch des Kirchenkampfes [The Protestant Church in the Third Reich. Handbook of the Church Struggle]. 1956.

Nitti, F. F. Flucht. Die persönlichen Erlebnisse eines politischen Gefangenen, der von der faschistischen Teufelsinsel Lipari befreit wurde [Flight. The Personal Experiences of a Political Prisoner Liberated from the Fascist Devil's Island of Lipari]. Year unknown.

Novak, V. Magnum—Crimen. 1948.

Papen, F. v. Der Wahrheit eine Gasse [A Path for the Truth]. 1952.

———. "Der 12. November 1933 und die deutschen Katholiken" ["November 12, 1933, and the German Catholics"]. A speech addressed to the Arbeitsgemeinschaft katholischer Deutscher [Working Group of German Catholics] at the Cologne Fair Hall on November 9, 1932. Published in Reich und Kirche. 1934.

Paris, E. Genocide in Satellite Croatia 1941–1945. 1962.

———. The Vatican against Europe. 1961.

Picker, H. Hitlers Tischgespräche im Führerhauptquartier 1941–1942 [Hitler's Table Talks in the Führer's Headquarters 1941–1942]. Edited by P. E. Schramm. 1963.

Pieper, J. Das Arbeitsrecht des Neuen Reiches und die Enzyklika Quadragesimo anno [Employment Law in the New Reich and the *quadragesimo anno* Encyclical]. 1934.

Poehlmann. Geschichte der sozialen Frage und des Sozialismus in der antiken Welt [The History of the Social Question and Socialism in the Ancient World]. Volume 2. 3rd edition. 1925.

Poliakov, L., and J. Wulf. Das Dritte Reich und seine Diener [The Third Reich and Its Servants]. 1956.

Posser, D. Deutsch-sowjetische Beziehungen 1917–1941 [German-Soviet Relations, 1917–1941]. 1963.

Pzillas, F. Die Lebenskräfte des Christentums [The Life Forces of Christianity]. 1960.

Revyuk, E. Atrocities in the Ukraine. 1931.

Roos, H. Geschichte der Polnischen Nation 1916–1960 [History of the Polish Nation 1916–1960]. 1961.

Rumpelstilzchen (d. i. A. Stein). Der Schmied Roms [The Maker of Rome]. 1929.

Scheinmann (Sejman), M. M. Der Vatikan im Zweiten Weltkrieg [The Vatican in the Second World War]. 1954.

Schmaus, M. Begegnungen zwischen katholischem Christentum und nationalsozialistischer Weltanschauung [Encounters between Catholic Christianity and the National Socialist Worldview]. 2nd edition. 1934.

Schneider, C. Geistesgeschichte des antiken Christentums [The Intellectual History of Christianity]. Volumes 1 and 2. 1954.

Schoenberner, G. Der gelbe Stern, Die Judenverfolgung in Europa 1933–1945 [The Yellow Star: Persecution of the Jews in Europe 1933–1945]. 1960.

Shuster, G. N. Like a Mighty Army—Hitler versus Established Religion. 1935.

Siebert, F. Italiens Weg in den Zweiten Weltkrieg [Italy's Path to the Second World War]. 1962.

Stauffer, E. Theologisches Lehramt in Kirche und Reich [The Theological Chair in the Church and the Reich]. 1935.

Theiner, J., et al. Die Einführung der erzwungenen Ehelosigkeit bei den christlichen Geistlichen und ihre Folgen. Ein Beitrag zur Kirchengeschichte [The Introduction of Enforced Celibacy in Christian Clergy and Its Consequences]. 1893.

Thomas, H. Der spanische Bürgerkrieg [The Spanish Civil War]. 1962.

Timmermans, R. Die spanische Revolution. Wie sie ist, warum sie kam [The Spanish Revolution. What It Is Like and Where It Came From]. 1936.

Tondi, A. Die geheime Macht der Jesuiten [The Secret Power of the Jesuits]. 1960.

———. Die Jesuiten, Bekenntnisse und Erinnerungen [The Jesuits, Confessions and Memories]. 1961.

Trend, J. B. The Origins of Modern Spain. 1934.

Troeltsch, E. Die Soziallehren der christlichen Kirchen und Gruppen [The Social Doctrine of the Christian Churches and Groups]. Volume 1. 1912.

Ude, J. "Du sollst nicht töten!" ["Thou Shalt Not Kill!"]. 1948.

Werner, M. Glaube und Aberglaube, Aufsätze und Vorträge [Faith and Superstition, Essays and Lectures]. 1957.

Winter, E. Rußland und das Papsttum [Russia and the Papacy]. Volumes 1, 2, and 3. 1960 ff.

Ziegler, M. Was sagen die Weltkirchen zu diesem Krieg? Zeugnisse und Urteile [What Are the World Churches Saying about This War? Attestations and Verdicts]. 1940.